The Riddle of the Sphinx

Essays on the Evolution of Consciousness

Published by Barfield Press

Books by Owen Barfield:

Poetic Diction: A Study in Meaning
Romanticism Comes of Age
This Ever Diverse Pair
Saving the Appearances: A Study in Idolatry
Worlds Apart: A Dialogue of the 1960's
Unancestral Voice
Speaker's Meaning
What Coleridge Thought
The Rediscovery of Meaning, and Other Essays
History, Guilt and Habit
Owen Barfield on C. S. Lewis
Night Operation
Eager Spring
The Rose on the Ash-Heap
The Riddle of the Sphinx: Essays
The Silver Trumpet

Translations:

The Case for Anthroposophy

Forthcoming new editions:

Orpheus: A Poetic Drama
English People
Short Stories
Poetry
Plays

www.owenbarfield.org

Owen Barfield

The Riddle of the Sphinx

Essays on the Evolution of Consciousness

Edited by Rory O'Connor

Barfield Press
OXFORD, ENGLAND

General Editor: Rory O'Connor

Published by Barfield Press, Oxford, England

First published by Barfield Press, Oxford 2023

A catalogue record for this book is available from
the British Library.

The Riddle of the Sphinx by Owen Barfield
ISBN 978-0-9569423-7-1 (hardcover)
ISBN 978-0-9569423-5-7 (paperback)
ISBN 978-0-9569423-6-4 (ebook)

Printed on paper with Sustainable Forestry Initiative
(SFI) accreditation.

Produced on behalf of
the Owen Barfield Literary Estate.

The Literary Estate promotes and safeguards the works
and intellectual legacy of Arthur Owen Barfield.

www.owenbarfield.org

CONTENTS

Editor's Introduction	ix
Note on Sources	xxxv
Form in Poetry	1
Greek Thought in English Words	9
Giordano Bruno and the Survival of Learning	28
Two Kinds of Forgetting	49
The Riddle of the Sphinx	68
Romanticism and Anthroposophy	77
Goethe and Evolution	93
Rudolf Steiner's Concept of Mind	102
The Many and the One	116
Israel and the Michael Impulse	136
The Nature of Meaning	157
Julian the Apostate	178
Equity	198
Why Reincarnation?	228
The Concept of Revelation	244
Meaning, Revelation and Tradition in Language and Religion	261
The Light of the World	281
Owen Barfield and the Origin of Language	305
Editor's Notes	327

EDITOR'S INTRODUCTION

FOR THOSE WHO know and admire the work of Owen Barfield, the publication of previously uncollected essays and lectures between the covers of a book, approximately a quarter of a century after his death, is an occasion for gladness. One of their reflections can be that a fresh opportunity exists for others — like themselves previously — to contend with the concept of an evolution of consciousness, to inform themselves regarding its nature, and then, it may be, to begin willingly to participate in its reality. This book is sent forth in that hope.

Regardless of the reader's level of familiarity with Barfield's writing, they will benefit in reading this volume, which contains essays written from 1920 till the early 1980s, by a mapping of its territory and a suggested route. Barfield himself, in both of his introductions to the two collections of essays published in his lifetime, *Romanticism Comes of Age* (1944, expanded 2nd edition 1966) and *The Rediscovery of Meaning* (1977), shows he is aware that there is some irreducible oddity in the endeavour of bringing together and making into one object essays written separately and episodically. Introducing the first of those collections, he metaphorically offers to the reader "to show him my diary and lend him my Baedekers",[1] with the suggestion that Barfield's personal path was one way, and perhaps the simplest way, to understand their coming together. In his second introduction, he writes about the essays that there is after all "an effective unity of content underlying the apparent fragmentation".[2] As can be imagined, this apparent problem might have been magnified by these essays being (with one exception) selected from what has remained unpublished in book form after those collections were published. Nevertheless, it arose quite naturally in the course of selecting them that, suitably ordered, they go a considerable way to illustrating *both* the unity and continuity of the process of the evolution of consciousness until our time and beyond, *and* also Barfield's personal path in understanding that process. It is as such that they will be introduced.

Owen Barfield's path towards understanding the evolution of consciousness began with an immediate, and common, personal experience: it was what he called the "felt change of consciousness" that came while reading lyric poetry. The poet's use of metaphor brings the reader to see the world differently.

My soul is an enchanted boat,
Which, like a sleeping swan, doth float
  Upon the waves of thy sweet singing...

"It is as though my own consciousness had actually been expanded", Barfield wrote about Shelley's lines: "henceforth the eyes with which I behold real boats and waves and swans, the ears with which in the right mood I listen to a song, are actually somewhat different".[3] While the feeling of the change of consciousness is transitory, these new perceptions abide as *knowledge*. The world about us becomes more *meaningful*. The first essay here, "Form in Poetry", analyses precisely how this comes to pass: words are given a specific liveliness through their imaginative combination. In Shelley's poem, the boat is enlivened by our knowing its enchantment, and in being compared to a sleeping swan we can readily picture the way it floats. A state of soul also comes before us, in which we may participate imaginatively. The essay was published in the *New Statesman* when Barfield was aged 21, and it is the case that he had significantly broadened and deepened his thinking about the lyric moment that creates new meaning by the time *Poetic Diction* was published when he was 29. What in the first instance had been a receptivity to the meaningfulness which poetry could draw forth from the world, had become a fully fledged theory of poetic diction as a form of knowledge. Nonetheless, the *mode* by which poetry could make a reader, in Barfield's term, *wiser*, is outlined in "Form in Poetry". Barfield accordingly in his early nineties recognised the essay as the "first symptoms" of what he called his "thinking about thinking".[4]

His discernment of an evolution of consciousness throughout the course of recorded history came through careful philological investigation of changes in the meanings of particular (Greek, Latin, earlier English) roots of our words, as used today, together with a closely reasoned account of how those changes had come to be. All of this was the necessary scholarly foundation for an understanding of how the processes of perception and thinking of ancient people was substantially different from ours. The evolution of consciousness, then, is a theory that in the past nature's phenomena had borne a spiritual countenance; that these spiritual qualities were directly perceptible by humanity. Nature as a whole had an "inside" perceptible by humanity, just as we have our inner lives, and can know something of others' inner lives, today. The history of language is the evidence for this and bears witness to that experience of nature. As Emerson had written:

> Every word which is used to express a moral or intellectual fact, if traced to its root, is found to be borrowed from some material experience. *Right* means straight; *wrong* means twisted. *Spirit* primarily means wind; *transgression*, the crossing of a line; *supercilious*, the raising of an eyebrow.[5]

At a stretch one could call these metaphors, in that they were unities of meaning between the ideal and the sense-perceptible. But there is the important distinction that they were not made by poets, and instead were immanent in nature. They were not formed by, but rather had formed, the human mind. In the course of this evolution, humanity has both become independent from nature in its thinking, and acquired a thorough inwardness and individuation which has been concurrent with an experience of apparently impassable separation from nature. The cultural record shows that even as this process was ongoing, man experienced, *knew*, himself to be the microcosm within the universal macrocosm. Barfield writes of seeing "the astrology, and especially the alchemy, of the late Middle Ages rather as a valiant attempt to arrest [the gradual fading away of the older participative consciousness] by preserving something of the old participation, while availing itself of the new impulse to think empirically and discover experimentally". The last vestige now of our participation in the phenomena of nature takes a quite different form, which is that it is only our mental intuition of what they are that allows our recognition of them at all. But this last vestige also is usually, for most practical and even theoretical purposes, forgotten.

Of necessity, though of greater difficulty due to the common view in our time of nature as having changed only through successive material states, this theory implies that *nature itself*, and not just the human mind, was substantially different than it is today. As disclosed by the history of language, the evolution of consciousness was at the same time an evolution of *phenomena*. This theory can be opposed to, and needs to be distinguished from, the conception that ancient people perceived and thought in the same way we do — that they were presented with phenomena and then attempted to arrive at explanations of these phenomena — but then arrived at erroneous conclusions, since scientific observation had not attained its present level.

"Greek Thought in English Words", collected here, among other things details one part of this evolution, and exemplifies how Barfield conceived it, the time when classical philosophy was in flower in Athens. This philosophy was in fact a critical factor in man's increasing conception of himself as a distinct reasoning being within nature. However, this took time, and Greek philosophical vocabulary continued to bear within it a suggestion that perception was or had been more closely bound up with thought — thought existing not in the mind only, but throughout the world:

> We may find it difficult to conceive of a time when the logical process of observing *phenomena* (things 'appearing' or 'seen') and forming *theories* to account for their relationship was unknown: yet the semantic development of the word θεωρία from its original meaning of mere contemplation or onlooking seems to confirm that this is so. [...]
>
> Both to Aristotle and to Plato the Greek θεωρεῖν meant, not hypothesis but contemplation. It expressed the act, not of a speculator, but of a spectator.

The development of logical process, an activity of the mind, is a step forward in this evolution from the experience of a cosmic Logos, which constituted both mind and nature:

> [T]here is really no way of translating words like λόγος, λογικός, λογίζεσθαι, as they are used by Plato. *Reason* is quite inadequate to convey to a twentieth-century imagination the cosmic process which Plato must have felt to be taking place — as much out in the world and among the stars as 'within' his own mind [...]. It was not until the 'analytic' method of thought arose with Aristotle that such a word as *logic* could begin to take on its modern meaning. Indeed its strictly technical sense cannot be traced further back than a passage in which Cicero uses the Greek phrase λογική τέχνη in reference to the syllogistic method. *Syllogism* itself is first found with that meaning in Aristotle's works, and so 'logic', that exclusively subjective process, is revealed to us as something which the mind only discovered when it began to turn outward to 'matter'.

Barfield consistently identified the period from the sixteenth century onward, concurrent with the scientific revolution, as when the subjective internalisation of the experience of the cosmic Logos to within the human mind reached its nadir. It continues in substance, taking different forms, till now. The Aristotelian understanding of logic recapitulating natural ideas or forms within the mind, was replaced by an understanding of innate ideas within the human mind, by which the human mind could apprehend abstract principles in nature. This too was succeeded by Locke's model of the passive mind as the receptor, through the senses and nerves, of impressions from the external world. And lastly there has been the ever increasing focus, continuing till today, on the physical brain formed by an accidental evolution as the sole seat of mental activity.

The loss of any consciousness of the human being as the microcosm within the macrocosm has led to an acute crisis in thought, especially from the nineteenth century onward, which finds expression throughout both the sciences and the humanities. This is so despite the fact that the scientific revolution, which was the precipitant of this crisis, was undeniably a forward step in thought. The initiative gesture of this revolution was the mutual exclusion of matter and mind marked by the philosophy of René Descartes. Matter, what Descartes called extended substance, could from the time of the scientific revolution be viewed essentially as an object of measurement and manipulation, which by the same token resulted in a new and laudably high value placed on accuracy, *precision*, in thinking. This is a gift which Barfield believed should be permanently taken forward with us. But precisely the dependability of scientific results produced in this way with regard to material phenomena obscured the fact that Descartes' model of space could not be hypostatised as the only valid one. Quantum physics, most authoritatively, began to suggest this in the twentieth century, but so did the implications of non-Euclidean (projective) geometry, and plant and animal morphology in biology. Barfield's study of extinct meanings within language itself had revealed a veritable "fossil record" of the presence of mind in space. Long before this, however, the setting in stone of a materialist picture of the world's phenomena led to a misconceived attempt to interpret the entirety of pre-history in material terms. On the basis of the geological fossil record and its understanding according to the Darwinian theory of evolution by natural selection, it was taken for granted that the human mind, a latecomer in history, had to have arisen from animal consciousness, locally within human brains. The undeniable boons of the Cartesian dispensation may adequately explain the failure to confront all indications that in fact mind had always been thoroughly entangled in space. But when Barfield quotes Darwin's admission that he was "almost forced to believe, *a priori* that articulate language has been developed from inarticulate cries", he is well aware that that *a priori* signifies simply a mental prejudice in favour of materialism. It is easy to be reminded of Barfield's suggestion that occasionally the evolution of consciousness simply results in "certain thoughts being 'in the air'". A primary reason for the persistency of materialism since the 19th century is simply that it is "in the air" of our thinking and experience.

As for the effects on the humanities of this intellectual crisis: however it may be with moral action, moral discourse is blighted by the loss of the grounding for the natural law, no matter how conceived. Literature is written and criticised as solely a subjective, or even merely personal, expression. As Barfield noted elsewhere, if caught within this web of materialist thought, one must finally answer the question, "Do I exist?" by replying, "No". It may be only a little consolation, or evidence rather of confusion, if the answer instead comes, "I don't know".[6] Natural science set this human humbling on its course through the removal from its considerations of the "occult qualities" (those not subject to measurement) in nature. By extension, the human individuality came to be included among these forbidden qualities. The mutual exclusion of matter and mind is superseded by a conception of mind as one possible metaphor for the material process taking place within the brain. Finally, the scientific spirit itself, considered apart from the technological productivity which has been its result, is itself potentially humbled by this thinking, since scientific *theorising* bears traces of the metaphysical speculation it had vanquished. "Two Kinds of Forgetting" and "The Riddle of the Sphinx" both diagnose this crisis in thought, analyse its symptoms, and outline possible prognoses.

Darwin's *a priori* does incidentally help to illustrate a point made by Barfield repeatedly through his work: the evolution of consciousness is something other than what we know as 'the history of thought'. He outlines the difference as follows: "A history of thought, as such, amounts to a dialectical or syllogistic process, the thoughts of one age arising discursively out of, challenging, and modifying the thoughts and discoveries of the previous one. [...] Many indications suggest that, in addition to the dialectical history of ideas there are forces at work beneath the threshold of argument in the evolution even of modern consciousness".[7] "Giordano Bruno and the Survival of Learning" details the outworking of what Barfield finds is fair (*pace* his great friend C. S. Lewis) to call a "Renaissance Impulse", and in "Romanticism and Anthroposophy" we learn something about romanticism as impulse. "Israel and the Michael Impulse" tells of a force at work both in modern and ancient consciousness.

There has been a point to all this. Humanity's loss of the experience of connection with the natural world, the apparent withdrawal of meaning, has been the condition of a new human *freedom*: freedom from nature, from custom, from the spiritual world itself. This has been accompanied by an awesome depth of responsibility.

Since the 20th century we are singularly responsible, not only for our own souls, but for others', and for the fate of the world. At this point, Barfield's first subject, the imagination, which he had always insisted was a means of knowing, but might still have seemed to be limited to an aesthetic realm, becomes of newly evident importance. For it is the imagination which in the long run determines perception, and our perception will determine our activity regarding nature and our fellow beings. Already a nature perceived purely as mechanism is acted on as such, at a price of much destruction. There can be no doubt as to the implications of this freedom and responsibility: Barfield writes elsewhere, with some apology for the expression, of humanity now having a "directionally creator"[8] relation to nature. Nature for so long time has breathed life into humanity. Now it is humanity's free decision whether to breathe life into nature.

So far unmentioned is one of those facts that tend to be known by those who have heard the name Owen Barfield: his discipleship of Rudolf Steiner, or perhaps more precisely of Steiner's method of knowledge and its results, anthroposophy. The extent of Barfield's debt to Steiner in developing theories of poetry as knowledge, and of language as revealing something of the true nature of evolution, were questions that, in his Preface to the first edition of *Poetic Diction*, he sidestepped. He encountered Steiner's work having already begun writing that important book, but Steiner had an influence on it which he acknowledged without wishing "to father upon him many of the views on poetry which I have expressed".[9] It seems reasonable to think of Barfield as "*using* [Steiner's] revelations"[10] as an aid in thinking about poetry and the history of language: which is precisely what Steiner expected others to do within their own domains of experience and expertise.

What was anthroposophy, for Barfield? In the first instance, he saw it as "a new and solid edifice of metaphysic" arising in succession to the relatively fragmentary, ungrounded romanticism of the late eighteenth and early nineteenth centuries. The images of human relationships, of the natural world, of ghostly presences, of the inner being of the human, in literary romanticism, had kept alive certain essential conditions of soul that were being perceived as illusory or meaningless in an atmosphere of pervasive materialism, practical and theoretic. The romantic vision was indeed one by which, as Wordsworth wrote in "Tintern Abbey", "We see into the life of things". But equally it was always harassed by the fear that this was "but a vain belief". In fact, there had been one figure who had taken a step towards a confident romantic metaphysic, who *could* begin to give an answer to the question, "*In what way* is imagination true?" J. W. Goethe's systematic use of the imagination in the scientific domain allowed him to perceive that the form of a plant is always metamorphoses of the leaf. Beyond this he could perceive the archetype of the plant-form itself, of which every particular species of plant is a metamorphosis. This was not an abstraction from particular existent plants, but a living idea, visible within every one of them. He also applied this faculty of perception to see, through their various parts, the unities within the spectrum of colours and within human and animal bone structures. By dint of Goethe's method, it is possible to perceive the organic wholeness of a phenomenon, rather than its atomised deadening. It is critical to note that this imaginal wholeness is at once fully apparent to perception in the phenomenon, and yet requires the use of the imagination finally to appear for the observer. It is in this sense that, as Barfield wrote elsewhere, we can think of imagination as "an ultimate mental activity that opposes, and transmutes into a kind of aesthetic or mystical contemplation, that absolute dichotomy between perceiving subject and perceived object on which our practical everyday experience (Coleridge's 'lethargy of custom') is necessarily based."[11]

Romanticism had been the first step in humanity's overcoming that separation from the natural world, which was a fresh and raw experience of the eighteenth century, but which the history of language discloses has been the completion of a process lasting three thousand years and more. There was however this critical difference: Goethe's renewed participation was not 'given' by nature, but was the product of a self-conscious engagement with its objects, determined and driven forward by his own individual will. Goethe's 'I' was breaking down the barriers between itself and the phenomena it sought out. The essays "Romanticism and Anthroposophy" and "Goethe and Evolution" are about the romantic ferment in which humanity's self-conscious participation in nature first arose. The latter was in fact delivered as a broadcast on the BBC Third Programme in 1949, accounting for a somewhat different tone, which may remind readers at one or two points of C. S. Lewis's radio talks on Christianity as published in *Mere Christianity.*

Since Steiner's theory of knowledge is the foundation on which anthroposophy and the spiritual findings associated with it are delivered, I have found it indispensable to include "Rudolf Steiner's Concept of

Mind" in this collection, though uniquely among those included here this essay is already available in one of Barfield's collections, *Romanticism Comes of Age*. As a summary of Steiner's epistemological writings, primarily *The Philosophy of Freedom* and *Goethe's Theory of Knowledge*, it is at once highly concise and detailed to a degree that it can be said that nothing that is essential in them is left unrecounted. The essay's inclusion was also essential because, to a much greater extent than in the two essay collections published during Barfield's life, this one includes essays intended for informed anthroposophical audiences, with anthroposophical conceptions assumed to a greater or lesser extent. This is true in particular of such essays as "Israel and the Michael Impulse", "Julian the Apostate" and "The Light of the World", though of others also. Clearly it is essential to indicate on what basis any of these conceptions could be said to be knowable. (The importance of *The Philosophy of Freedom* in particular is the understanding, shared by Barfield, that for the person who thinks and acts freely in the way that the book illuminates, anthroposophy may flow to them: that they may develop their own "wisdom of man". And it was for this reason that Steiner himself said that it would outlast all his other works.)

For how is it that we could come to know anything of the world beyond what is given to us in perception; which incidentally may include many qualities, not immediately apparent to the senses, of phenomena familiar to us from everyday life? To take a few matters arising, and taken for granted as answerable in the affirmative, in this collection: Are there members of the human body beyond the visible physical body? Can anything be said about the potentiality of reincarnation and of human existence between death and rebirth? Is there anything to be said with certainty about the orders of angels and its, and our, adversaries? One adds "with certainty" merely to emphasise that, in using the word *know*, it is of course essential that this would be beyond the possibility of subjective illusion. As a last, important, question: on what basis could we say it is possible to develop a relationship with these beings, these realities?

Steiner's implicit answer to these questions, about the potential of perception in these domains, begins by drawing attention to the constitutive nature of thinking in our perception of reality. Thinking itself has ordered things such that we are subjects looking into a mass of objects: it is after all the only thing that allows us to conceive ourselves as subjects in the first place. As we have seen, imagination, a form of thinking, can breach that frontier temporarily enforced by thinking. In the meantime, the ordinary world, as commonly recognised by us, is made of percepts and concepts which are, so to speak, compacted together. It is in fact concepts, arrived at by thinking, which allow us to recognise what is before us, whatever it may be. "We owe it to our concepts that we perceive a world of shapes, forms, 'things' at all", Barfield wrote. Thinking is of course our activity, but it is only one part of reality. We may therefore "reason back" from this truth to the realisation that *there is* a 'given' world beyond our conceptual determinations. However, it cannot be approached with our inveterate habit of forgetting the thinking which already constitutes reality as it is apparent to us, and instead thinking 'about' it as if it were wholly independent of us — a habit of thought which is now revealed to us precisely as a subjective illusion, albeit one almost universal in our time.

Our activity of thinking is, customarily, bound up with the physical world and with sense-perception. But we can be certain that thinking is separable from these bindings, since, in a primordial way, it has already ordered the physical world for us, made comprehensible our sense-perception. In this sense, thinking is in fact a spiritual activity: as Barfield writes, quoting Steiner, it is "that factor in man 'through which he inserts himself spiritually into reality'". It is therefore possible to have what Barfield calls here "a strengthened thinking", a pure, sense-free thinking, which would of necessity, given thinking's constitutive forming of perception, "result in widening the field of *perception* or *observation* themselves". Or as Steiner had already put it in *The Philosophy of Freedom*:

> The human being must simply *await* what will arise as perception along his life's path. The only question could be whether, from the point of view that results purely out of intuitively experienced thinking, it can justifiably be expected that man would be able to perceive, besides what is sense-perceptible, also what is spiritual. This can be expected. For although *on the one hand* intuitively experienced thinking is an active process taking place within the human spirit, *on the other hand* it is at the same time a spiritual perception grasped without any physical organ. It is a perception in which the perceiver himself is active, and it is an activity of the self which is also perceived.[12]

As Barfield's mention of "a strengthened thinking" suggests, this awaiting of new perception is an *active* waiting, to which a discipline of thinking taught by Steiner was directed. The first step in this enhanced cognition, free of the familiar senses, is called Imagination, in which the student puts images with a real spiritual content before her mental eye. There is indeed an inherent spiritual depth in those images. The *activity* in their coming before the student, on the other hand, is hers alone, rather than that of other beings or of the dreaming subconscious mind, and it needs to be recognised by her as such; by the same token, she must be able to cease this meditative activity at any point and return to the rest of life. This is because the 'I' must be in control: congruent with Goethe's renewed participation in *natural* phenomena, this human, free, willing is a requirement for modern participation in purely spiritual phenomena. The second step in enhanced cognition is called Inspiration. Steiner describes this as a facility of being able to 'read' the relations between the spiritual beings whose substance is represented in the imaginative pictures — a reading achieved in part by dismissing the pictures the better to relate to the beings. In the lecture to the Lindisfarne Association included here under the title "The One and the Many", Barfield outlines some elements of these stages of higher cognition, and in "Romanticism and Anthroposophy" clothes them in pictures drawn from the work of Wordsworth.

It is evident in his Introduction to *The Rediscovery of Meaning* that Barfield distinguished between those essays of his written for a general audience, and those written specifically for an audience familiar with Steiner. This was a distinction of approach, rather than substance. It was because he sought to lead people to Steiner that he usually began with any given issue in its own terms. Those written for a general audience might, for example, illustrate an historical period within the evolution of consciousness; or a problem attendant on science limiting its investigations to what can be perceived by or inferred from the senses; or an aspect of contemporary social existence — and then advise emphatically towards their end that these considerations are given their proper context, and best illuminated, by Steiner's spiritual science. Whereas those written for an anthroposophical audience begin with that assumption. Nevertheless, it was at times Barfield's practice to present Steiner's findings "cold" to the general public — most successfully in *Unancestral Voice*, in which the scholarly-poetic Burgeon, more or less a stand-in for Barfield, encounters the Meggid, who plainly presents spiritual realities to him that match Steiner's findings.

Even if it is granted that there may be a sound epistemological basis for an openness to the findings of spiritual investigation, the inclusion of essays which assume the validity of spiritual science presents an apparent difficulty as well as an obvious substantial opportunity. As to the opportunity: simply put, it is straightforwardly to present to the reader a small amount of those results of Steiner's spiritual investigation which Barfield advised were so illuminating, without qualification. In that act, there is already the first step in overcoming the apparent difficulty. For after all they are only a presentation. "Think these thoughts without believing them", Barfield once quoted Steiner as saying, and himself added:

> I cannot think it is unduly paradoxical to say that it is really a kind of betrayal of the founder of anthroposophy to believe what he said. He poured out his assertions because he trusted his hearers *not* to believe. Belief is something which can only be applied to systems of abstract ideas.[13]

Those unfamiliar with Steiner can approach these essays in that spirit, but at the same time may notice another experience, which Barfield had. In the last essay collected here, "Owen Barfield and the Origin of Language", he records that "[t]he often surprising things that Rudolf Steiner reported with such confidence as the findings of his spiritual research" had acted on him "in the same way as did poetic or figurative language". This was "the same sort of change of consciousness" as occurred to him while reading poetry, with the significant difference that it was the imaginal content of Steiner's findings taken on their own terms, rather than the metaphorical suggestiveness of poetry, that had this effect. Those who have already read Barfield or Steiner can take the findings reported in essays such as "Israel and the Michael Impulse" and "Julian the Apostate" as pictures of specific stages in the evolution of consciousness, and then perhaps as springboards for spiritual research. Anyone who to date has not encountered the results of spiritual investigation, may in the first instance find that these essays operate on their consciousness in the way Barfield describes.

It was after all the dearest wish of Barfield's public life that his readers would take seriously and act on his invitation to them to familiarise themselves with Steiner's findings. In this they could assess for themselves their capacities to shed light on the world as it is already known to the reader and potentially to inspire beneficial action in the ongoing moment, which is the first way open to the reader to adjudge their validity. Those capacities are of course one way to adjudge their truth, and "Equity" is included here as exemplifying them. Moved by the misery of the Great Depression, Barfield interested himself in economics, and was co-translator of Steiner's lecture series *World Economy* into English.[14]

Anyone with a passing awareness of contemporary economic life will recognise the description in "Equity" of the "morbid symptoms displayed by the economic life of the world today" caused by "the tendency of capital to accumulate in the form of land-values". A redescription of economic life in Steiner's terms, as described by Barfield — with capital, essentially a creature of spirit, conceived as being in a polar relationship to nature — allows the practical, but today scarcely heard, suggestion that "it is not merely morally but economically necessary that [...] the capital so accumulated should be placed at the service of the *spirit* and thus allowed *indirectly* (that is *via* its disbursement on educative and other spiritual activities) to flow back into the land and into further production". Steiner's lecturing on the economy was only one of the seeds he planted in practical life, with others in education, agriculture, medicine and countless other fields. Barfield was particularly interested in Steiner's art of movement, eurythmy.

A number of the essays treat of portions of humanity's religious history. "Israel and the Michael Impulse" outlines the nature of the archangel's hope for humanity in the time of ancient Israel and in ours. "Julian the Apostate" tells the story of that deeply spiritual pagan in the time of early Christianity, and of the reasons in the spiritual world for his tragic fate. "The Concept of Revelation" approaches the title's topic through the lens of the evolution of consciousness. "Meaning, Revelation and Tradition in Language and Religion" brings us to a deeper understanding of the meaning of the first verse of St John's Gospel. Underlying these essays is the view that while many religions have seen the Godhead — sometimes in an obscured way, sometimes more clearly — as having a threefold nature, "What is peculiar to Christianity is the nexus that it acknowledges between the Second Person of the Trinity and a certain historical *event in time*".[15] History, Barfield held, must be seen by us as involving an evolution of consciousness, if the meaning of Christ's presence on Earth is to be recognised in its full significance.

The last two named essays build on this understanding of the religious significance of history, to point to the ongoing potential for revelation in what other thinkers might have dismissed merely as literature. Regarding the study of what had come to be called hermeneutics, Barfield wrote, humorously but truthfully, of having discovered on his arrival to America that he was regarded as "something of an authority, in a department of academic study of which [I] had never heard!" While previously hermeneutics had referred exclusively to interpretation of the Bible, in the twentieth century it had come to refer to a study of symbolism in language generally. Barfield's motion within this field of study can be summarised as drawing our attention to the fact that its broader domains only extended the scope within which the potential for revelation should be attended to — and that in fact this, within the medieval scholastic tradition, had always been understood. "Meaning, Revelation and Tradition...", in its summary of a tradition of thinking that was able to investigate the coming into being of each word "even just before its birth", and of Jesus' parables about the Kingdom of God as taking the form of the transformation of a sensible "likeness into something transcending likeness", is a subtle, powerful invitation to think non-materialistically, symbolically, purely spiritually.

For the removal of one possible misunderstanding, given the centrality of Christianity in these essays, it is well to emphasise that anthroposophy, which I described in the first instance as an epistemological theory and method, and then in a fuller way as a consciousness of the nature of humanity, is clearly not to be thought of as another Christian confession. (And indeed all may benefit from learning of Barfield's conception of the evolution of consciousness, regardless of religious perspective.) Steiner noted that he had come to his knowledge of the Christ's incarnation and what he called the Mystery of Golgotha through the same form of intuitive supersensual perception as he used in the rest of his spiritual research. From his own perspective, which he hastened to acknowledge was more modest, Barfield simply wrote that

> [i]t is perfectly possible to accept as true such an account of the evolution of consciousness as is deducible from these essays as true without relating it specifically to the events recorded in the Christian gospels. On the other hand once it *has* been accepted, one may come to feel that such a special relation is almost self-evident.[16]

Finally, the special relationship of Barfield's thought (and of Steiner's) to Christianity is evident: the incarnation of Christ was the turning point in all history, the moment that the infinite I AM united Himself fully with the Earth, making this possible also for humanity. With Christ's help, we are neither to be dragged down into a mechanical sub-natural state, nor to float in an unearthly spirituality above the world. Rather we have the capacity to be free, conscious, spiritual beings, fully present on earth, and fully engaged with spiritual life. "Love is the consciousness of survival in the act of self-surrender", Barfield once quoted R. L. Nettleship as writing.[17] To say Christ has made that possible on Earth is also, for instance, to say that He has made possible the renewed conscious participation in nature practised by Goethe, as well as the new modes of cognition brought to light by Steiner. Essential to all history, Christ's presence, in affording the human a loving inwardness which can will the good, even as the Earth has lost its inwardness in our perception, has nevertheless peculiarly anticipated the need of our time.

Regarding the editorial notes which appear at the end of this book explaining references in fifteen of the essays, there is only a little to say. Barfield is a highly referential writer, naming the sources of inspiration of an argument, or the instances of a trend being described, with which the reader can engage further. Since, however, the argument at any given point is not dependent on familiarity with these references, in the great majority of cases they can safely be left for the reader to pursue at will and at leisure, with no need for annotation. It is no doubt a little shaming to us, but it will also be comprehensible to contemporary people, that my question has been: "Will what is being said here make full sense to anyone who does not have the internet readily to hand?" With that guideline, phrases in languages other than English, whether ancient or modern, are annotated. So also are terms that derive specifically from Steiner's intellectual patrimony. Once again, Steiner's terms are annotated with an eye to the stumbling-block, if left unremarked, that they may pose to readers unfamiliar with them. There is also the slight hope that, in providing a basis on which to read Barfield's essays, they may prove an inspiration to engage with the concepts and realities named — that they will at least be found, to at least a small degree, to inspire some change of consciousness. These annotations are made to aid general comprehension, and also comprehension specifically in the context of the essay, since often the topic requiring brief explanation will have been explored by Steiner from a number of different perspectives in the course of his lecturing. They are by no means definitions in the dictionary sense. I have also occasionally made a note to advise the reader where Barfield has expanded elsewhere on a theme outlined briefly in these essays. All footnotes to these essays were written by Barfield himself.

It only remains to explain the book's title. Before the ancient Egyptian and Greek initiates, it is said, a being would come in vision. It had something of the form of the lion, something of the bull, and had the wings of the eagle. What, who, was this being? Sitting with, working on, puzzling over this curious, insistent figure, the initiate came to realize that this being, the Sphinx, represented the evolutionary development of the human being. (This human evolution, incidentally, had assimilated and balanced the inner nature of these different creatures, not only their outer forms — as well as preserving the distinctively human being, represented by the human head in the sculpture of the Sphinx at Giza.) The initiate could in truth ultimately say of the Sphinx: "This being is I myself, as in my deepest being I have developed over long periods." There is of course another riddle of the Sphinx, the one solved by Oedipus, which goes, "What walks on four legs in the morning, on two legs at noon, and on three legs in the evening?" The answer, "the human being", hinted at the Sphinx's concerns. But it is the former riddle, that of *the nature of the Sphinx itself*, that Owen Barfield has in mind, when he writes in the essay from which the book derives its title: "What was, or rather what *is*, the meaning of anthropos?[18] Asked originally by the Sphinx, this question was answered in the Mysteries not in the indicative but in the imperative mood: *gnöthi seauton* — know thyself!" The evolution of consciousness has been comprised of evolving answers to the question, "What is the human being?" As these essays attest, Owen Barfield saw that now particularly free, perceptive and creative answers are called for, from each person. Such answers can take their start in the recognition that the form of consciousness, the type of thinking, the *world*, familiar to us are each only one of many that have existed; and in fact that a further evolution of these is now due.

Rory O'Connor
Dublin, Ireland
November 2022

Rory O'Connor is a writer who has assisted the Owen Barfield Literary Estate for a decade and is now General Editor for the Barfield Press.

NOTES

[1] *Romanticism Comes of Age*. Oxford: Barfield Press, 2012, 3rd edition, p. 1.

[2] *The Rediscovery of Meaning*. Oxford: Barfield Press, 2013, 2nd edition, p. 3.

[3] *Poetic Diction*, Oxford: Barfield Press, 2010, 4th edition, p. 47.

[4] Barfield makes this remark in a recorded interview included the documentary film *Owen Barfield: Man and Meaning*, which was produced and narrated by G. B. Tennyson. Encino, CA: OwenArts, 1996.

[5] R. W. Emerson, *Nature*, Chapter IV, 1836. Quoted in Landon Loftin & Max Leyf's *What Barfield Thought*. Eugene, OR: Cascade Books, 2022, p. 36.

[6] *The Rediscovery of Meaning*. Op. cit., p. 227.

[7] *Saving the Appearances*. Oxford: Barfield Press, 2011, 3rd edition, pp. 72–73.

[8] *Saving the Appearances*. Op. cit., p. 151.

[9] *Poetic Diction*. Op. cit., p. 2.

[10] This phrase appears in "Anthroposophy and the Future", originally published as an essay in the magazine *Towards* 3.1 (Fall 1987): 32–35, 49–50.

[11] *Romanticism Comes of Age*. Op. cit., pp. 24–25.

[12] *The Philosophy of Spiritual Activity*. William Lindeman, translator. Hudson, NY: Anthroposophic Press, 1986, pp. 243–244. *The Philosophy of Spiritual Activity* is an alternative title for *The Philosophy of Freedom*, which is a literal translation of the German, and by which it is best known.

[13] *Romanticism Comes of Age*. Op. cit.: p. 94.

[14] It is currently available in that translation in a volume titled *Rethinking Economics: Lectures and Seminars on World Economics* (Great Barrington, MA: SteinerBooks, 2013: pp. 1–182).

[15] *Saving the Appearances*. Op. cit.: p. 195.

[16] This passage is in the essay "Philology and the Incarnation", printed in *The Rediscovery of Meaning*, op. cit.: pp. 338–350.

[17] This is quoted in "Death", an essay originally published posthumously in *VII: An Anglo-American Literary Review* 25 (2008), pp. 48–60.

[18] Greek. "The human being."

ACKNOWLEDGMENTS

For their friendship and encouragement in the period that this book was being edited I thank Jean Callanan, Paul Carroll, Anthony McCarthy, Eamon O'Callaghan, Christopher Reburn, Hussein Sarhan, Gosia Stach, Richard Watchorn and Egle Zinkute.

For helpful comments which improved this introduction I thank Gabriel Schenk and Jac Hielema. They are also included in the first category for thanks. Any remaining errors and infelicities are my responsibility alone.

I take this opportunity to express my appreciation for my parents Joanne and David, and for Ian and Sally, and for Brede O'Connor.

For assistance in obtaining essays written by Owen Barfield, I am grateful to staff at: the Weston Library, Oxford; the Library of Trinity College Dublin; Rudolf Steiner House Library, London; and the Marion E. Wade Center at Wheaton College, Illinois. I am endebted to the late Jane Hipolito for her exhaustive Bibliography of the Published Writings of Owen Barfield, and also for her example in preparing work by Owen Barfield for publication, as an editor for the Barfield Press.

I owe special thanks to Owen A. Barfield, trustee of the Owen Barfield Literary Estate, publisher at the Barfield Press, and the writer's grandson. His initiative in suggesting to me that I edit this collection, and his patience and trust as well as friendship and encouragement while I undertook it, have been invaluable.

NOTE ON SOURCES

"Form in Poetry": *The New Statesman* Vol. 15 (7 August 1920)

"Greek Thought in English Words": *Essays and Studies 1950*, G. Rostrevor Hamilton (ed.).

"Giordano Bruno and the Survival of Learning": *Drew Gateway* Vol. 42 (Spring 1972)

"Two Kinds of Forgetting": *The Nassau Review* 4.2 (1981)

"The Riddle of the Sphinx": *Arena* 19 (April 1964)

"Romanticism and Anthroposophy": *Anthroposophy: A Quarterly Review of Spiritual Science* 1.1 (Easter 1926)

"Goethe and Evolution": *The Listener* Vol. 42 (1 Dec. 1949). Text of a talk given on the BBC Third Programme.

"Steiner's Concept of Mind": *The Faithful Thinker: Centenary Essays on the Work and Thought of Rudolf Steiner, 1861–1925*, ed. A. C. Harwood. London: Hodder and Stoughton, 1961. Also published in *Romanticism Comes of Age* 3rd ed (Barfield Press: Oxford, 2012).

"The Many and the One": Archive of Owen Barfield, Special Collections, Bodleian Library, Oxford, catalogued under the title "manuscript lecture notes on anthroposophy and the evolution of consciousness, given to the Lindisfarne Association, 1982"

"Israel and the Michael Impulse": *Anthroposophical Quarterly* 1.1 (Spring 1956)

"The Nature of Meaning": *VII: An Anglo-American Literary Review* Vol. 2 (1981)

"Julian the Apostate": *Anthroposophical Quarterly* 6.2 (Summer 1961)

"Equity": *Anthroposophy* 7.2 (Midsummer 1932)

"Why Reincarnation?": *The Golden Blade*, 1979

"The Concept of Revelation": *VII: An Anglo-American Review* 1 (1980)

"Meaning, Revelation and Tradition in Language and Religion": *The Missouri Review* 5.3 (Summer 1982)

"The Light of the World": Supplement to *Anthroposophical Movement* Vol. 31.2 (Feb. 1954)

"Owen Barfield and the Origin of Language": *Towards* 1.2 (June 1978); 1.3 (Dec. 1978)

FORM IN POETRY

Pater's tranquil insistence that "all art constantly aspires towards the condition of music", cutting, as it did, a new path through the wilderness of sentimental criticism, has led, nevertheless, to some confusion of thought among those who would follow this path too far. It is a confusion that is especially marked in the conception of poetry which some modern art-critics are developing. "Matter" and "form" in poetry are often defined from false analogies with the other arts and then sharply distinguished in such a way that criticism carried to its logical conclusion becomes a mere parody of itself.

In a picture, says the critic, what does the "story" matter? Of what importance — artistically — is the photographic accuracy of its representation of nature? It is the form, and the form only, that matters, the blending of the colours and the significance of the lines. Then he turns to poetry and discusses it in the same terms. The meaning behind the words, any message that they have for the brain is treated as "matter", while the euphonious arrangement of them, the music of stress and cadence is "form". There are aesthetic experts who have carried this so far as to assert that the intellectual content of a poem is actually a burden which obstructs its aesthetic appeal. Hey-diddle-diddle ranks as an idyll, and we seem to hear them saying that all poetry constantly aspires towards the condition of musical nonsense.

Analogies between different forms of art are valuable in so far as they help to increase appreciation (the *raison d'être* of all criticism), but they are never entirely satisfactory, and, where they are falsely drawn, must do more harm than good. It is, then, worth while examining closely this question of form in poetry.

It is not in its wide distinction between matter and form that such criticism as the above misses the mark, but in its interpretation of these two words as applied to poetry. What do we mean by poetic form? What is it in poetry that is analogous to that constructing, that fashioning or combining, of material which seems to be the essential feature of the other arts? Now, a word is the final objective record for each person of the whole series of thoughts or sense-impressions received by him every time he has spoken or heard that word. Repeat it, and certain of these thoughts or sense-impressions are revived in his memory — associations are called up which, ever since he first learnt the word, have been rearranging and colouring themselves subconsciously in his memory. When two or more words are heard or read in juxtaposition, the set of associations clustering round the first word is immediately brought into touch with that different set, which grows and spreads from the second in such a way that some of their innumerable ramifications must intermingle in the mind. Moreover, each word reacts delicately upon the other, emphasising some of its associations, blurring some, and eliciting from the recesses of the subconscious mind, many which in any other context would have slept undisturbed. It is just this blending and harmonising of remembered impressions that constitutes true form in poetry, and it is here that poetry satisfies our aesthetic sense, our desire for and emotional appreciation of that form.

The marriage of epithet and noun presents the simplest illustration of this. The poet who places epithet and noun in a new and beautiful relation creates in us a new "state of memory" — a "form" which the emotions instinctively recognize as having aesthetic significance.

> And I made a rural pen
> And I stained the water clear...

says Blake in "The Piper". What a vapid colourless word "rural" can be! "Rural scenery", "rural neighbourhood" — the phrases have an idiotic guidebook sound about them! That is because in such chords there is too great a consonance — the harmony of them is trite and outworn. Blake, the artist, joins "rural" to the word "pen" and so strikes a beautiful discord; for the two words have only their remotest harmonics, as it were, in common — distant, bell-like reverberations of themselves, which meet and mingle undetected in the memory, till the epithet becomes a thing full of life, infinitely suggestive.

Of this particular corner of poetic form — the choice of epithet — perhaps Milton is the absolute master:

> Sometimes with *secure delight*,
> The upland hamlets will invite...

The "pert fairies", the "dapper elves", or the "lubber fiend" — who can forget them? And there are a thousand other examples. Or think of Keats' magic use of the word "rich":

> Or if thy mistress some rich anger shows...

and

> Now more than ever seems it rich to die...

This "form" or harmonious arrangement of the memory which has been exemplified in its simplest aspect is the body of each line and of the whole poem. It is the body of such a couplet as:

> She *ran* upon the *platforms* of the *wind*
> And laughed to hear the fireballs roar behind.

It is the body of a whole poem such as Mr Yeats' "Lake Isle of Innisfree".

I have chosen only the more startling romantic examples, but the truth is one that underlies all real poetry, and there are times when naked simplicity is of a greater *formal* beauty than romance. It will be clear that there is not in a poem the same wholeness of form and interdependence of the parts as there may be, say, in a picture. Detached lines and paragraphs retain their significance in isolation in a way that is not comparable with any other art. Sometimes a sonnet or very short lyric may be an almost indivisible creation — such, for instance, as Mr de la Mare's "Here lies a most beautiful lady" — but it remains true from the strictly aesthetic point of view that "there is no such thing as a long poem" — only a connected series of short ones.

The poet's material, then, is memory. He fashions and rearranges it, as the sculptor fashions his marble or the musician rearranges vibrations in the air. He expresses his individuality not so much in his choice of words as in his combination of them, in those particular associations out of all the innumerable ones that each word is father to, which, by his arrangement of them, are set vibrating most intensely in the memory. Thus Milton, who, like Virgil, was essentially a "language-poet", tends to bring out the historical, almost the philological, personality of the words he uses:

> A daughter fair
> So buxome, blithe, and debonair...

or

> I come to pluck your berries harsh and *crude...*

while Keats picks out from their texture the more purely sensuous threads with such art that he can make a grocer's catalogue big with romance:

> While he from forth the closet brought a heap
> Of candied apple, quince, and plum, and gourd;
> With jellies soother than the creamy curd,
> And lucent syrops tinct with cinnamon....

or, again,

> Full on this casement shone the wintry moon
> And threw warm gules on Madeline's fair breast...

Think how Milton would have used the word "gules"! His line would have had the ancient flavour of heraldic lore; it would have affected us like some gorgeously illuminated manuscript.

Enough has been said to show that form in poetry is not merely synonymous with its music. Then what is the position of music — that quality in poetry to which some people would confine its whole aesthetic appeal? It is a part of this form, and an indispensable part. First, the actual mechanical rhythm, poetry's primitive foundation, is a *sine qua non.* There can be no poetry without it, though there may be musical or beautiful prose. Its function is to raise the mind — by almost physical means — to a certain level of appreciative excitement or exaltation. It is like the richness of colour in a picture or the timbre of the note in music. At this level, too, combinations of words or ideas which might normally appear forced and unreal are accepted without demur by the imagination; and it is the one thing which explains the toleration — for whole periods at a time — of an inflated "poetic diction" such as that which burdened the unfortunate eighteenth century in England. But music is something that transcends all this. It is a beauty fashioned by instinct out of alliteration, assonance, and all the varying cadences that arise from the delicate superimposing of the natural speech-rhythm on a regular verse-rhythm. This music is quite inseparable from what I have described as "form", for an unmusical phrase can never even "mean" the same as a musical one. The finer and more elusive of the word-associations are not elicited and blended in the same way, so that the state of memory produced by one is different from that produced by the other. Moreover, phrases of a *different* music must convey a different meaning. For example, an epithet following its noun does not mean quite the same as it does in its normal position in front. Once again, Milton is the storehouse from which we can draw the best examples:

> In service high and anthems clear…

or

> Meadows trim with daisies pied…

or, best of all,

> Teiresias and Phineus, prophets old…

The difference is inexplicable and varies with each example but it is undoubtedly there.

It is possible — just possible — that this effect of the music upon the meaning is traceable to some remotely onomatopoeic reminiscence that still lingers unconscious in the language. Conscious, recognizable onomatopoeia, however, exists side by side with music; it is not a part of it.

> Forlorn, the very word is like a bell
> To toll me back from thee to my sole self…

It is not only because they are onomatopoetic that these lines are musical, for music is something greater than imitation.

Nevertheless, it is true that music in poetry, inseparable as it is from form, has a certain value as well. We can say of a refrain such as "Hey nonny nonny"[1] or "Whipsy-diddley-dandy-dee"[2] that it is or is not musical. But even in such cases as these the music has a special value in its own context. "Hey nonny nonny", as it stands alone, has a certain music in it and no sense. By itself it is musical nonsense; yet it requires some effort to imagine a poem composed entirely of variations on the two words "hey" and "nonny". Put the refrain in its context, and at once its music has become a part of the music of the whole song, besides which it now expresses *by its music* what it is meant to express — something which is the opposite to "sounds of woe". Similarly, on lower levels, "Whipsy-diddley-dandy-dee" has a certain air of *abandon* about it, which serves well enough to express the rather self-conscious "dogginess" of that uxorious young batrachian! It is useless, then, to point to some of Shakespeare's songs as examples of musical nonsense. It is just because they are musical that they are not nonsense. Their music is their sense and has its own effect on the arrangement of the memory, dealing perhaps with the subconscious rather than the conscious associations.

These are the things that go to make up form in poetry. It might seem at first sight that, after all, it does not matter very much — that the various elements of poetry will remain the same, whatever names you find for them or however you alter their classification. It is true that the old labels or rather the old way of distributing the labels were good enough, so long as everyone clearly understood what these labels meant. But words change their meaning. They are changing them all the time as surely and imperceptibly as men are changing their skins. Art critics begin to put the word "form" into inverted commas; soon it comes to mean something slightly different; then the inverted commas are dropped, and confusion is inevitable, unless our ideas and especially the terms in which we express them are carefully readjusted. Moreover, it is through these readjustments themselves that criticism gradually approaches nearer to the truth. It can never go all the way; but definitions, generalisations, epigrams containing half-truths are all like so many searchlights playing upon an airship at night. The airship can never be seen as clearly as in the daytime; its upper half can never be seen at all. Nevertheless, the more searchlights the better, for if the latest beam falls on a spot already illuminated, then that spot is made a little brighter; if it reaches to some part hitherto unlit, then there is light upon one more facet of the unknowable; we are one step nearer to perfect appreciation.

GREEK THOUGHT IN ENGLISH WORDS

There is so much of it, that I had better begin by defining the limited scope of this essay. I am not, then, concerned with words like *drama*, *episode*, *paragraph*, *climax*, *hysteria*, all of which may be considered as pointers to history in general, rather than to the history of thought in particular. Nor again with little etymological poems like the "nut-leaved" (καρυόφυλλον) *gillyflower* or the "swallow-wort" (χελιδόνιον) called *celandine*, nor with the dubious divinity latent in *panic*, nor the snug immortality (ἀθανασία) that nods to us in the familiar *tansy*. All these words are derived from Greek, and so are many of those with which I shall attempt to deal; but not all. I am concerned with Greek thought, still traceable in an English word, whether or not the word itself is a Greek derivative.

On the other hand the history of Western thought is so complex and interpenetrating, that there may well be few abstract words of any sort in which omniscience, or even erudition, would fail to detect a Greek influence at some point in the historical processes which produced their present-day meaning. The vocabulary of the English New Testament is an obvious example. I shall limit myself to cases in which the Greek influence is *directly* traceable.

The facility with which the English language goes on creating imaginary Latin and Greek words to meet the expanding needs of science and philosophy seems to me to bring with it one disadvantage. Indispensable as such comparatively recent labels as *centralization*, *positivism*, *cleptomania*, *anaesthetic*, etc., undoubtedly are, it is a pity that their increasing plethora should tend to mask the historical strength and dignity of genuine Latin and Greek formations — of old words like *essence*, *intelligence*, *hypothesis*, *mechanics*, *analogy*. Many educated people would be surprised at the antiquity of some of these modern-sounding terms; they would be surprised to learn that *hypotenuse* and *isosceles* date back to the misty origins of Pythagorean philosophy, while *astronomy*, *grammatical*, *phenomenon*, *economic*, *cosmogony*, *physical*, *theory*, *hypothesis*, *eclipse*, and many others — that is to say the Greek compounds of which they are anglicized forms — were all in use before Plato began to teach. I propose to notice more particularly a handful of English words which owe either their origin or some essential part of their meaning to the Greek philosophers.

The first of all is, of course, *philosopher* itself — a word believed, according to Liddell and Scott, to have been coined by Pythagoras as a label for himself and his followers — "lovers of wisdom". *Cosmos* is another example of a word which goes back to the Pythagorean school, carrying our minds along with it to the "shapeliness" and harmony which these early philosophers perceived reigning in the universe. Among the words for which Liddell and Scott give no earlier quotation than Plato, and which may possibly, therefore, have been created by him, are *antipodes* (*Timaeus*), *criterion*, *enthusiasm*, *dialectic*, *theology*, *mathematical*, *synthesis*, and *analogy*, while we seem to owe to Aristotle *energy*, *ethics*, *physiology*, *fantasy* and *fancy*, *synonym*, *entelechy* and, of course, *metaphysics* — which is a mere catalogue title for the treatise written next after the *Physics*.

Now many of these words are extremely important landmarks in the history of consciousness, denoting as they do either new modes of intellection or a more exact and conscious application of modes already in force before their appearance. Thus, the interest is not merely philological. Examining these common English words, we are reminded, for instance, of the rapidity with which the intricacies of Greek philosophy grew up out of the old mythological outlook that preceded it; we find them indicating with some precision the gradual evolution of intellectual faculties whose enjoyment we are apt to take for granted, faculties which anthropologists will sometimes even project back into the minds of the most primitive peoples. The naturalistic theory of myth, for example, is based on the assumption that "pithecanthropus erectus" confronted a sunrise with the same sort of curiosity that the apple aroused in Newton. It is a useful imaginative exercise, therefore, to try and strip our mental apparatus of all that part of it which is due to the employment of such words by generations of intellectual forebears, and then to see what is left. We may find it difficult to conceive of a time when the logical process of observing *phenomena* (things "appearing" or "seen") and forming *theories* to account for their relationship was unknown; yet the semantic development of the word θεωρία from its original meaning of mere contemplation or onlooking seems to confirm that this is so; while the two words *analogous* and *analytic*, the one invented, as we may believe, by Plato and the other by Aristotle, make an excellent starting-point for an imaginative reconstruction of the whole of the logical faculty.

Plato and Socrates, like most of the philosophers before them, dealt with feelings and thoughts, and even words, to some extent as though they were living beings.

They related them to one another in accordance with what they conceived to be their own intrinsic natures, proving their points by *analogy*, and by *etymology* (i.e. the relation between words and things); it was only later, when men began to have a different feeling of the nature of thought, and of their own relation to the thoughts which passed through their minds, that this kind of reasoning came to be criticized as mere verbal quibbling. Thus, there is really no way of translating words like λόγος, λογικός, λογίζεσθαι, as they are used by Plato. *Reason* is quite inadequate to convey to a twentieth-century imagination the cosmic process which Plato must have felt to be taking place — as much out in the world and among the stars as "within" his own mind — when he spoke of τὸ λογιστικόν or contrasted νοῦς and ἐπιστήμη with δόξα.[1] It was not until the "analytic" method of thought arose with Aristotle that such a word as *logic* could begin to take on its modern meaning. Indeed its strictly technical sense cannot be traced further back than a passage in which Cicero uses the Greek phrase λογική τέχνη in reference to the syllogistic method. *Syllogism* itself is first found with that meaning in Aristotle's works, and so "logic", that exclusively subjective process, is revealed to us as something which the mind only discovered when it began to turn outward to "matter". In analysing its environment, it seems, and submitting itself humbly to the results of observation, the mind first began to feel its own shape and parts, much as the fingers discover their relation to one another when they are trying to fit themselves into a glove.

The rich legacy bequeathed by Greek philosophy to the English language is further masked by the fact that many of its terms have come to us in the form of Latin translations. For example, the simple *quality* and *quantity*, obvious as they seem and absolutely indispensable as they are to our thinking, are Latin translations* of two Greek words invented by Plato and Aristotle or one of their respective contemporaries. These are ποιότης, which it looks as if Plato himself coined† to express the notion of "of-what-sortness" or "quiddity", and ποσότης ("how-much-ness"), which was used by Aristotle. Among the Latin words which appear to be conscious translations of terms in special use among the Greek philosophers down to and including Plato are *qualitas*, *aer* [air], *essentia* (οὐσία), *idealis* (ἐπ' ἰδέᾳ or ἐπ' εἴδει), *individuum* (ἄτομον), *vacuum* (τὸ κενόν), and *equivocalis* (ὁμώνυμος). When we come to Aristotle, we find a much greater number. *Quantitas* has already been mentioned, and there are in addition *subjectum* (ὑποκείμενον), *actualis* (ἐνεργείᾳ), *potentialis* (δυνάμει), *substantia* (ὑπόσταοις), *quintessentia* (πέμπτγ οὐσία), *proprietas* [*property*] (ἰδίωμα), *accidens* (συμβεβηκός), *praedicamentum* (κατηγορία), *deductio* (ἀπαγωγή), *inductio* (ἐπαγωγή), *moralis* (ἠθικός), and almost certainly *definitio* (ὁρισμός).

For about two thirds of these extremely useful expressions Cicero is responsible. He tells us more than

* Qualitates igitur appellavi, quas ποιότητας Graeci appellant, quod ipsum apud Graecos non est vulgi verbum, sed philosophorum; atque id in multis. Dialecticorum vero verba nulla sunt publica, suis, utuntur. Et id quidem commune omnium fere est artium; aut enim nova sunt rerum novarum facienda nomina aut ex aliis transferenda. Cicero: *Academicae Quaestiones*, i, 25.

† ...τὸ μὲν πάσχον αἰσθητήν ἀλλ᾽ οὐκ αἴσθησιν ἔτι γίγνεσθαι, τὸ δὲ ποιοῦν ποιόν τι ἀλλ᾽ οὐ ποιότητα; ἴσως οὖν ἡ ποιότης ἅμα ἀλλόκοτόν τε φαίνεται ὄνομα καὶ οὐ μανθάνεις ἀθρόον λεγόμενον. Plato, *Theaetetus*, 182A.

once how he had deliberately set himself to render this service to his country, and it is often possible to find the exact passage in which, usually with some comment of half-humorous apology, he converts the Greek into Latin. Thus, we owe to his efforts *quality*, *individual* (for it was formed by the Schoolmen from his *individuum*), *vacuum*, *moral*,* *property*, *induction*, *element*, and probably *definition* and *difference*, though only in two cases — *individual* and *moral* — have we made the best possible use of his services, by retaining the Greek originals, *atom* and *ethical*, and adopting Cicero's words alongside of them as doublets with a different shade of meaning. Cicero also enriched his native vocabulary with many translations of Greek words in use among later Greek philosophers but not found in Plato or Aristotle — particularly the Stoics, whose ethical doctrines were soon to take such a firm hold on the intellectual life of imperial Rome, and whose metaphysic remains even today deeply imbedded in our thought. Such are *notio* (ἔννοια or πρόληψις),† *comprehensio* (κατάληψις), *infinitio* (ἀπειρία),‡ and *appetitio* (ὁρμή).

It is not easy to determine the date of the others. Some were probably translated by obscure Greek schoolmasters in Rome, and others by medieval Schoolmen whom it would be a long labour to identify. For the rest, *accidens* is found in Seneca, *essentia* and *substantia* in Quintilian, *idealis* in Martianus Capella (A.D. 425), and it seems possible that *praedicamentum* was the work of St. Augustine.

* Eam partem philosophiae "de moribus" appellare solemus; sed decet augentem linguam Latinam nominare "moralem". *De Fato* I.

† Notionem appello, quod Graeci tum ἔννοιαν tum πρόληψιν dicunt (*Topica* 7, 31).

‡ Infinitio ipsa, quam ἀπειρίαν vocant (*De Finibus* i, 21).

But more interesting in a great many ways than the appearance of new words is the penetration of new meanings into the old ones. When we are dealing with ancient literatures of which only a fragment is still extant, we can often date these elusive phenomena and trace them to their sources more exactly than the words themselves. If, for example, we can never be quite sure that such a word as ἀνάλογος[2] was not used until Plato used it, we need have no doubt about the new *meanings* which his writings, and no others, have injected into words like θεωρία, μέθοδος,[3] μουσικός,[4] and ἰδέα — or into φιλεῖν and καλός, and through them, into the English *love* and *beautiful*. Of the words subsequently borrowed into English, which were re-baptized in the same way by Aristotle, *syllogism* has already been mentioned, and one could add *category*, *poetic*, *politic*, *axiom*, *problem*, *synthesis*, *mathematical*, *dynamic*, and others.

Some knowledge of the semantic history of such words is practically essential to an historical understanding of our Western outlook. Certainly we no longer feel, with the earlier etymologists, that by finding out what a word once meant we can learn what it means or "ought to mean" now. Yet, for this very reason, it is of great interest to trace out the way in which the modern meanings of such important instruments of thought have been arrived at; to try and see what our ancestors made them signify before us and what we have done with the legacy they bequeathed. What, for instance, of *ideas* – those curious abstractions which, in spite of their spaceless quality, we can scarcely avoid thinking of now as flitting about somewhere "inside" our heads? Once again the history of the word seems to carry us back to a time when the human mind could have no such experience, when it could not think of its own thoughts, or "apperceive", as the psychologists used to say; and once again Plato and Aristotle appear to have played an important part in the development of that faculty.

Until Plato's time the word *idea* (from ἰδεῖν, to see) meant the form or appearance of a thing. Most people are familiar enough with the later Platonic doctrine of Ideas to know that they were understood by Plato, not as something which existed solely in his own mind, but as eternal Beings which stood behind the ever-changing forms of material nature. Distrusting the information gained from the senses because of the obvious transience of all sense-phenomena, the Academics would only give the name of knowledge (ἐπιστήμη) to the contemplation by the human soul of these underlying and undying Ideas. Aristotle, who was Plato's pupil, took over from him this doctrine of Ideas and proceeded to refashion it more in accordance with his own metaphysical outlook. He insisted that the ἰδέαι or εἴδη,* as he preferred to call them, were, as we should say, immanent, that they existed *in* the objects and could have no being apart from them. In order to get at them, it was necessary not so much to be initiated into the Mysteries and to sink yourself in philosophic contemplation of the eternal, as to investigate nature herself with all the means of accuracy at your disposal.

It is convenient here, to say a word or two concerning the word *theory*. Both to Plato and to Aristotle the Greek θεωρεῖν meant, not hypothesis but contemplation. It expressed the act, not of a speculator, but of a spectator.

* Plato had also used εἶδος as a synonym for ἰδέα, but less frequently.

It meant, not the result of the investigation of nature but the investigating, or rather, the beholding itself. In his *Psychology*, Aristotle makes a special use of the verb θεωρεῖν. The word which Plato used for knowledge (ἐπιστήμη) he seems to relegate to an unconscious or sleeping phase of the soul. The "knowledge" which the soul possesses ὡς ἐπιστήμη is potential only. But in the process of contemplating particulars this is changed into knowledge ὡς τὸ θεωρεῖν, and it is this which is the soul's entelechy. It is in this process that she may truly be said to awaken. It will be seen that such a meaning, although nearer to the modern meaning than Plato's, is still a very long way from it. The word appears to have come into English through medieval Latin translations of Aristotle. But the earliest example the Oxford Dictionary records of its use in the commonest modern sense of a *particular* hypothesis or speculation is at the end of the eighteenth century. It would involve too long a digression to do more than suggest that Goethe was endeavouring, in his scientific writings, to restore a less superficial meaning to this ancient and honourable term; particularly when he said, speaking of Nature: "Her phenomenon *is* theory, if only we can find it."

To revert now to the word *idea*, this does not seem to have been borrowed by English writers until the dawn of the Renaissance, when Lydgate used *Idee* with a definite Platonic allusion; and the earliest uses in English are all literary and allusive. Thus, it is often spelt with a capital letter, as by Spenser in his *Hymns* to *Love* and *Beauty*, or by Drayton who used *Idea* as the title for a sequence of love-sonnets. But by the end of the sixteenth century the word had gained a firmer footing in the English language. For example:

> Xenophon in his Ciropaedia... having... under the person of Cirus, framed an idaea or perfect patterne of an excellent prince...

In such a sentence as the above, which is quoted from the Oxford Dictionary, it is noticeable that the word is used — probably metaphorically — to describe a pattern *existing in the mind of the writer.* Soon it acquired also the sense of a standard or principle to be aimed at, and the word *ideal* was adopted at about the same time. Meanwhile we find Shakespeare, and others, using it to express an image or picture retained by the memory:

> Th' Idea of her life shal sweetly creepe
> Into his study of imagination. ...
> — *Much Ado* IV, i, 226

while for Milton it has already weakened so much that it implies little more than a conception of something that ought to be done:

> That voluntary Idea, which hath long in silence presented itself to me, of a better education... than hath yet been in practice.

But now the philosophers were to take hold of the word again. In 1690 John Locke wrote in the introduction to his *Essay on the Human Understanding*:

> I must here in the entrance beg pardon of my reader for the frequent use of the word *idea*, which he will find in the following treatise. It being that term, which, I think, serves best to stand for whatsoever is of the understanding when a man thinks, I have used it to express whatever is meant by *phantasm*, *notion*, *species*, or *whatever it is which the mind can be employed about in thinking*; and I could not avoid frequently using it.

He certainly could not; and after reading a few chapters of the *Essay*, we have no difficulty in realizing the part played by seventeenth-century philosophy in giving to the word that wide and colourless meaning of "any concept", which it has retained since the eighteenth century.

Yet the doctrine which these philosophers were actually combating was no longer that of the objective reality of ideas, but that of innate ideas (κοιναὶ ἔννοιαι) or, to use Cicero's word, *notions*. These were held to be present, subjectively, in every individual mind, from the date of birth; for without them, it was thought, the human mind would never have been able to apprehend abstract principles. As to the Platonic, and objective, or semi-objective, meaning, perhaps the most striking thing about the biography of the word in English is the rapidity with which this was discarded. What was the cause? We must look for it in the outlook of the age in which this word was borrowed, and this we can examine most easily by penetrating behind it.

Like the Greek philosophers themselves, Cicero, and others who translated their terminology, would commonly, instead of creating a new word, employ a Latin one already in existence. In so doing, they often drastically altered its meaning. We can, for example, trace the influence of Greek philosophy in our word *universal*, adopted from the Latin *universalis*, which was used by Quintilian to translate the Aristotelian καθολικός.* *Matter*, which reached us through French from the old Latin *materia*, plainly embodies the new meaning given to that word by Lucretius and other Roman writers who employed it

* Praecepta, quae καθολικὰ vocant; id est (ut dicamus quomodo possumus) universalia, vel perpetualia. Quintilian II, 13, 14.

to translate the Greek ὕλη, and its older, purely Roman, and severely practical meaning is perceived in the later French *matérial*, and of course, our English derivative, *material.* Among the Latin words, subsequently adopted into English, which Cicero renewed with draughts of Greek thought are *elementa* (found constantly in Lucretius, but used by Cicero to translate Aristotle's στοιχεῖα), *definire* (ὁρίζειν), *differre* (διαφέρειν) (old meaning "to put off" or "delay"), *instantia* (ἔνστασις), and *scientia* (ἐπιστήμη). *Scientia* in Latin had been used to express the knowledge or consciousness of some particular fact, never absolutely for *knowledge* or *science.* In the same way Cicero employed *imago* — a bust or statue (generally of an ancestor) — to translate the Greek εἴδωλον,* which was popular among the Stoics in the sense of a mental image. No doubt it is partly due to this that we find Virgil and Horace using *imago* for "phantom" or "ghost", and we may suppose a sort of fusion of both meanings in the new verb *imaginor*, with the derivative *imaginatio*, which occur in Pliny and Tacitus.

But perhaps the most interesting of all these words is *species*. Derived, like ἰδέα, from a verb meaning "to

* ...imagines, quae εἴδωλα nominant, quorum incursione non solum videamus sed etiam cogitemus. *De Finibus* I, 21. Cicero is referring to the peculiar Democritan theory of perception, which explained sight as caused by the impact on the eye of films or husks thrown off in endless procession from the surfaces of objects. Those "images" were also supposed to penetrate through the pores of the body to the mind, thus causing mental impressions. εἴδωλον had been used by Homer for "phantom", by Plato and Aristotle for images reflected in the water, etc., and so for unreal mental fancies. The technical sense which Cicero translated into *imago* is due to its use by the Stoics; the theological, which we have adopted with the word, to its use in the Septuagint. Bacon's attempt, in the *Advancement of Learning*, to revive its psychological reference (*idols of the cave, idols of the market-place, idols of the theatre*, and *idols of the tribe*) was never taken up.

see", and possessing accordingly the meaning of "form" or "appearance" (in late Latin a pretty girl was *virgo speciosa*) it was seized on by Cicero to translate the Platonic idea. In his *Academicae Quaestiones* (I. viii. 30) we find him writing:

> Quamquam oreretur a sensibus, tamen non esse iudicium veritatis in sensibus. Mentem volebant (sc. Academici et Peripatetici) rerum esse iudicem: solam censebant idoneam cui crederetur, quia sola cerneret id, quod semper esset simplex, et unius modi et tale quale esset. Hanc illi ἰδέαν appellabant, iam a Platone ita nominatam, nos recte *speciem* possumus dicere.[5]

Cicero does not seem to have stressed the difference between the Academic and Peripatetic schools, and so, in the natural course of events, *species* came to be regarded as the received translation of the Aristotelian εἰδος. But what is especially curious is that Aristotle's third century commentator, Porphyry, and after him the early Schoolmen, apparently transplanted this term out of his Metaphysics and into his Logic. At any rate, according to the Oxford Dictionary, the Latin *species* first appears in Scholastic philosophy as the second of Aristotle's predicables (κατηγορικά). Aristotle himself in his *Topics* only recognizes four: γένος (*genus*), ὅρος (*definitio*), ἴδιον (*proprietas*) [property], and συμβεβηκός (*accidens*). This system was modified by Porphyry, who omitted ὅρος and inserted εἶδος (*species*) with διαφορά (*differentia*).

A new term had accordingly to be found to convey the wider metaphysical meaning of ἰδέα or εἶδος, and the Schoolmen fixed upon *universale*. For years the contest raged between the three rival schools of thought,

Platonic Realism, with its doctrine of "Universalia ante rem", Aristotelian Realism ("Universalia in re"); and Nominalism ("Universalia post rem"). But we are the less surprised to see Nominalism carrying the day at last in the majority of minds, when we know that in the third century of the Christian era, a commentator like Porphyry had already unconsciously indicated that he could not help taking a more subjective view of "species". And this fact does suggest that, with all the exceptions,* anticipations, and throwbacks, besides a sort of general recapitulation in the Middle Ages, there has been a more or less regular historical progression in the metaphysical outlook, the *Weltanschauung* of the Western world.

In Aristotle's system — after Plato's death — the Ideas are dragged down from heaven into nature; then, in the Middle Ages, they move, as abstractions, out of nature into the classifying and "naming" mind of man, where they are soon firmly entrenched by the increasing subjectivism of Descartes, Berkeley and Kant. When the natural science of the eighteenth and nineteenth centuries began to question the dogma of a "special" creation it was, of course, carrying the matter a stage further. For, after first evolving a subtle but useful distinction between physiological and morphological "species", it announced that to those who took long enough views, there were really no such things as species at all. "All", in Empedocles's phrase, "was one"; and the species were only "categories" invented by the mind of man for its own convenience. At the beginning

* Parmenides, for instance, one of Socrates' dialectical opponents, displayed decided Nominalistic tendencies.

of Plato's career, and afterwards again in the Middle Ages, your opinion of "universals", of which *species* was only one, was expected to be consistent with itself. If you wished to believe that the species Lion existed before or with individual lions, you also believed that the species Triangle existed before or with individual triangles, and that the same was true of Chair and chairs. Plato himself, however, by the time he wrote *Timaeus*, had apparently ceased to consider the existence of any Ideas, other than those of ζῷα (animal or vegetable creatures) and of the four elements. Philosophy had thus achieved, by the end of his life, an *implicit* distinction, at any rate, between logic and ontology. It remained for the Dark and Middle Ages to entangle once more, by misinterpreting Aristotle, the twin threads which the Greeks had almost succeeded in unpicking. By endeavouring to prove empirically that the difference between a lion and a lamb was of the same artificial and "nominal" nature as the difference between a chair and a table, the nineteenth-century biologists raised the old question once more in a form which made it seem a burning issue; and, for a time, at all events, few educated men could remain wholly indifferent to the problem of the "origin of species".

It was, I suppose, at about the time when the ἰδέα of Plato and the εἶδος of Aristotle were finally disappearing into the Darwinian *species*, that the Latin word which Cicero had used to translate their ἐπιστήμη finished its metamorphosis into our hard-worked present-day "*Science*". Here is another of those interesting parallels between the native term and the classically borrowed equivalent, or near-equivalent, in which the English language is so rich: *science* and *knowledge*. I have already indicated that there are other and more refined parallels to be absorbed between the Greek word and its Latin equivalent, both of which have often been anglicized with more or less divergent meanings. We may compare *individual* and *atom*, *moral* and *ethical*, *potential* and *dynamic*, *universal* and *catholic*, *predicament* and *category*. And I have been speaking at some length of *idea* and *species*.

Perhaps the English word *kind* bears much the same relation to *species* as *knowledge* does to *science*. It is a simple word, not very precise but much richer in suggestion than its parallel. It has not been bullied and argued about in the way that so many of the classical borrowings have been and therefore seems out of place when we want to suggest anything systematic. The "origin of kinds" would not do at all. On the other hand, how much poorer the language would have been if, in welcoming Cicero's *species* with both hands, we had altogether abandoned its Greek prototype *idea*!

With this reflection I find myself already over the borders of the pleasant, if dangerous, realm of might-have-been, and I cannot quite forbear some further speculations — speculations which take their rise in linguistics, but lead beyond it. I have mentioned Cicero's use of *scientia* — a word with a more limited meaning — to translate ἐπιστήμη. The particularity of the Latin term seems to have continued in two different ways to attach to its English derivative. We reflect a pragmatical and Roman attitude to "knowledge", when we speak of such things as "domestic science" or the "science of boxing": meaning thereby a systematic study of some skill or calling intended to lead to its practical mastery. On the other hand, when *Science* is used today to signify purely theoretical knowledge, its meaning is limited in another and, I suggest, confusing way. For it signifies not merely systematic knowledge (which would in itself be a limitation) but knowledge acquired in a particular way. It implies for most people — and strongly suggests for all — knowledge acquired by the same method as that by which knowledge of physics and mechanics is acquired, the exactness of which depends on measurement. Yet such a connotation is in fact quite inappropriate to many of its most characteristic references, for the viability of this method varies enormously, I might almost say grotesquely, between one so-called "science" and another. There is indeed a sort of graduated scale of fitness.

It is well adapted to the science of mechanics, slightly less well so to physics, less still to biology, much less to medicine or sociology, and to psychology hardly at all. I believe much harm has resulted from the long and desperate struggle to jockey all these realms of enquiry with the strait-waistcoat of *science*. To the extent that inquiries cover the morphology or behaviour of living beings, above all when the beings concerned are human (and therefore include the inquirer himself), both their effectiveness and their exactness depend less on tabulation and more on such things as imagination, insight and self-knowledge. We need a word to distinguish, for instance, the equipment of a successful psychologist from the unsystematic "knowledge" of human nature which endues many people whom no one would dream of calling psychologists. Most of us number such people among our acquaintance. Shakespeare, Goethe, Sir Walter Scott and many other writers have left monumental records of the sort I have in mind. Yet — however often we may find in some casual sentence from (let us say) the Waverley Novels, a penetration into human motivation and human self-deception, about which practicing psychologists often appear to be more ponderous rather than more exact — the distinction still remains between a systematic and an unsystematic study of such matters. I have pointed out that the English language had been using *species* for a long time before it went back to the source and borrowed its prototype, *idea*. Is it very fanciful to imagine a more enlightened age in which medicine and psychology and the like would be recognized for what they are, neither *sciences* at one end, nor vague *knowledges* at the other, but — *epistemies*?

I sometimes wish the well of English would not go on being quite so undefiled. Nowadays, when writers make a raid of this sort on the treasure-house of Greek thought they will insist on remaining macaronic and italic. Otherwise a borrowing of the very kind I have just been suggesting — but this time from Hellenistic Greek — would actually have been effected, I believe, within the last decade. Between the all too systematic associations of *charity* — trailing clouds of poor-law and blankets — on the one side and the all too ambivalent *love* — meaning anything from Hollywood to the Bhagavad Gita — on the other, certain theological writers have shown an increasing tendency to introduce the Pauline *agapé*. Any thoughtful Christian must, I think, agree that this is all to the good, for here is a depth and body of essential meaning unblurred as yet by irrelevancies; this is all to the good; but why not *agapy*?

Quo Musa tendis?[6] And yet speculations of this kind are not perhaps quite as idle as they may appear at first sight. It is not necessary, and it is probably fallacious, to attribute much causal significance to the limitations of a nation's vocabulary. *Causa sine qua non*[7] perhaps, but hardly *causa causans*.[8] But forms of expression, whether or no they help to shape the forms of thought, are facts. And if you are inclined to wonder and reflect, it is better to reflect on facts than to reflect only on other people's reflections. It is well on a summer day to climb a high hill and take an extensive view of the varied face of nature; but it is also well to kneel on the grass and look long and closely at the growing point of a flowering plant — buttercup, stitchwort or even *tansy*, it does not matter which. A wide prospect is good, but so also is a certain depth of insight into particular goings on. Indeed the one is needed to give life and substance to the other. So it is with nature; and so it is, I believe, with the mind of man.

GIORDANO BRUNO AND THE SURVIVAL OF LEARNING

WITHIN THE DOMAIN of literary criticism one of the changes that has come about in my time is a kind of re-establishment of Rhetoric as a respectable category. I expect it began earlier; but it is noticeable that in 1936 Professor I. A. Richards chose, as his title for a collection of essays, *The Philosophy of Rhetoric*. For further examples: Erich Auerbach's *Figura*, much of which was subsequently incorporated in *Mimesis*, first appeared in German in 1944; and in 1957 there was a good deal about Rhetoric in that long and interesting work, Northrop Frye's *Anatomy of Criticism*. I suppose the whole *Scrutiny* development and, later, the New Criticism, can be seen as part of the rehabilitation process, though I am not sure if they made use of the actual word.

The term began to recover its dignity when it began to be realized how much its meaning had changed. It had come to mean, and still meant when I was growing up, simply Oratory; and by that time *any* kind of oratory was beginning to be regarded as ornamental and therefore phoney. One could perhaps say that oratory disappeared from the British Parliament (Churchill being the exception that proves the rule) at about the same time as Rhetoric began to re-appear in critical theory. Its status as a category began to improve, as it came to be better understood how much more than what we mean by "oratory", how many other disciplines, the term Rhetoric covered in Antiquity, and throughout the Middle Ages — and in a diminishing degree for two or three centuries more. Our predecessors often said "rhetoric", where we should say "literature".

It is, I think, also becoming more and more appreciated that the *contracted* meaning of the term, representing as it did a kind of etiolation of the category it stands for, reflected, not just the substitution of one system of terminological classification for another, but something more like a change in people's whole experience of words and ideas and the relation between them. If that is so, the change itself, and therefore the history of Rhetoric, can hardly fail to be interesting. For instance, in E. R. Curtius's *European History and the Latin Middle Ages* there is a brief but pregnant passage on the *Confessions* of St. Augustine, in which the relation is considered between their real *meaning* on the one hand, and on the other hand their *style* — which Curtius describes as that of "antique artistic prose". Is it a relation of contrast only? Do we experience, as we read, the new wine of Christian, or Judaeo-Christian, inwardness struggling helplessly in the old bottle of Roman forensic oratory and its tricks? Oddly enough we do not. It is astonishing — and it is a fascinating literary experience to feel — how snugly and effectively the agonising polarities and contradictions between God and man, between virtue and sin, between good and evil, between nature and grace, have adopted and revitalized those counterbalancing periods and pointed antitheses (the technical skills of *isokolon*, *antitheton*, *homoioteleuton* and the rest), which had long become the principal concern of Greek and Roman literature. In short, continuity rather than substitution is here revealed, certainly as the instrument, perhaps as a *condition* of semantic metamorphosis.

Or one could take the topic — which has even become the psychological problem — of figurative language:

simile, metaphor, symbol. These have been written about and worked over not only in poetic theory (much of which has been concentrated on Metaphor as the very sparking-plug in the internal combustion system called Imagination), but also, from the semantic point of view, as a prime factor in the history of language and indeed of consciousness itself. All very true, but it all began with the Art of Rhetoric and the attention its teachers gave, among much else, to what they called "figures of speech", useful sometimes for ornament and sometimes for persuasion.

There was one other device, to which a good deal more attention was paid by the professors of Oratory than to "figures of speech". Already in classical times, and then down to and including the Renaissance period, it was written about and worked over in something the same way as was to occur later with figurative language. This was the technique of memorizing, which is so important for a speaker. How I envy those lecturers, to whom I sometimes listen, who continue happily and fluently for sixty minutes without any written assistance; and how ashamed I always feel of my own voluminous notes! But I can at least *have* the notes, or script, and have them not too conspicuously evident — a matter of much greater difficulty before the invention of paper. The practical importance of mnemotechnic in the Art of spoken Rhetoric, or Oratory, hardly needs emphasizing. But as with figures of speech (only much earlier), the study of it led to consequences altogether transcending the aims of ornament and persuasion.

Yet, unlike figurative language, this is an aspect of rhetoric which has received very little attention in my time. The Art of Memory seems to be an art that stopped short in the cultivated courts of the Renaissance. But now, as to its development down to and including that time, it is possible to read all about it in a book called *The Art of Memory*, by the Reader in the History of the Renaissance in the University of London, Dr Frances Yates. It was published in 1966; and I strongly recommend anyone who has not already done so to read it. I should be glad to think that, whatever I may have succeeded or failed in doing, I have won it some more readers.

Memory is in the first place, not something we do, but something that happens to us. The *art* of memory is the methodology of artificially stimulating it, so that it becomes something we do as well as something that happens. By tradition this methodology, amid a rich variety of detail, has always been focussed on two central devices: that of Places and that of Images — *Loci* and *Imagines*. Verbal memory, or "learning by heart", as we say, is one thing; but the politician, the advocate or the lecturer without notes had also the problem of fixing in his memory the serial order of whole sections of his discourse and the transitions from one topic to another. For this purpose he was recommended, in the earlier and simpler form of the art, to visualize a building, say a house with a series of rooms (or it might be a theatre) and to suppose himself walking through the house from one room to another. These were the *Loci*, or "Places"; and the next thing was to fill them. Within each room, or disposed about the whole house in its corners and niches, you had to invent, and then to visualize sharply an *image* of some sort: perhaps a statue, perhaps a friend with some outstanding characteristic, perhaps a scene — such as a flogging or a murder — each of which was vividly associated in your mind with something you intended to say, and even with the feeling you would put in to what you were saying.

I have never seriously tried it myself. Such experiments as I have made indicate that it is very hard work and would take up a lot of time, and it is so much easier to make notes and refer to them. But one experience I do have, which easily convinces me that images of place, and particularly of movement from place to place to place, have a strong psychological link with the strength of memory. For reasons into which I need not enter, I sometimes endeavour, at the end of the day, to remember the events and experiences of the day — and even to recall them in inverse order from evening to morning.[1] This I find very difficult. I am always having to go back and fill in the most irritating gaps. With one exception. If the day, or any part of the day, has been spent in travelling — it doesn't matter whether by train or car or on foot — there is no difficulty whatever. Everything falls smoothly in place, in the right order, and with nothing left out. Some further evidence of the link may be found in the fact that Aristotle used the word "topoi" (meaning "places") for the Heads of Discourse — and this has entered firmly into our language in the words *topic* and *commonplace*.

As to the Images, with which the Places were to be occupied, although statues could be employed, it was strongly recommended that they should be *dynamic*. I mentioned the instance of a violent scene. In drama, in motion, in gesture or in some powerful emotion they suggested, they should be (it was taught) *Imagines agentes* — *active* images — if they were to prove really effective; if they were to be effective, that is, in bringing about the transition from natural memory to artificial, or achieved, memory; or, one could say, from passive memory to active memory.

All this is common ground among those who have written on the subject, though it is ground that is not very often trodden. It has also long been known that, at the time of the Renaissance, the passion for Mnemotechnic suddenly swelled in such a surprising way that actual buildings were constructed, to embody the fancied ones. What is new, I believe, in Dr Yates' book is her fully documented, and illustrated, account of the extraordinary "Memory Theatres" of Giulio Camillo and Robert Fludd, and her persuasive arguments for the light which a further study of these could be expected to throw on the design of Shakespeare's Globe Theatre. That, and its underlying argument, which is that the attention given in that time to Mnemotechic (like the attention given in our own to figures of speech) developed in such a way as to transcend its original object. It is this developmental aspect of the subject which I find especially interesting, and which I should like to look at a little more closely.

The Art of Memory is very much concerned with the integration of concepts, drawn originally from Mnemotechnic, into the whole way of thought of a great many prominent thinkers of the Renaissance. Very much; but also very modestly; inasmuch as the author repeatedly emphasizes the need for further work on the subject. Among these thinkers the one who is singled out as the most relevant, and whose writings are accorded the fullest treatment, is Giordano Bruno. It should be added that, as the author of an earlier work, *Giordano*

Bruno and the Hermetic Tradition, Dr Yates is an authority on Bruno; I should suppose the leading authority in the English-speaking world.

Bruno was born in 1548 in Nola, near Naples. He was trained as a Dominican and no doubt received a thoroughly scholastic education from the monks of his convent. At a comparatively early age he fled, first from his convent and then from Italy, and his short life was spent in an uneasy series of sojourns in France, England and Germany, concluding with eight years in the prisons of the Inquisition before he was burnt as a heretic in 1600. It is somewhat of a mystery how, in the course of such a disturbed and restless life, he managed to think as deeply and to write as voluminously as he did. His stay in England endured for something less than two years between 1583 and 1585. Although he aroused resentment in Oxford, which then (as now) had its own antiseptically exclusive brand of philosophy, he was welcomed in London in the enlightened circle that included such figures as Fulk Greville, Sir Philip Sidney and Edmund Spenser. When he left London, it was for Wittenburg; and it has even been argued, not on that ground alone, that he is the prototype of Shakespeare's Hamlet. However that may be, it is doubtful if he ever actually met Shakespeare, who would have been about twenty years old at the time. Of his influence on Spenser, especially evident in the Cantos of Mutability, which conclude the *Faerie Queene*, there can however be no doubt. A number of Bruno's Italian works (he wrote in both Latin and Italian) were published while he was in England, including the *Cena de la Ceneri*, or *Ash-Wednesday Supper*, the account of a philosophical dialogue which took place in Fulk Greville's house in London.

Bruno also published, while he was in England, a book in Latin, which has a very long title that starts with the words *Ars Reminiscendi* and is usually referred to as the *Thirty Seals*. It was followed a few years later by a work on Images called *De Imaginum, Signorum et Idearum Compositione* ("On the Composition of Images, Signs and Ideas"). These are two out of five major works by Bruno, which can be loosely described as "works on memory". I have selected them for reference, because their titles alone (taken in conjunction with what has been said here already) give some indication of their relevance to what I would call the "underlying theme" of Dr Yates' book. The theme is in fact mainly threaded on Bruno, and is developed by showing how precisely the Art of Memory was the mental framework of his whole adventurous metaphysic.

Yet he was not the only philosopher of whom that might be said. Ramon Lull is another outstanding example, and the chapter in the book on Lullism as an Art of Memory is indispensable. Incidentally I do not think anyone who set out to master the philosophy of Bruno — a formidable task — would get very far if he were not prepared to give some preliminary attention to Lull; and very little such attention appears to have been given in my time. But I have had to confine myself to Bruno, and indeed have said little enough even about him. I really have no time to do more than add that the book has immeasurably strengthened and confirmed the tentative picture I had already formed in my own mind of Giordano Bruno, with his voluble and meteoric flittings through Europe, as a kind of philosophical torchbearer of what I shall venture to call the "Renaissance Impulse".

It is with that impulse, and its relation to memory, that I am primarily concerned. I myself first came to it — or I came *at* it — as I suppose most of my contemporaries did, through the Romantic Movement; or, again, let me say "the Romantic Impulse", and I shall be saying something about this word "impulse" a little later. The intimate link between the Romantic Impulse and an intensive study of Shakespeare has often been noticed, especially as regards the growth and development of the concept of Imagination; and it has been nowhere perhaps been better drawn out than in Logan Pearsall Smith's essay on "Four Romantic Words" in the collection called *Words and Idioms*. Lessing, Schlegel, Goethe, Schelling, Coleridge are, I suppose, the great names, though plenty of others were involved. One can hardly survey the literature and criticism of the Romantic period without coming to see Shakespeare too as a torchbearer for Europe, though in rather a different way. Not in his case by travelling, not even during his life at all, but two hundred years after his death, he was the torchbearer certainly of something, but of what? Should we say of the Renaissance impulse itself, an impulse that was not to be fully revealed or realized until later on, in the eighteenth and nineteenth centuries?

That the comparison is a fair one is suggested by the fact that Bruno's name, too, was one to conjure with among the great ones of the Romantic philosophy. It is true that not all those who were enthusiastic about him actually *knew* very much about him. But not all those who were enthusiastic about Shakespeare actually knew very much about Shakespeare. The thought of him was somehow an inspiration; so that Schelling, for instance, could write a philosophical Dialogue and call it "Bruno", although it is not actually about Bruno at all. Bruno was indeed much more concerned with the philosophical than with the poetic imagination. *The Art of Memory* describes part of the *Thirty Seals* as "a kind of a manifesto of the primacy of the imagination in the cognitive process". It is not surprising therefore to find that Coleridge devoured all of Bruno's writings that he could lay hold of. To Bruno he attributed his own leading thought, or rather idea, of universal polarity, and there is a mysterious passage in the *Biographia Literaria*, where he acknowledges the debt, which he says he shared with Schelling, to "the polar logic of Giordano Bruno". It was in point of fact an attempt to pursue the implications of this reference, and to assess the actuality of Coleridge's debt to Bruno that led me on to scrape such acquaintance as I can claim with the writings of Bruno himself.[2]

Readers of C. S. Lewis's volume on the *Sixteenth Century* in the *Oxford History of English Literature* are sure to remember his brief digression on the word "Renaissance", in which he argues with his usual cogency that it can properly mean no more than the "Revival of Learning" in the technical sense — the substitution, for instance, of a classical style in Latin prose for a medieval one. It should suggest, not Bacon and Shakespeare, but Gabriel Harvey and Erasmus. At least, if it were still used with that limited reference, the word would have *some* meaning; but, as it is in fact commonly used, the word has no real meaning at all. It is the name, he says, for a fictitious entity ("some character or quality supposed to be immanent in all the events") — and for the emotional overtones which that non-entity has gradually been collecting around itself.

Roughly speaking, his case is that there was no such thing. Dr Yates, in a number of passages, draws the opposite conclusion. For her, by the time Giulio Camillo had built his wooden Memory-Theatre, "something has happened within the psyche, releasing new powers"; as the result of which "there is a new Renaissance plan of the psyche". Not merely has there in fact been a Renaissance, but it sprang from something that can legitimately be called an impulse. Furthermore this impulse is inseparable from the emergence into a clearer light of consciousness of both the experience and the concept of the faculty of Imagination — or better say the activity of Imagination. Moreover it was just this new Renaissance plan of the psyche that set on fire the poets and the philosophers of the Romantic Movement.

What is particularly interesting is that, in emphasizing as she does the element of novelty in the Renaissance mentality, the author nevertheless rejects the commonplace view. What happened was not a sudden decision, arrived at out of the blue, to repudiate the whole culture of the Middle Ages and put something new in its place. Quite the reverse. We are shown the new Renaissance "plan of the psyche" growing in all detail, and by gentle gradations, out of the old medieval plan; and this at the same time as we are also being shown the practice of Imagination emerging from the Art of Memory.

If she is right, as I believe she is, it must follow that, so far from the Renaissance being merely coterminous with the Revival of Learning, that predominantly academic aspect of it has been, if anything, overstressed. The men of the Renaissance period themselves are partly responsible for this, since many of them stressed it so heavily at the time. Bruno on the other hand was one of those who were aware, even while it was happening, that there was more to it than that — who felt deeply that "something had happened within the psyche". And yet it is also Bruno, whose philosophical development brings out so clearly that other truth, which Lewis emphasized, namely, that the relation between the Renaissance and the Middle Ages was by no means one of absolute contrast. With all his insistence on novelty, and all his exuberant boasting about the outstanding originality of his own contribution, there is never any doubt that Bruno is building on foundations — on a "plan of the psyche" — derived originally from Greek and Hebrew philosophy, but developed further by such immediate predecessors as Ramon Lull and Nicolas of Cusa. It is Bruno who brings out most evidently the fact that the Renaissance was less a Revival than it was a Survival of Learning. And this is also a truth that has been gaining fuller recognition in the last few decades. One thinks, for instance, of Johann Huizinga's *The Waning of the Middle Ages*. It is particularly instructive to compare Bruno's attitude to the authority of the Past with the sometimes almost puerile iconoclasm of Francis Bacon.

There are three things, I would suggest, which can be brought home to us by study of Bruno. The first is the paradox that, while the Renaissance intellect is not nearly as new as we had thought, the Renaissance *impulse* was, if anything, newer than we had thought. And, as a corollary to this, that that impulse is primarily evident in the emergence of Imagination as a personal psychic activity and the awareness of it as such. (And here I would add, in parenthesis, that, when we call the Romantic Movement the Romantic Revival, it is this last that we are really thinking of — not just the revival by Mrs. Radcliffe and Sir Walter Scott of a taste for medieval trappings.)

The second thing is, that this new impulse did not arise somehow from nowhere, but was the transformation of a much older impulse. I use the same word at this stage, leaving aside for the moment the question whether, before its transformation, it should properly be called an "impulse" at all.

The third thing is, that this transformation amounted to, not the substitution of new matter for old, but something much more like a change of *direction* — "basic changes of orientation within the psyche", in Dr Yates's term. And perhaps it is this third aspect, above all, which is particularly evident to us within the mind of Bruno, in the shape of his passionate adherence to the new Copernican astronomy. He was not merely already a Copernican when many were still committed to the Ptolmaic system; he was a man positively drunk with Copernicanism — so drunk that it permeated his every thought. Immanuel Kant is often referred to as the inaugurator of a "Copernican revolution" in psychology. I suspect that, when the history of philosophy is better understood, he will be seen as merely recording it; and that, if we want to observe the revolution actually *happening*, we shall do better to attend the wedding ceremony, in the mind of Bruno, between Copernican astronomy and the Art of Memory. In the mind of Bruno — and of course elsewhere; but very conspicuously indeed in Bruno.

I have been speaking about an "impulse", about the Renaissance impulse in particular, and about the "transformation" of an impulse. What does the word mean? For it must not be forgotten that to extend its meaning in this way beyond the psychology of the individual, and to employ it as a term of history, raises — or, if you like, it begs — some very deep questions, questions which it will be quite impossible for me to argue. All I can do in the time remaining to me is to offer a few observations.

In the first place, then, to use the word "impulse" at all in *any* context is to pass from a psychology of the conscious to a psychology of the unconscious, or sub-conscious, mind. It assumes, what some would deny, that at least there *is* such a thing as unconscious mental movement or pressure. In the second place, to use it as a term of *history* implies much more. It implies, firstly, that the unconscious mind is super-individual and, secondly, that it has a history. Or, if we accept R. G. Collingwood's view that the term "history" is only applicable to events accompanied by purposive thought, then we must say that the unconscious mind has, not so much a history as an evolution. In other words, we cannot conscientiously use the word "impulse" as a term of history, unless we assume that, in addition to the process we call "history of ideas", there has been a history of the unconscious mind underlying those ideas.[3] I generally call this an "evolution of consciousness", since, as Herbert Spencer noticed, if we are going to associate unconsciousness with mind at all, we must just lump the logical contradiction. In his own words: "Mysterious as seems the consciousness of something which is yet out of consciousness, we are obliged to think it."

Not that the writers and critics of the English-speaking world have shown much sign of bothering about the logical contradiction. It is not the sort of thing they do bother about. Or much sign of denying an unconscious mind. On the contrary! And here I think I must allow myself a brief digression on something else that happened in my time. By and large, the literary fraternity have been content to let others do their thinking for them. At a critical juncture in the twentieth century, there was perhaps one Johnson,[4] but unfortunately there was no-one even remotely approaching the calibre of a Goethe, a Schlegel, a Coleridge. If there had been, much might since have gone very differently. Even without that... a competent man of letters may not be a philosopher; but he need not necessarily be a mere quidnunc. Faced with a sensational novelty, our writers might (one would have thought) have had the courage and the wit to attempt some sort of dispassionate appraisal by bringing it to the bar of their own philosophical heritage. In the '20s, on first hearing the hot news from Vienna, they might, for instance, have looked at the chapter called "The Unconscious Soul" in a book on the psychology of poetry, which had appeared in 1866: E. S. Dallas' *The Gay Science*. They might even have re-pondered Chapter XII of the *Biographia Literaria* and the long tradition on which it draws concerning a "consciousness which lies beneath or (as it were) *behind* the spontaneous consciousness natural to all reflecting beings". Instead, they just swam around, gaping — and gaping wide enough to swallow the gospel according to Sigmund Freud hook, line and sinker. Can I be mistaken? My recollection of the 1920s and '30s is of one unseemly rush to see who could fall flattest and quickest before the common idol. It was rather like the moment when the music stops in the children's game called Musical Bumps. And thirty years later, in 1960, it was not a member of the literary fraternity, but a man with predominantly scientific interests, Lancelot Whyte, who took the trouble to do a little elementary research and publish a book called *The Unconscious Before Freud.*

The distinction between an evolution of consciousness (that is, of the *un*conscious) and a history of ideas is an important one. The leading characteristic of the latter is continuity — the *gradualness* of any change that occurs; the leading characteristic of the *former* is the interruption of long periods of continuity by briefer ones of comparatively abrupt mutation. It was, I think, Lewis' learned and clear perception of the essential continuity of European thought from classical times down to the seventeenth century that engendered his scepticism about "the Renaissance". And that continuity is indeed evidenced both by the history of the Art of Memory and in the writings of Bruno. On the other hand the very sudden development of the art, amounting to a transformation, just at the time that we allocate to the Renaissance, and especially its development in the mind of Bruno, may be seen as the outward sign of an inner *dis*continuity.

Now we assume, if we use the word "impulse" as a term of history, that there is an evolution of consciousness underlying the history of ideas. Moreover, the fact that this evolution operates *within* the historical period, and thus in the short run, precludes us from equating it with *biological* evolution. C. S. Lewis was consistent in this, as in most things. He was perhaps the most consistent man I ever knew. His refusal to admit the existence of a Renaissance "impulse" (as distinct from the intellectual revolution, which he also denied) was integral to his general principle of anti-historicism; which is, in substance, the denial of *any* evolutionary process continuing into the historical period. He held very firmly that either there is no such process or, if there is, it is quite impossible for us to know anything about it.

Incidentally, it has always been something of a mystery to me that we seemed to meet somehow in my little early book *Poetic Diction*, of which he held, and continued to hold, a very high opinion, although it is mainly concerned with demonstrating an evolution of consciousness from poetic to prosaic, from universal to individual, from macrocosm to microcosm. In point of fact I have spent most of my literary life — in so far as I can be said to have *had* a literary life — in variations on that theme and that demonstration. And I feel this is sufficient justification for what I now propose to do; which is to assume its acceptance in the rest of what I have to say. One cannot always stop to argue, and a lecturer is entitled to say to the sceptics in his audience: "It will do you no harm to assume for a quarter of an hour what I have been convinced of all my life and have moreover argued at painstaking length in half a dozen books."

Assuming, then, an evolution of consciousness from universal to individual: inner experience will have been, in its earlier stages, more a passive reflection of the outer processes of nature herself than anything originating within the organism. It will inevitably have been of a pictorial, or imaginal, description; and the element of inwardness, which entitles it to be labelled "consciousness" at all, will have been inseparably bound up with the pictures themselves. But a picture with an element of inwardness is just what we mean by an image or figure. To borrow from Auerbach's *Mimesis* an expression he is using in a slightly different context, in primitive perception you have a situation, where "the sensory occurrence pales from the power of the figural meaning". Only it will be a figurative meaning, not supplied or produced by the individual mind experiencing it, but given in the experience itself. And this sort of experience is rather an extension of life itself, of the universal life of nature, *into* an individual organism than it is any separated mental life of the organism itself.

To return to the Art of Memory, one of the German words for "memory" is *Erinnerung*, or "inwardising". And it is fairly clear that a perceptual image remembered has already moved a step further into the individual organism than one which merely lights up in the moment of actual perception and vanishes again the moment actual perception ceases. Memory is thus a key factor in the interiorisation, of which the whole evolution of consciousness (I am assuming) consists. But even then the remembered images are still, to begin with, *passive* products of the life of nature as a whole. They are in no sense the *activity* of the individual.

Work on the memory, cultivation of the memory, on the other hand, is an activity originating from within the individual himself. And such an activity becomes more and more necessary in the measure that the natural *life* inherent in the passive memory-images grows weaker, as the history of mankind progresses, with the result that they fade more and more easily. Moreover it is just this weakening of the universal, or macrocosmic, life that has made a more individual mental life begin to be possible. One could perhaps put it that what was formerly the *pulse* of life in general has become the *im*-pulse of an individual mind. I believe it is somewhat in this sense that we should be thinking, if we are to describe the Renaissance impulse as the "transformation" of a former impulse.

This is not what the book, with which I have made so free, actually says, but it is what, to me at least, it strongly suggests; presenting, as it does, the genesis of Imagination as a kind of metamorphosis of the older psychology of Inspiration; and doing so in terms of Bruno's cosmology of macrocosm and microcosm. For, as the author shows, it was in Bruno's mind more than anywhere else that the *imagines agentes* of the Art of Memory coalesced with traditional macrocosmic imagery, such as the Elements, the Planetary Spheres, and the Signs of the Zodiac. Thus, her book is also valuable for the new light it throws on such historical matters as iconography and typology. Clearly there were, in the Middle Ages and for some time afterwards, not only the great stone cathedrals, at which we can still gaze, but also those "invisible cathedrals of memory", to which access is more difficult for us.

By the time of Camillo and Fludd and their "Memory Theatres", this coalescence of dynamic subjective images with the traditional macrocosmic imagery, which we find so often in the cathedrals of stone, had already started taking place. Their "theatres" were not conceived as practical devices for making oratory more efficient, but rather as groups of images with which the mind of the spectator could unite itself and, in doing so, rejoin, so to speak, the macrocosm out of which it had itself been originally constructed. The Globe Theatre itself was so designed as to be not merely circular, but "global" in this sense also; and we hear an echo of that in the Prologue to *Henry V*.[5]

Quite apart from historical interest, "the role of the art of memory in the formation of imagery" (to quote Yates once more) has important psychological bearings, if it can help at all towards a better understanding of the true nature of that popular mystery, the "creative imagination". Have we reflected enough on its connection with memory? One thinks of Coleridge's discernment of a "law of the passive fancy and mechanical memory" in the *Biographia Literaria* and of his consequent distinction between Fancy and Imagination. Much has since been written on the distinction between Fancy and Imagination, but very little on that "law of the passive fancy and mechanical memory", on which it really depends.[6]

If there were a little more time, I should have been disposed to hazard a few speculations of a more practical nature. Because there is more than one other context, in which one could consider "the survival of learning", especially at a time when we are beginning to hear ominous talk in some quarters of "the dissolution of learning". One could think of it historically, but in relation to the future rather than the present. Thus, there is currently a good deal of bewilderment concerning the true aim of education, and still more concerning the best methods of attaining it. Most enlightened people are agreed that, whatever it is, the true aim of education is not the amassing of remembered information — that (to borrow another bit of Coleridge's terminology) its object is to develop heads that are "springs" rather than "tanks". Can you teach creative imagination? In America at least they seem to think you can. But can you teach it, or can you teach anything, except *by way of* information? Is not that what teaching and learning actually *mean*? Is not the true aim of education, not the substitution of undirected whimsy for information and learning, but rather the survival of learning transformed? The question whether memory itself is susceptible of some kind of transformation must, I think, be relevant here. If we felt it was, should we be quite so sure as most educationists seem to be that it is idiotic to make children memorize what they do not yet understand? Perhaps there is even something to be said for teaching a little Rhetoric?

I do not of course mean to imply that mere study of the history of memory will hand us on a plate a new and better theory of education. I shall be more than content if I have succeeded in suggesting two things at all convincingly: first, that perhaps after all the mystery of memory is no less deep than the mystery of creative imagination; and secondly, that, if that is so, then it will bear some further reflection. We are, for instance, fond today of using the word "seminal" for the kind of thought we feel to be creative. But we do not often reflect that our metaphor carries historical as well as genial implications, inasmuch as a seed owes its creative energies to the past no less surely than it bestows them on the future. One sometimes feels that whatever in heaven and earth was not known by one or more of the Greek philosophers was known by their mythology. In that mythology it is not Madam Oedipus, nor is it some fancy goddess called *Genesis* or *Poiesis*, who is mother of the Muses. It is Mnemosyne.

TWO KINDS OF FORGETTING

LOOKING AT THE letter of invitation that brings me here I see that, in addition to naming the overall theme of your studies, "Continuities and Discontinuities in Modern Consciousness",[1] it asks the specific question: "Are there assumptions within your discipline that cause the work of the past to be ignored? Are there factors external to the discipline that have had that effect?" So, taking my discipline to be the nature and significance of language, I think I will begin by recounting a little bit of history, which not only furnishes a concrete example of a major assumption within the discipline, arising from a factor external to it, but also illustrates the startlingly shallow foundations on which such assumptions sometimes prove, on inspection, to be based.

At about the time, in the second half of the 19th Century, when T. H. Huxley was popularising the evolutionary theory of his contemporary Charles Darwin, another contemporary figure, hardly less — or perhaps more — familiar to the educated world at the time than either Huxley or Darwin, though (unlike theirs) his name scarcely rings a bell of any sort in the ears of our own contemporaries, was busy popularising the historical or evolutionary contemplation of language. It was the recent advances in the study of oriental languages, especially Sanskrit, which had given a new turn to that contemplation by virtue of the fresh light it shed on all the Indo-European languages, including of course English; and the man to whom I am alluding is the oriental scholar Max Müller.

There may still be a few persons about who are vaguely aware of Müller's prolific output of essays and lectures under such titles as *Biographies of Words*, *Essays on Language and Literature*, *Essays on Mythology and Folklore*, *The Science of Language*, but you would need a very fine-toothed comb to find one who had ever heard of his encounter with Darwin and Darwinism. Müller did not question the primary Darwinian thesis, that the human form has evolved, or emerged from animal forms. What he did refuse to accept was the tacit corollary that human *consciousness* has biologically emerged from animal consciousness, and therefore that human speech has ("must have" was of course the way that Darwinians actually put it) somehow or other emerged from animal cries. As a conscientious student of language and of the development of meaning, he told Darwin that, whatever else his theory of evolution explained, it could not possibly explain the origin of speech. And speech is of course the endowment that most obviously distinguishes the human being from the rest of the living world.

When I say he "told" Darwin, I am speaking literally. For he not only delivered a series of lectures to the Royal Institution in 1873 under the title *Mr. Darwin's Philosophy of Language*, but he sent the pamphlet in which they subsequently appeared to Darwin himself and afterwards called on him. "He listened most attentively," wrote Müller, describing the interview, "he asked questions, but raised no serious objections. Before he shook hands and left me, he said in the kindest way, 'You are a dangerous man'." Moreover, after reading another essay of Müller's two years later Darwin wrote to him: "...though some of your remarks have been rather stinging, they have all been made so gracefully, I declare that I am like the man in the story who boasted that he had been horsewhipped by a Duke." But that is not all. In an earlier letter to Müller, written after reading the lectures I have referred to, there is a still more revealing admission:

> He who is fully convinced, as I am, that man is descended from some lower animal is almost forced to believe, *a priori*, that articulate language has been developed from inarticulate cries; and he is therefore hardly a fair judge of the arguments opposed to this belief.

The words *a priori* are italicized, no doubt because they are in Latin, but when we reflect on the momentous consequences for Western thought in almost every department of it and on the depth to which it has penetrated our whole imagination of the past, we may feel that we should have reasons of our own for italicizing them, even if they were in English. I mentioned the shallowness of the foundations underlying some influential assumptions. It is widely assumed that, since the scientific revolution, conformity to reason has been the acid test for determining the soundness of any theory. History will no doubt one day pronounce on how far that assumption was justified, and I am not suggesting that it is wholly unjustified. What can, I think, be said is that, as far as the received theory of the origin of humanity in an emergent biological evolution is concerned, it is *not* justified. It is clear enough from the above that the light of reason was not Charles Darwin's guiding star. You can find a further account of the whole encounter in Nirad Chaudhuri's life of Max Müller published in 1974 under the title *Scholar Extraordinary*.

Actually it was precisely the issue of reason which determined Müller's opposition to any application of the

Darwinian theory to the origin of language. Incidentally he was well acquainted with — in fact he later translated into English — Kant's *Critique of Pure Reason*. "No speech without reason: no reason without speech" was the conclusion to which he insisted any faithful student of language is compelled by his own reason. And, however intelligent some animals are, or may become by training, the light of reason itself is not participated by the brute creation.

What Müller had exposed, though it went largely unnoticed at the time, thanks to the fascinating simplicity of Darwin's theory, was the fallacy, to which I have already alluded, of inferring from biological evolution to a parallel evolution of consciousness. Physical bodies of animals appeared on the earth before physical bodies of men; therefore human consciousness grew out of animal consciousness. What could be more obvious? So long of course as you refrain from examining it. It was this unquestioned assumption which did so much harm to the whole historical study of language. In the early days it entailed that anyone inclined to speculate on the origin of speech was expected, as a matter of course, to devise some new way of solving the spurious problem of how animal cries could have turned into speech. There was a "bow-wow" theory, a "pooh-pooh" theory, and so forth. That sort of thing has largely gone out of fashion; but it is still the incubus of this largely unquestioned assumption which, more than anything else, prevents a genuine insight into the true nature of language, an insight without which all speculation on its origin is of course frivolous. Because it closes — and even when it does not close, it obscures — the only avenue by which such an insight can possibly be reached, namely, the approach from within language itself. Language is, more than anything else, the vehicle of human consciousness; and if you want insight into human consciousness and its evolution, you will get it by studying what is going on, and what has been going on, *within* human consciousness, not by studying what goes on outside it and drawing all manner of inferences therefrom.

In order however to shed any useful light on the kind of questions I understand you to be deliberating, I am persuaded that we must now leave behind the special domain of language and look back behind Darwin and into his background. And if one diligently enquires how it came about that Darwin's *a priori* assumption prevailed so easily over the demands of reason, he comes, rather surprisingly, to another *a priori* assumption. The drama of an exclusively biological evolution requires a stage for its performance. If you postulate a history of living organisms changing and developing into their present forms by virtue of their responses to a separate environment, you must first postulate such an environment. And you must further assume that it has remained substantially unchanged over an enormous tale of years. There is no doubt (if you wish to verify it, you need go no farther than the article on "Evolution" in the 13th edition of the *Encyclopedia Britannica*) that Darwin's biology could never have come about without Lyell's geology. And if you take the trouble to look back at the period when geology first began to wear its modern dress, you find that it too is based on an assumption; in this case an assumption that did not slip in unnoticed, but which was consciously and deliberately adopted. Inasmuch as it is an assumption — or theory, if you prefer — about the past, and past events are not susceptible of experimental verification, it is also an *a priori* assumption, and was acknowledged by Lyell to be so. I refer, of course, to the doctrine — or perhaps "maxim" is the more accurate term — which was called, until its *a priori* status was forgotten, "uniformitarianism": the maxim, namely, that what we today ascertain to be the laws of nature have always existed and have never changed. Call it what you will — assumption, theory or maxim — it is the arbitrary foundation on which our whole familiar world-picture of a solid earth substantially as we have it today — the mountains perhaps a bit higher, the rains a bit more torrential, but substantially as we have it today — having existed for billions of years before we were born — the indispensable foundation on which that whole world-picture reposes.

Here too the assumption carried a momentous corollary. As biology and physiology went on to assume that mind must have evolved in parallel with body and brain, so geology and palaeontology went on to assume that, in the history of the earth, and indeed of the universe as a whole, inanimate preceded animate matter. Right or wrong, I believe it would be difficult to exaggerate the part these two assumptions, taken together, play in the whole structure of modern thought. It is not just the life-sciences. Dig a little way beneath the surface and you find them everywhere, in anthropology, no matter where you look. As C. S. Lewis once put it:

> It's probably the deepest-ingrained habit of mind in the contemporary world. It's behind the idea that our morality springs from savage taboos, adult sentiment from infantile sexual maladjustment, thought from instinct, mind from matter, organic from inorganic, cosmos from chaos.

He added: "It always seems to me immensely implausible, because it makes the general course of nature so very unlike those parts of it we can observe." We do, of course, see all round us every day the living turning into the lifeless. What we never see is the lifeless turning into the living.

I have just said "if you dig a little way beneath the surface". I notice, on referring again to the letter of invitation which constitutes my terms of reference, that the particular aspect of your overall topic which you are focusing on this term is described as "systematic forgetting". I found that phrase a bit puzzling. What is systematic forgetting? It cannot surely mean forgetting deliberately undertaken (as a "system" is deliberately constructed), because that cannot be done without making yourself remember whatever it is more clearly than ever! I can only interpret it as signifying a forgetting which is the result of a process of conscious thought of some kind; as distinct from that unsystematic forgetting, which I will come to later, and which is the result of prolonged inattention. The former, on the other hand, I take to be the process by which what began by being conscious does not fade right out but gradually becomes sub-conscious. And in this sense I think the presence throughout the Western mind of the two assumptions I have been speaking of, together with the absence of conscious attention to them, may properly be seen as the product of systematic forgetting. The assumptions themselves are almost forgotten; the fact that they are assumptions is entirely forgotten, still more of course the fact that they are *a priori* assumptions, and all that remains above the mental surface is the deeply-ingrained habit of mind, of which

Lewis wrote. They have ceased to be thoughts and become merely the *way* men think about other things.

I did not include linguistics in the examples I gave of disciplines affected by them, perhaps because a good deal had already been said about language. Now that the Darwinian assumption is ingrained, we no longer hear much of flighty speculations on the origin of human speech. The effects have gone much deeper. Man is a tool-using animal, so runs the argument, sometimes explicit but more often implicit. He began to become man because he began using tools, and language was the most useful tool of all. Thus, if we wish to investigate language really scientifically, we must conceive it as a tool for practical, and ultimately technological, ends. And so on. It has gone so far that there is even a school of thought which holds that a truly objective inquirer into language must omit meaning altogether from his considerations. More recently the computer has been brought in; and, as you know, this analytico-mechanical conception of language has fed back into philosophy — another omission from my list. The total effect has been incalculable. It is probably putting it too strongly, but I must confess that, whenever I personally am favoured with a glimpse into what seems mostly to be going on in the academic world under the names of both linguistics and philosophy, I get the impression of a separate class of mandarins, imperturbably aloof from the ordinary run of men and playing games of skill with a set of intellectual and scientific toys.

And here there is something I find very interesting. Just as it was among those who had studied language from within, notably Max Müller, that the most convincing, however ineffective, opposition to the

Darwinian assumption itself arose, so, now that the assumption has become ingrained, it is from within the same discipline that it is being most dangerously undermined. Historical penetration into language and its roots in consciousness, of which Müller, with his combined interest in language and mythology was a conspicuous pioneer, has been carried much farther since his day, with the help of subsequent advances in anthropology and archaeology as well as in philology itself. For some time now a number of thinkers, of whom Ernst Cassirer is probably the best known, have been pointing out that there is really no question of speech having originated in the responses of tool-using organisms to an already established environment, an environment which we should recognize as our own if we could be spirited into it. On the contrary, the world about us — the only world we can perceive and know — came into being *along with* language, of which it is at least as much the effect as it has ever been the cause. And an important development here has been an increasing realization that we must look for the source of language in myth, in the mythic consciousness, and not, as Müller rather crudely speculated in his observations on metaphor, for the source of myth in language.

What is not yet realized, is the unavoidable conclusion which this discovery entails. And the reason why it is not realized is that it flies in the face of a third ingrained assumption to which I now come. Perhaps in this case it cannot be called an assumption with quite the same justification as the other two. At least it is not, as they are, an *a priori* assumption, because it is not, as they are, concerned solely with an imagined, but unobservable past. I am referring to that heterogeneity or dichotomy between mind or consciousness on the one hand and body or matter on the other, which is generally called "Cartesian", because it was first so clearly and positively formulated by René Descartes. Hardly a mere assumption, like Darwinism and Uniformitarianism; rather a discovery that is indeed one valid way of thinking about the world and ourselves, a discovery that has been amply borne out by its subsequent applications, since it is at the root of all technological development. Hardly a bare assumption, since it brought with it a new valuation, almost a new conception of *accuracy* in cognition, notably of course *quantitative* accuracy; but a conception which has spread, with beneficial results, from the sphere of natural science into that of the humanities. I have no doubt, for example, that we were largely indebted to it for that new impulse, leading to new discoveries, in philology of which I spoke near the beginning of my lecture.

What *is* an assumption, an assumption that was made by Descartes himself and has been retained by most Western minds as their overriding reality-principle, is the corollary that it is not only a valid and fruitful way of thinking about the world, but the only cognitive and veridical way of doing so. From this aspect it is indeed not less, but rather more than an assumption. Inasmuch as it is far more deeply ingrained than are even the other two I have mentioned. In fact it is a kind of threshold, which even the most honest and penetrating thinkers will do *anything* rather than cross. It is in my opinion the reason why the unavoidable conclusion that follows from that discovery of the *concurrent* development of consciousness and the objects of consciousness is so very very rarely drawn even by the discoverers themselves.

I mean the conclusion that that part of reality, which we rather equivocally refer to as "consciousness", though we have long been in the habit of intending by it the sub-conscious and even the unconscious as well — all that which we experience otherwise than through the senses, or which (to put it succinctly) comes from within and not from without — is not to be thought of as a series of units encapsulated in a series of human organisms, but rather as the inside of the world as a whole. An inside which, like the inside of anything else, is inseparable from the outside, though the distinction between the two remains obvious enough.

Now, if we go back four or five hundred years in history, we find that this way of perceiving and thinking of the natural world was taken for granted, in both the sciences and humanities, as firmly as it opposite is taken for granted today. Moreover we find that it was taken for granted, not as the result of specific ideas or theories first mooted, then accepted and then systematically forgotten, but because it was the way in which men had thought about the world ever since they began to think at all. Why then has it disappeared so completely, or almost completely, from among us?

It is in answer to that question that I suggest it is worthwhile looking more closely at the complementary process of *un*-systematic forgetting. In dealing with systematic forgetting I ventured to focus attention very specially on three names, Darwin, Lyell and Descartes. I hope I made it clear that I was using them as labels, rather than putting forward their owners as the sole causes of the theoretical notions and assumptions associated with them. Important contributory causes they certainly were. But the French philosophers had been suggesting the animal origin of humanity long before Darwin, and Lord Monboddo and others had brought the doctrine to England. In the same way the Cartesian diremption of a mechanically determined nature from an individual observing mind antedates Descartes, as an unclearly formulated way of thinking. Butterfield made that clear enough in his *Origins of Modern Science*. Nevertheless the labels are convenient and not altogether misleading.

Systematic forgetting is an aftermath of thinking rather than of failure to think. Custom and education together bring it about that an idea entertained and accepted, perhaps enthusiastically accepted, by one generation becomes in a subsequent one a sub-conscious assumption that forms part of its common sense. Unsystematic forgetting on the other hand is a kind of atrophy from disuse. Ideas and ways of perceiving that were familiar to former generations are forgotten because the attention that was once directed to them has so long been directed elsewhere and away from them. And so, with the same object of focusing on particular examples rather than indulging in vague generalities, it may be useful to have a look at three older ways of thinking, now largely forgotten as a result of the diversion of attention to the ways I have labelled Darwin, Lyell and Descartes.

Before Descartes being was not held to be coterminous with existence. It was almost universal habit to think of birth, life and growth in terms of a potential existence becoming actual. What was still only potential was not unreal simply because it was as yet imperceptible. And by Aristotle's time this way of thinking had crystallized into a philosophy, a psychology and a science all based on the most intricate conceptions of *actus* and *potentia* and the varying relation between them. All this was swept away by the Cartesian dichotomy. Everything that is objective is perceptible to the senses. And so, as time passes, the imperceptible becomes the unreal. How completely it was swept away, so that the denial of potency was regarded as so obvious as to be simply common sense is well illustrated by a principle of interpretation which was laid down as one of a number of legal maxims. I don't know when it first appeared in the law books, but it is still included as a recognized maxim in contemporary lists; and it is as follows: *De non apparentibus et non existentibus eadem est ratio*; which I suppose is best translated: "Anything that is invisible is assumed not to exist". And so, for science as for law, the potential is not to be thought of as real. There is no such thing as potentiality, only the abstract possibilities and probabilities of subjective calculation.

Alongside the elimination by Descartes of *actus* and *potentia* as a mode of thought can be placed, I think, the final obliteration by Lyell — or Lyellism or Uniformitarianism — of another mode which was equally integral to educated thought in general at least down to the Renaissance: the conception of man as, both physically and psychically, a microcosm within the macrocosm, from which he takes his origin and with which he remains linked, not only by such material means as gravitation and perception, but also organically and immaterially — from within, in fact, as well as from without — linked more in the manner of an embryo within a womb than in the manner of an insect crawling over the surface of a sphere. Any such conception has been effectively obliterated by a long-term fixation of attention on the Lyell picture of a macrocosm, with no inside to it, in existence for millions of years before not only man himself but *any* kind of consciousness, any kind of inside, had come to pass.

And Darwinism: is there any older way of thinking and feeling which Darwinism has been especially instrumental in obliterating? The question almost answers itself. The conviction that man not only owes his origin to a Being, or a state of being, higher and greater than himself, but also that he has cut himself adrift from that origin by his own self-will, seems to have been with the human race almost as an integral part of its constitution from the beginnings of civilization. The paradise imago in one form or another — whether as the *Saturnia regna* of classical mythology, or in various older oriental versions, or in the myths and traditions of primitive races surviving today, or in the form most familiar to us, the Old Testament account of the "Fall" of both man and nature from a primal state of innocence into its present predicament — in one form or another it was surely almost a part of human nature, until it was replaced by that imago of something emerging accidentally out of nothing, which I suppose is the prevailing twentieth century cosmology.

I have distinguished three forgettings, but of course they have overlapped with and supported one another. In the mode of *actus* and *potentia*, the potential can become actual, only because it is itself preceded by an actual. If there is no actual perfection anterior to the potential perfection (the "perfectibility of man" they called it in the nineteenth century, out of which our ubiquitous and appallingly vague notion of "progress" arose), then there can be no macrocosm, no greater world at once transcending and generating the little world our self-consciousness has detached from it. You cannot have a fall, without there being a height to have fallen from.

Nor is it only in these general respects that they overlap. The biologist's inability to deal with *form* in organism, arises no doubt from his inability or refusal to conceive a blossom as both immaterially and really potential in a seed, but that refusal and that inability derive much of their rigidity from the inveterate background picture of a world of forms having emerged in the first place from formless matter and having developed simply by a series of mechanical interactions. The same could be said of the truly grotesque obsession of some neurologists with the physical brain, as not only the condition but the cause of waking consciousness, and their conviction that in exploring its tissues they are exploring, and will some day "explain" consciousness itself. Indeed the inability to distinguish between a condition and a cause, between *causa sine qua non*[2] and *causa causans*,[3] is one of the most conspicuous blind spots which the forgettings have brought about. But I believe, if we had the means of exploring the sub-conscious, we shall find this particular obsession greatly strengthened by a Darwinian overlap. As thus: just as we investigate consciousness in its early stages by examining fossil remains, measuring brain-cavities and so forth, so we investigate present-day consciousness by examining the brain itself.

For some time now there have been increasing signs of the losses as well as the gains beginning to be realized. It is pointed out here and there, for example, that the accurate knowledge we owe to post-Cartesian science is achieved only by excluding all those parts or aspects of reality that are not reducible to abstract quantities. Books appear with such titles as *The Perennial Philosophy* or *The Lost Word*. This within the humanities. Elsewhere the consequential deficiencies are beginning to force attention to themselves, whether or not they are also recognized as losses or forgettings. I don't know that that need matter much. When we look back from our world of accuracy without meaning into that older world of meaning without accuracy, we are not bound either to relinquish our habit of accuracy or to resuscitate the old terminology. Provided that, let us say, the life-sciences come to recognize that *De non apparentibus et non existentibus eadem est ratio* really won't do, if form is to be apprehended, and that reality includes an immaterial component, it does not matter whether they come again to speak of *actus* and *potentia* or whether they envisage a principle, such as that of "holism", as a new discovery.

There are these signs then, but they are still very very tentative. Neither the proponents of holism nor the ecologists, with their healthy impulse to integrate man once more into the surrounding world of nature, seem able to take the only way that can lead to a truly intimate knowledge or a truly organic integration. And it is the same with the advanced philosophical physicists. They speak of indistinction between observer and observed, and some of them even go so far as to suggest that we must abandon our obsession with a Cartesian dichotomy. But read a little farther and you will find them still *imagining* in the Cartesian mode, still reifying anything the self could experience as not-self. The unsystematic forgetting has proved so very total. The systematic has gone so very deep into the sub-conscious. I spoke just now of a kind of threshold which even the most honest and penetrating thinkers will do anything to avoid crossing. *De non apparentibus* rules the imagination even when it is rejected by the intellect. There are very very few who can accept that the inside of the world as a whole is made of the same stuff as that inside of our organisms and our brains, which we call consciousness. Julian Jaynes's book *The Origins of Consciousness in the Breakdown of the Bi-cameral Mind* is a depressing example of the way in which trains of thought leading in that direction are wrecked by assumptions to the contrary left lying on the rails. I recall, in my own discipline, the pleasure I felt in becoming acquainted with Noam Chomsky's notion of generative grammar. The very word "generative" was like a breath of fresh air with its suggestion of a creative Word. And then you go a little further and you discover that by "generation" he simply means the physical configuration of the brain!

I remember once reading of a simple riddle, or intelligence-test, for children. A traveller in a part of the country he does not know comes to a crossroads, where the signpost has been uprooted and is lying on the ground. How can he use it to find his way? The answer is of course that he knows the place he came from and if he replaces the signpost with the name of that place pointing to it, it will also show him the way forward to where he wants to go. Perhaps it is the task of the humanities to replace the signpost, so that it points correctly to the past, and for the sciences to take the way forward into the future. But I missed any suggestion of such a creative relation between past and future, when the battle of the "two cultures"[4] was joined a few years ago.

Yet besides forgetting there is also remembering. Remembering! We might conclude by pausing on the word itself. The German poet Novalis observed, in an aphorism on the nature of words, that there are two kinds of etymology, the genetic and the pragmatic. The genetic is the kind that can be securely established from documentary evidence, the kind you find in Skeat's etymological dictionary. Pragmatic etymology, by contrast, may be irresponsible and even flighty, but may nevertheless contain a germ of unprovable truth since we can never be sure what accidental resemblances of sound, what perceived or fancied analogies of meaning, together with those underlying psychological drives that have sometimes been called "folk-etymology", have played their part in the forming of a word at some period in its history. A good example of pragmatic etymology was afforded by the adventurous spirit who pointed to the relation between the noun "thing" and the verb "to think", as revealing a truth once realized but long since forgotten, namely, that it was a species of thinking in the first place which brought into being the world of recognisable things. A Max Müller or a Skeat would of course have nothing to do with it. Yet close resemblances in sound are a fact, however they came about, and are not necessarily wholly accidental, because their causes cannot be documented. And so, as Shirley Sugerman has pointed out in her book *Sin and Madness*, remembering — and certainly the kind of collective remembering that is correlative to unsystematic forgetting — may also be thought of with a hyphen, as "re-membering".

At all events what I have been trying to suggest to you — no doubt with a good many obscurities and irritating short cuts — may perhaps be summarized as follows. As Heraclitus realized long ago, when systematic thinking had just begun to emerge from unsystematic, there are two kinds of thinking: the divine light of reason, which Darwin preferred to ignore, the κοινός λόγος[5] one in all and waiting to be appropriated by each, and the ίδια φρόνησις,[6] which is the same light possessively appropriated and readily distorted by each, "everyone to his own way". That is why there are two kinds of forgetting. Secondly, that by taking some trouble to remember just what has been forgotten we may come again to distinguish the one kind of thinking from the other. And lastly, that to distinguish one from the other is also to realize that, just as our skin-bound physical frame is a member of the spatial world of bodies and things, so our seemingly isolated little spark of self-consciousness is a member of a greater world of spirit and of spirits, to which that other world owes its existence in the first place.

THE RIDDLE OF THE SPHINX

> When the man said THAT IS SUBLIME, he appeared to be making a remark about the waterfall... Actually he was not making a remark about the waterfall, but a remark about his own feelings.

These words appeared in an English Literature textbook for schools, published about a quarter of a century ago, and when the late C. S. Lewis delivered his Riddell Lectures on *The Abolition of Man*, his text was that schoolbook and his theme the argument, that to treat all values as subjective entails in the end abolishing all values.

The view that poetry and literature in general, whatever they purport to refer to, are in fact referring solely to the author's feelings first began to gain general acceptance in English literary circles with the publication of I. A. Richards' *Principles of Literary Criticism* in 1925. I am not at the moment concerned to argue against this doctrine, but simply to point out that its emergence coincided roughly with an attempt being made elsewhere to exclude what is called "metaphysics" from the realm of scientific theory. The arguments for and against both positions are not dissimilar. Thus, if Richards' opponents have since pointed out that unfortunately the "emotive" power of a poetic statement depends precisely on our interpreting it as an objective reference to something *other* than emotion itself, we have also heard Karl Popper objecting, in his *Logic of Scientific Discovery*, that scientific laws cannot be reduced to elementary statements of experience and that positivists, in their anxiety to annihilate metaphysics, unfortunately annihilate natural science itself along with it.

Owing to the predominantly figurative nature of the language of poetry, by way of metaphor and symbol, "the truest poets are the most feigning". Richards' problem was to satisfy himself and his readers that poetry is valuable, even within the framework of a behaviourist philosophy, in spite of the fact that most of the statements it contains are manifestly untrue. But this could not be done without raising, and not only for poetry, the whole issue of the multiple significance of figurative language. A metaphor, for instance, considered semantically, is not one statement but at least two. It is a "vehicle" (the literal meaning — usually untrue) containing a "tenor" (the metaphorical meaning). What, if anything, does the tenor affirm? What is it about? Is it in any sense veridical? Such are the questions which have exercised a good many minds over the last fifty years.

But so also has a very similar question in the domain of science. With the collapse of the imaginal "models", on which classical physics largely relied, and the apparent disappearance of any ultimate atomic principle there has arisen, as a live issue, the question: what are physical *theories* (as distinct from singular predictions) about, or what, if anything, may they be said to affirm? For the sub-microscopic realm to which they must increasingly be applied is no more accessible to the senses and the understanding based on them than is the tenor, as distinct from the vehicle, of a linguistic metaphor.

To enquire however into the nature of figurative language is to enquire into the nature of language itself; that is to say, into the primary instrument of expression, information and communication. For the *pons asinorum*[1] of etymology is the discovery that the meaning of virtually every word we use can be traced back to a time when it had a metaphorical or at all events a figurative significance. The precise relation between vehicle and tenor in the case of such a word as *pneuma* at the time when it meant both "wind" and "spirit" may be, and frequently is, disputed; but the fact that it *was* a vehicle with a tenor remains beyond question. Words themselves in fact are symbols — a term on which attention, both historical and epistemological, has long been focussed with about equal intensity from the three directions of literature, philosophy and science.

The answer to the question about the origin and growth of meaning which was given during the period when classical physics reigned undisputed is very similar to the way in which classical physics answered its own questions about the nature and constitution of the material universe. Language was assumed to have commenced with a number of "literal" words, each having a single objective reference, whose meanings were later developed and extended subjectively by combination and metaphorical application, until they produced the infinitely delicate and varied cosmos presented by almost any modern civilized literary language. Similarly the physical cosmos was assumed to be founded and built up from a number of identifiable atoms, electrons, elementary particles — no matter what, but stable entities of one kind or another. Moreover all objectivity was deemed to depend on the existence of these stable entities. For classical physics had already succeeded in transferring from the objective to the subjective domain all else of which the external world appears to consist — its beauty, ugliness, colours, shapes, sounds, even its very solidity.

My purpose is to suggest that the recent outcry about a divergence between two cultures[2] is largely misconceived, and that the various educational reforms proposed as remedies will remain inadequate as long as they continue to be based on the very assumptions that have brought about the real disease. The culture of the West is not two parallel lines but a single twisted skein. The physicist's conclusion that qualities are subjective was not a scientific happening only. It led to the treatment of values (expressed, because the symbolical nature of language compels it, in terms of qualities) as correspondingly subjective. Behaviourism, begotten by nineteenth century science on twentieth century philosophy, impinged effectively, as we have seen, on literary criticism and, through that, on the education of the young in literature and the humanities.

Among the intelligentsia the progressive elimination of values from literature has already progressed a good deal further in the manner foretold. It has, for instance, become the rule that nothing whatever may be condemned, and that the "values" of a Marquis de Sade or of a Genet are entitled to as respectful a hearing as those of a Socrates or a St. Francis of Assisi. Possibly this is an exaggeration, but a Londoner, with his monotonous week-end diet, may be pardoned for forgetting that there are places in Europe where literary critics are still permitted to denounce inhumanity because it is unhuman.

The author of *The Abolition of Man* did not base his argument on Christianity or even on Theism. What he detected as fatal was, not the disappearance of God, but the disappearance of "the doctrine of objective values". It is a doctrine that has been given many different names — in the West it once took, among others, the form of a "natural law" presumed to be innate in man and nature alike. If it was *lex naturae*, the law of nature, it was at the same time *jus gentium*, the law of nations, because also of human nature itself. This same natural law was to have formed the basis of the positive international law which Grotius was already hoping, and we have still failed, to establish. Instead, the whole doctrine of objective values, and with it the concept of a stable and objective humanity, was analysed away during the period now closing, in favour of that other doctrine of objective stable entities, particulate in nature and literal in language. But these were conceived to be objective precisely because they were non-human.

What we have since been witnessing is the analysing away of the stable entities themselves; the researches of Cassirer[3] and others into the origin and growth of language destroying the prevalent notion that there was once a literal language with exclusively objective (non-human) reference, as surely as the cloud-chambers of microphysics destroy the prevalent notion of stable material particles.

The disappearance of the presumed solid ground, whereon rested both the cosmology of the nineteenth century and the doctrine of subjective values to which it gave rise in the twentieth, is also not a scientific happening only. It at once compels and makes easier the re-examination of some other assumptions that have long prevailed in the realms of literature and science alike. To give one example: while physics has concluded that all that is qualitative in nature is subjective (that is, mental), other sciences such as geology and biology, accepting that conclusion, have nevertheless remained content to continue postulating on a pre-historic earth the evolution of forms of animal and plant life identifiable only by the very qualities with which no mind as yet existed to endow them. We should now be able to see that, if the physicist is right in treating quality as "merely" human, it must follow that historical research from within into the origin and growth of language is at least not *less* relevant to any valid theory of natural evolution, including the origin and descent of homo sapiens, than the exclusively external approaches of contemporary biology and geology.

After all, either qualities are purely subjective manifestations or they are not. Yes or no. If yes, evolution must, for that reason, have been from the beginning as much a mental as a material process. But if no, then the grounds on which we were led to abandon the original doctrine were in all sincerity mistaken. Because it was involved with a non-Cartesian outlook on space and with the notion of man as a microcosm, the original doctrine of objective qualities and values has generally been criticized since the scientific revolution as "anthropocentric".[4] It *was* anthropocentric. But, in case we should have discarded its truth along with its errors, we may pause to reflect also on what it was not. It was not *prosopocentric*,[5] as our own cosmos of values has now become. Whatever anthropos meant to the medieval artist, writer or natural scientist and to his Greek predecessors, it did not signify a jaunty, or a terrified, little personality bounded by birth and death and presumed to re-emerge from nonentity at about seven-o'clock every morning. What then did it mean? What was, or rather what *is*, the meaning of anthropos?

Asked originally by the Sphinx, this question was answered in the Mysteries not in the indicative but in the imperative mood: *gnōthi seauton* — know thyself! To cease altogether from hearing the question and from endeavouring to answer it with moral choices, with artistic creation and with the disinterested pursuit of truth is virtually to cease from being a man. It is, more particularly, to drop the question out of which all art, literature, philosophy and science were born. Yet there are those who are resolving to drop it. The least obvious but most conclusive evidence of human entropy is the fact that more and more representatives of both "cultures" are found intentionally closing their ears to that very question.

In science, it was the disinterested pursuit of truth that led, in the first place, to the abolition of objective quality in nature. Today, I have suggested, the same pursuit can only lead humanity back to the perennial question. Yet how many there are who would rather abandon the pursuit than follow its lead! Science, according to the positivists among its votaries, "no longer wants to understand but only to describe".

And literature? The flight from meaning in poetry followed on the elimination of quality from nature. Not immediately, it is true. The best of the Romantics resisted and, instead of closing their ears, strove to answer the perennial question both with their poetry and with their thinking about poetry. The Parnassian revolt, when it came, was at the same time an actual effect of the scientific revolution and its analogue in the history of art. For the French Symbolists turned and fled what the Romantics had resisted and attacked — a world without quality. Their aim (in which they partly succeeded) was self-preservation; and who shall judge them for pursuing it? They deprived poetry of all cognitive significance, though not yet of all objective reference, since a Neo-Platonic sense of man as microcosm still hovered, as its vague tenor, behind much of their imagery. The English and American Imagists, who followed them, sedulously disinfected the poetic image of the last lingering vestiges of any such universal and objective meaning as the term "symbolism" connotes. They aimed at purifying the linguistic vehicle from any tenor whatsoever, so as to make it convey precisely, and only, some immediate personal experience of the author at some particular moment. The poetic image became identified with the prosopocentric image; and poetry, and literature in general, entered inevitably on their present course of degeneration into the insipidities of private anecdote.

By the logic of their own development the disinterested pursuit of scientific truth and the disinterested pursuit of art "for art's sake" have combined to bring us face to face with the choice before which we stand; and the true frontier is not drawn between literature and art on the one side and science on the other, but between this choice and that. It is rubbish to class as concerned with "the humanities" men of letters who merely vie with one another in finding new ways of delightedly presenting anthropos as meaningless; and to exclude from that class a scientist who maintains that "all thinking men are interested in the problem of understanding the world — including ourselves, and our knowledge as part of the world". What matters today is, not the two cultures, but the *trahison des clercs*[6] that would destroy them both.

There *is* a gulf, and a rapidly widening one, but it yawns between responsible men of letters and men of science on the one hand and, on the other, the fribbles in both camps who are happy to cock a snook at the Sphinx and get the biggest kick they can from producing either slicker and slicker gimmicks or sicker and sicker and sicker poems, stories and pictures. It is stretched, not between culture and culture, but between culture of any sort and anarchy, culture and chaos, between *gnōthi seauton* and the abolition of man.

ROMANTICISM AND ANTHROPOSOPHY

I.

"Time and again in the world's history," wrote the late Sir Walter Raleigh, "where East meets West, the spirit of romance has been born." What are the modern meanings of those two popular words *romance* and *romantic*? The longer we try, the more impossible we shall find it to compress them into any kind of formula. Definitions are wholly inadequate to such potent and evocative terms; if we wish to get at their fulness, we must approach them historically, examining what they have been made to signify at different times, and in different contexts, since they were first introduced into the language.

As the Roman Empire gradually declined, more and more of the provincials acquired the technical status of Roman citizens, and the blood of the original Latin race was thus mingled with that of the Celtic tribes who covered most of France, Spain, and Great Britain. At some point in this process the discrepancy between the correct 'Latin' spoken by professional Roman orators or written by learned historians and elegant poets, and the 'low Latin' spoken by the common people on the outskirts of the Empire, became sufficiently marked for people to become conscious of it. If you spoke the colloquial dialect, which had grown up spontaneously between Roman and barbarian lips, you were said to speak '*romanice*', and it is from this adverb that the English word *romance* is ultimately taken. As is well known, in course of time this popular dialect split into several, which diverged more and more widely, developing separate individualities according as the peoples who spoke them grew apart into separate nations, until they at last became recognizable as the modern languages of Italian, French, and Spanish — languages which we still group together under the appellation of 'Romance.'

The next important step in the meaning of our word was taken when men began to invent and to commit to memory or writing those old medieval tales — a curious blend of literal history, Celtic myth, esoteric Christianity, and other elements — which the French called 'romans' and English critics of the Renaissance *Romances*. To such critics the chief feature which distinguished a Romance from other forms of literature was the interaction in its plot of wonder-working supernatural agencies — fairies, sorcerers, giants, and similar mythical relics, which, with the rise of literary criticism, came to be regarded as the poetic 'fictions' of the authors. More and more, as time went on, the remoteness of these tales from all that now appeared to be the *reality* of life impressed itself on men's consciousness. At the close of the sixteenth century Cervantes had satirized romance in the immortal figure of Don Quixote; and during the next hundred-and-fifty years or so the general growth of rationalism and scepticism, and — in England — a violent reaction against the fanatical element in Puritanism, contributed to throw literature of this fantastic nature — whether it were the old tales themselves or modern imitations of them — into disrepute. Hobbes, for instance, protested in 1650 against the introduction of "impenetrable armour, Inchanted Castles, invulnerable bodies, Iron Men, Flying horses…" and Shakespeare's plays were looked upon as 'barbarous' or 'Gothic' in their extravagance.*

* Oxford English Dictionary. sb. *Romantic*.

It was at about this time that the adjective *romantic* was born, and it was used, as might be expected, chiefly in a disparaging sense. Very soon, however, its meaning unfolded a little further. It was applied to human beings, to people whose light heads were supposed to be filled with these Romances, of which they had read too many. Finally, by a yet further development, it was employed to characterize aspects of Nature of a kind among which 'Romances' were usually set. The connection is clear. In the eyes of readers who had stocked their hearts with the sentiments and their minds with the scenes of romance, such scenes — uncouth mountains, or wild, waste landscapes — possessed a romantic glamour and fascination which to the normal eighteenth-century gentleman was quite opaque, and which he accordingly found ridiculous. The romantic *impulse*, however, was quite strong enough to survive ridicule. Isolated more and more completely from the outside world by the desiccating encroachments of 'pure reason', it was to grow in strength and following, until it blossomed at last into that great outburst of fresh human thought and feeling which is known to us as the Romantic Revival.

Meanwhile, towards the end of the eighteenth century, we have seen how the adjective *romantic* had, as it were, two sides to its meaning. On the one hand it was applied to tales which were alive with medieval colour and witchery and to human imaginations which had fed on such tales; on the other, to Nature herself, as she could be perceived in the light of such an imagination. And now this word, and the ideas it contained — together with some other important æsthetic terms, such as *creative*, *originality*, *genius*, were borrowed or translated from the English language by Continental thinkers.* In this country, where they had originated, they had already been the subject of some haphazard speculation; in Germany they were taken up with an enthusiasm amounting to fury. Out of the chaos of the *Genieperiode* or *Sturm und Drang*, as it is now commonly called, a vast metaphysical æsthetic was erected on these foundations by her poets and philosophers — a body of thought and impulse, of which what one may perhaps call the poetic essence trickled back to us across the North Sea through the enthusiasm and the imagination of Samuel Taylor Coleridge.

From now on — fertilized by their contact with French and German genius — we can watch these two complementary meanings of *romantic* coming out into complementary expression in two significant English personalities — those of Coleridge and Wordsworth.

Discrimination between the two poets must not be taken in any rigid sense. Both aspects of Romanticism appealed strongly to both of them; but, taking their work as a whole, it is clear enough now how Coleridge found his inspiration more particularly in the *inner* workings of romance, in its direct effect on the human imagination; while Wordsworth spent his life rather in discovering and expressing those sublime feelings which hearts so attuned can draw from Nature. Thus, as the two meanings of the word *romantic* are complementary, so these two personalities seem also to have been complementary. They found each other out in the world; they formed, for some time, a close friendship; and out of that friendship the impulses for much of their best

* *Four Romantic Words*. L. P. Smith. Clarendon Press, 1924. (Society for Pure English. Tract. No. 17), from which much of the material in the preceding part of this essay is derived.

work sprang. In the volume called the *Lyrical Ballads*, which they published conjointly in 1798, "it was agreed", writes Coleridge afterwards:

> that my endeavours should be directed to persons and characters supernatural, or at least romantic; yet so as to transfer from our inward nature a human interest and a semblance of truth sufficient to procure for these shadows of imagination that willing suspension of disbelief for the moment, which constitutes poetic faith. Mr Wordsworth, on the other hand, was to propose to himself as his object, to give the charm of novelty to things of every day, and to excite a feeling analogous to the supernatural, by awakening the mind's attention to the lethargy of custom, and directing it to the loveliness and the wonders of the world before us. ...

And it is recorded by both poets that the idea of producing such a volume at all grew naturally out of the fact that Coleridge was writing — discussing it with Wordsworth as he went along — that poem, of all poems in the English language, into which there is distilled the very essence of witchery and faery — "The Ancient Mariner". They attempted to collaborate, but it was soon found that Wordsworth's poetical bent led him along a different track. Accordingly the *Lyrical Ballads* were projected, in which, alongside of Coleridge's "Ancient Mariner", we find Wordsworth seeking rather to express the "sweet lore which Nature brings"; and describing in "Tintern Abbey" how

> The sounding cataract
> Haunted me like a passion: the tall rock,
> The mountain, and the deep and gloomy wood,
> Their colours and their forms, were then to me
> An appetite; a feeling and a love,
> That had no need of a remoter charm
> By thought supplied. ...

And so gradually, out of the Romantic impulse, Wordsworth came to build up that misty yet sublime conception of the human soul, which he afterwards embodied less lyrically but more philosophically in the *Prelude*.

> We receive but what we give,

Coleridge had written

> And in our life alone does Nature live. …
> And would we aught behold of higher worth. …
> Ah! from the soul itself must issue forth
> A light, a glory, a fair luminous cloud
> Enveloping the Earth.

Wordsworth, though he would not have said that we receive from Nature "but what we give", was yet vividly aware of the extent to which susceptibility to her influence depends upon the history and training of the soul. It was this knowledge based firmly on his own experience, which made him feel, to a degree which has sometimes been censured, the importance of his own inner biography. Thus, the alternative title of the *Prelude* is the *Growth of a Poet's Mind*, and in that long poem Wordsworth gives shape to all his most intimate and significant memories, seeking to lay his finger on the various early experiences which had contributed to fashion his imagination. This he did, not out of futile self-importance, but because his was an imagination which to the visible world of Nature could

> add the gleam,
> The light that never was on sea or land,

one which had power to generate that "auxiliar light", which, as he notes in the Second Book of the *Prelude*,

> Came from my mind, which on the setting sun
> Bestowed new splendour; the new melodious birds,
> The fluttering breezes, fountains that ran on
> Murmuring so sweetly in themselves, obeyed
> A like dominion, and the midnight storm
> Grew darker in the presence of my eye.

Such a light — and especially at the beginning of the nineteenth century — was not meant to be hid under a bushel.

Now while, as we saw, the *growth* of this impulse — the impulse to perceive with new and conscious delight a living spirit in Nature — is indeed connected historically with the imaginative life that burgeons in the old Romances, yet the impulse itself, once it had reached the outer air of self-consciousness, quickly overstepped such narrow limits. Thus the Romantic Revival is also intimately connected with the re-discovery by men like Goethe and Coleridge of the surpassing greatness of Shakespeare. And in the *Prelude* fairy-tales and Romances are only *one* of the many influences which Wordsworth records as having shaped his imagination. Here, as elsewhere, he describes how it fed also on the great mythologies of the past, on literature and art, and in particular on all tender human experiences and sympathies:

> The clouds that gather round the setting sun
> Do take a sober colouring from an eye
> That hath kept watch o'er man's mortality;

And he tells us, again, how all these influences, and the moods which they have induced, accumulate and gather force, until the soul,

> Remembering how she felt, but what she felt
> Remembering not, retains an obscure sense
> Of possible sublimity, whereto
> With growing faculties she doth aspire,
> With faculties still growing…

II.

I have tried in the foregoing to isolate two elements in the meaning of the words *romance* and *romantic*, and to show how they developed historically and how they finally found a peculiar expression in the personalities of Coleridge and Wordsworth. There are other elements, but for the moment these must suffice. What one cannot help noticing today about Romanticism is that it is all a little vague and vast and shadowy. Perhaps it is for that very reason that this word *romantic* has long been the nucleus, together with such counter-terms as *classical* or *realism*, of violent and heated discussions in æsthetic circles throughout Europe. And perhaps it is partly as a reaction against all this that there should be abroad at the moment a fairly pronounced feeling that Romanticism, at any rate as metaphysic, is a failure. Its potentialities seem to have been left hanging in the air, its numerous loose threads ungathered; and the would-be Romantic who, in his youth, may have come under the spell of Wordsworth, Coleridge, Shelley, Keats, is faced, as he grows up, with the alternative of attempting to write second-hand romantic verse, or losing himself in the obscure and self-contradictory mazes of German transcendental philosophy.* So, at any rate, it seemed until recently.

Even today, few people are aware that, towards the close of the nineteenth century, Dr Rudolf Steiner began to erect on the foundations laid by that prince of Romantics, Wilhelm Goethe, a new and solid edifice of metaphysic. With what unspeakable relief one discovered this new channel, into which the deep creative impulses awakened from their ancient slumber by romance, only to be choked back into the unconscious by the ubiquitous determinism of twentieth century thought — into which these could pour themselves without fear of check, and without the risk of soaking away through banks too weak to hold them — leaving nothing behind but a few puddles of promiscuous sentimentality!

Let us look, for a moment, at the two first stages of the 'supersensible cognition', to which Dr Steiner pointed the way. He named them Imagination and Inspiration, and in his various writings he sought to give indications of their nature from a thousand different points of view. In Imaginative Cognition, he taught, one acquires, as it were, a picture-consciousness; it is analogous to the consciousness men have in dreams, and in it the great spiritual facts of life and creation come before the soul in the form of pictures. Formerly the human soul lived instinctively in this kind of consciousness, and the great myths of the past are but lovely crystallizations of its waking dreams. Today, Imaginative Cognition can be recovered — with the added element of full self-consciousness — partly by definite exercises in

* A third possibility — fashionable at the moment, and carried to orchid-like perfection by the late M. Marcel Proust — is to indulge in minute and dilettante reminiscences of one's earliest childhood.

concentration and partly by letting the imagination dwell on these myths and on the historical events of the spirit which underlie them. And it is just these elucidations, from within, of the historical events and processes in the spiritual evolution of man and of the Earth which once found pictorial expression in the myths — it is just these which are scattered in such star-like profusion throughout Dr Steiner's writings.

We notice also that in Imaginative Cognition the *memory* plays an all-important part. It is strengthened and vitalized in such a way that the individual's past life lives in his consciousness as an organic whole. He feels his biography as the time-body of his ego, just as his flesh and bones are its space-body. Steiner was always careful to insist that the experiences which come as the result of this kind of cognition are all experiences *created by the individual himself*. At this stage, we do indeed — as Coleridge wrote so sadly — "receive but what we give"; and the knower is deluding himself if he takes such experiences as messages from a spiritual world outside himself, just as the author of "The Ancient Mariner" would have been deluding himself if he had seen that the greybeard loon actually walking into his drawing-room.

It is only at the next stage (though the two need not be reached in strict chronological sequence) — that of Inspiration, that he begins to experience the spiritual reality underlying the world of Nature, to perceive and feel the manner of its working in flower and animal, in earth and water and sky. It is not that nobody else receives intuitions of a lofty and spiritual nature from the living beauty of this Earth; but that in Inspiration, as it is defined and inculcated by Rudolf Steiner, one lives with the Spirit of the Earth in a specially vivid and secure way — one has relations with Nature which differ from the ordinary ones as a great poet such as Wordsworth differed from the ordinary man.

Now all genuine art is the result of some degree of supersensible cognition — though the artist may not be fully conscious of this — and it is natural that Romantic poetry, which is of such recent birth, should have shadowed forth in its development just the method of attaining to such cognition which is suited to our times. Accordingly we find it pointing quite clearly to a progress through imagination to inspiration; we find this progress in the history of the very meaning of the word *Romantic*; we find it in the development of a new and strong feeling for Nature in Coleridge and Wordsworth, not only in the separate life of each poet, but also in the relation between them. Coleridge brooded on the remains of Celtic and other myth contained in medieval faery romance, on esoteric Christian doctrine, and on modern transcendental philosophy. His imagination, thus nourished, could produce such astonishing concatenations of pictures as "Kubla Khan" and "The Ancient Mariner" (it is also remarkable how the poetic level of "Christabel" immediately drops, when that poem seeks to pass from a chain of suggestive imagery into simple narrative). Moreover, his imagination could play with lambent flames around the genius of Wordsworth, offering him its native magic, as a kind of wand, with which to charm the spirit forth from Nature into the majestic harmonies which we all hear. One thinks at once of the tremendous simplicity of such lines as

> The silence that is in the starry sky,
> The sleep that is among the lonely hills.

where, as has been well said, Nature herself seems to take the pen from the poet's hand and write with it.

This was indeed a significant friendship; one beneath whose mild exterior there is audible such a hum of mighty workings that none but the deaf could think it accidental. For it had brought about one of those momentary impacts between an inner human world and an outer Nature world, of which the varied recurrence is the very rhythm of the history of the labouring Earth. East and West had kissed again, we feel, at Alfoxden, and once again Life was the fruit of their union.

Much of that Life we absorb into ourselves today, without knowing whence it comes. If we would help to make it more abundant for those who come after us, we must seek to understand the meaning of Imagination and Inspiration. And as a beginning towards this, it may be useful to English people to be able to trace their incipient workings in the English poets of the Romantic Revival. In particular, throughout the fourteen books of Wordsworth's *Prelude*, are the subtly interwoven strands of these two modes of consciousness discernible. To begin with, the very subject of this poem makes us feel to what an extent memory, strengthened by meditation, was, in Wordsworth's case, the well-spring of imagination. One is reminded of the famous "Ode on Intimations of Immortality from Recollections of Early Childhood", and again of Wordsworth's remark in his essay on *Poetic Diction* that the memory, if left to itself, will do most of the necessary poet's work of selecting and arranging experience. In the *Prelude* itself we find such passages as:

so wide appears
The vacancy between me and those days
Which yet have such self-presence in my mind,
That, musing on them, often do I seem
Two consciousnesses, conscious of myself
And of some other Being.

and

The days gone by
Return upon me almost from the dawn
Of life: the hiding-places of man's power
Open; I would approach them, but they close.
I see by glimpses now; when age comes on,
May scarcely see at all; and I would give,
While yet we may, as far as words can give,
Substance and life to what I feel, enshrining,
Such is my hope, the spirit of the Past
For future restoration.

In Book 5 the poet describes at length a curious day-dream which came to him, as he was sitting by the sea reading *Don Quixote*, and musing

On poetry and geometric truth,
And their high privilege of lasting life,
From all internal injury exempt.

Obsessed with the mournful thought that the external creations of man must all perish, he dozes and fancies himself lost in a boundless, sandy plain, across which an Arab approaches him, mounted on a dromedary, and carrying a stone in one hand and a shell in the other. The stone, said the Arab, is Euclid's *Elements*, "and this [the shell] is something of more worth". The poet holds it to his ear, and it gives forth

A loud prophetic blast of harmony;
An Ode, in passion uttered, which foretold
Destruction to the children of the earth
By deluge, now at hand.

Wordsworth walks on beside the Arab, thinking he has found a guide, but looking back he sees a great ocean of waters gathering to engulf them both. The Arab hurries on ahead to bury the books before the world is drowned, and the dreamer awakes in terror. Here is a remarkable Imagination, whose symbolism — the Arab, with his stone and shell — is made a good deal clearer by the study of Anthroposophy. And leading on from such experiences as these, we find the poet seeking to give expression to others, not really expressible in words — to moments when the pictures, as it were, "go out", and the purely spiritual experience of inspiration is left in its nakedness. Thus, in the First Book, he describes the night on which, as a boy, he had rowed by moonlight on a lake; suddenly memory reveals to him how the shapes of the mountains had then entered into his heart:

my boat
Went heaving through the water like a swan;
When, from behind that craggy steep till then
The horizon's bound, a huge peak, black and huge,
As if with voluntary power instinct,
Upreared its head. I struck and struck again,
And growing still in stature the grim shape
Towered up between me and the stars, and still,
For so it seemed, with purpose of its own
And measured motion like a living thing,
Strode after me. ...

but after I had seen
That spectacle, for many days, my brain
Worked with a dim and undetermined sense
Of unknown modes of being; o'er my thoughts
There hung a darkness, call it solitude
Or blank desertion. No familiar shapes
Remained, no pleasant images of trees,
Of sea or sky, no colours of green fields;
But huge and mighty forms, that do not live
Like living men, moved slowly through the mind
By day, and were a trouble to my dreams.

It would be possible to quote any number of passages bearing on the same theme. But at present I am content if I have contrived to indicate one of the historical connecting links between Romanticism and Anthroposophy, and to hint intelligibly at the way in which Anthroposophical activity can take up the Romantic impulse into itself and endow it with fresh life and youth. In conclusion I shall quote one more passage from the *Prelude*. Wordsworth is describing his walk across the Simplon pass and how, upon enquiring the way of a peasant, his party suddenly realized that they had "crossed the Alps" without knowing it:

Imagination — here the Power so called
Through sad incompetence of human speech,
That awful Power rose from the mind's abyss
Like an unfathered vapour that enwraps,
At once, some lonely traveller. I was lost;
Halted without an effort to break through;
But to my conscious soul I now can say —
'I recognize thy glory': in such strength
Of usurpation, when the light of sense
Goes out, but with a flash that has revealed
The invisible world, doth greatness make abode,

There harbours; whether we be young or old,
Our destiny, our being's heart and home,
Is with infinitude, and only there;
With hope it is, hope that can never die,
Effort, and expectation, and desire,
And something evermore about to be.

GOETHE AND EVOLUTION

If we say that Goethe looked on man as a part of nature, there is a deceptively familiar ring about the last part of the sentence. "So do I", most people will reply. Neither a Darwinian, nor a Behaviourist nor a Marxist will have any quarrel with him on that score; and most Christians will agree after making the distinction between a state of nature and a state of grace.

And yet there is a very great difference between what Goethe meant and what most people mean today when they speak, or think, of man as being a part of nature. When we say it, we have at the back of our minds — most of us — what I will call the outside of man, his flesh and his bones and his brain — all in fact that we can perceive of him through the senses during his life or after his death. And we think of all this as having developed by gradual process from a world in which there were once no men and at an earlier stage still no animals, and so forth. Whatever he thought about this process, Goethe also believed that the inside of man was a part of the inside of nature. There are of course those who contend, or appear to contend, that man has no inside, in the sense in which I am using the word. They say that his consciousness, including his thoughts, is a bodily process analogous to secretions. But I do not think I need pause to consider if they are right, because it follows, if they are not wrong, that there is no such thing as being right or wrong but only secretions and a making of noises. Our business is with Goethe.

If anyone entirely unfamiliar with Goethe's outlook on man and nature asked us today how he could come at some notion of it, what should we tell him? I think I would begin by referring to a realm of experience with which most people nowadays have a nodding acquaintance, though it had not been heard of in Goethe's day. I would tell him to think of the Unconscious. If he directed his mind to the whole vague network of thoughts and assumptions involved in such a phrase as Jung's *Collective Unconscious* — and it is nothing to my immediate purpose whether Jung's theories are true or not — I think the words 'inside' and 'outside' would begin to be clothed with meaning, and he might begin to appreciate the difference between 'man' — and nature too — as Goethe thought of them, and man and nature as the natural sciences investigate them.

Here I should like to observe that, whenever I myself begin to feel a bit comfortable with nature, there is always someone ready to hurry along and tell me that I am trying to get back, or am getting back, or have already got back, to the womb. I have heard this so often in one form or another that I am quite sure it must be true; and I am very sorry about it. May I however just point out that the first step usually taken by practical men engaged in a practical undertaking is to establish themselves in a thoroughly well-warmed headquarters.

Was Goethe then an introvert? Mainly interested in ferreting about among those half-formed emotions and impulses and huge creative forces which move in a mysterious way within us, we are told, as the forces of nature drive us and shape us from without? Not for a moment. He was intensely interested in outsides. He was the most exact and conscientious observer of plants and animals and the physical structure of man — especially his bones. Nothing delighted him more than the loan of an elephant-skull. He seems to have been about as good at borrowing other people's bones as Coleridge was at borrowing other people's books; and at least one rather aggrieved letter, which is still extant, suggests that he was not always much better at returning them. Incidentally I think Charlotte von Stein has been a little unfairly treated by some of Goethe's biographers. The intellectual and active life of that lady between the years 1775 and 1786 must have been something of a marathon. When she was not mugging up Spinoza in Latin as well as German — or inspecting musty skulls, she was always liable to get an urgent request from Goethe for "mosses of all sorts, if possible with the roots — *and wet*".

In the same letter Charlotte speaks of a new book which makes it probable that men were originally plants and animals. And this brings me to the hardest part of my task. For I have to try to describe the origin of something new in the world of thought. Or rather — which makes it still harder — something then new, but now very familiar to us all. I do not mean a theory. The absence of that is easy enough to look back on. No, I mean an image or construct, a meaning, a *Vorstellung*, a *Bild*, as the Germans say — whatever word or phrase you choose, as long as you grasp that it is not a theory I am talking about, but rather the raw stuff about which theories are formed.

What is it which, more than anything else, cuts us off mentally from the year 1749? It is the presence, implicit or explicit in practically all our thinking about everything, of this mental image of development, or evolution (for the two are really synonymous). I am not speaking of any particular theory of evolution; nor only of the evolution of species, but of 'development' in general, including the development of the individual from procreation to maturity. I am asking you to withdraw your mind from such things as arguments between Huxley and Wilberforce, or between Darwinians and Lamarckians and to direct it to the thing they were arguing about — this mental image, so familiar to us now, and yet, in itself, so strange, of one form gradually changing into another form and yet somehow retaining identity. This was the new thing that came into men's minds between Goethe's birth and his old age. This is still the important thing. By comparison with it the theory of, for example, natural selection, however true it may be, is little more than a stunt. For that was simply the transference to one set of observations of a well-established way in which men were already thinking about another. Whereas evolution *simpliciter* was a new *way* of thinking. And like all such new ways, its introduction was an act of man's image-making faculty; sometimes called imagination. It sprang, not from theorising but from direct observation.

What is the best way to get inside the skin of a man whose state of mind or feeling on some matter is quite alien to me — alien, because it lacks something which I take for granted? The best way is to find a something else about which I feel as blank as he does about this. Jones's emphatic refusal of all kinds of salad-dressing is so incomprehensible to my taste that I begin to feel he is an affected ass. I get irritated with him. But the moment I stop thinking about salad-dressing and concentrate on rice-pudding, I find myself standing open-eyed in his shoes, and he is once more a man and a brother. The same device may be used for slipping on the mental shoes of a bygone age. Do you want to imagine what the new idea of 'development' looked like to an age in which the word 'evolution' merely meant what Sam Weller called "swelling wisibly"? In which it meant what is now called *emboîtement*, the doctrine that the entire animal or, in man, an entire *homunculus*, is contained in miniature in the primary cell? If so, my advice would be to stop thinking about evolution and think, instead, about something which we regard as absurdly unscientific and romantic: Greek mythology, if you like. I believe Rossetti once told William Morris that it was absolutely impossible for him to feel any interest at all in anyone whose brother was a dragon. Perhaps you feel that the whole world of gods and furies and naiads and so forth is so remote and preposterous that you cannot take it seriously even as fiction? Well, if not, choose something else that you *do* find queer. What I am trying hard to suggest is the intellectual ferment which was required in order that what we call 'evolution', instead of being as unfamiliar to us as Greek mythology (or whatever else you have chosen), should become something we simply take for granted. For in that ferment Goethe, as is clear from his correspondence, was a very active ingredient indeed.

I am not well enough read in the works of eighteenth-century biologists throughout Europe to be able to assess with confidence the precise importance of the part played by his imagination in creating or realising the idea of evolution; and I rather wonder who is. My own guess would be that it was a pretty important part; but it is not my case that, but for Goethe, we should never have heard of evolution — or, as he called it, metamorphosis. What I am concerned with is the form which the idea took, or rather retained, in his mind. For that is very different from most of the forms it has taken since. About as different, I would say, as a motor-car driven under its own power by one of the skilled workers who designed it is from the same motor-car hitched to a pair of oxen and used in the good old way as a luxury farm-waggon.

To understand Goethe's view of nature one thing is needful and that is, to understand what he meant by *Urphänomen*. These archetypal ideas or phenomena,[1] which realise themselves, he held, in the ever-changing forms of organic nature, are indeed the heart of the matter. They are the 'inside' of nature of which I spoke earlier; but — and this is all-important — they are as much inside man as they are inside nature. If therefore you call them, as Schiller did, ideas, you must remember that Goethe insists they are objective ideas. If you say, "Well then, they are not ideas but real entities", then you must not forget that nevertheless they are subjective. *Sinnlich-übersinnlich*[2] he said they were and he insisted that they were perceived rather than thought about, but perceived by the mind instead of by the senses. And this perception which depended on love and a devoted self-surrender as well as on accurate observation was a kind of communion.

It is not an easy notion and many people have regarded it as nonsense. I do not think so myself, and that is why I was at such pains to try to set before you the pure idea of evolution — or, as we had now better call it — metamorphosis. Because, if we have managed to hold in our minds the pure idea, or mental image, of metamorphosis itself, as distinct from the theories that have been woven round it, we have, I believe, taken the first step towards perceiving one of Goethe's *Urphänomene*. For metamorphosis, so apprehended, is really the *Urphänomen*, the archetypal phenomenon, of the whole of organic nature, of life itself.

The scientific works of Goethe were fully edited and annotated at the end of the last century by Rudolf Steiner. If you are in doubt whether investigations based on any such principles could ever lead to practical results, you should acquaint yourself with the way in which they were subsequently developed both by Steiner himself and after his death by his followers in such matters as medicine, agriculture and elsewhere. Of course it is only a beginning, but I happen to have the best of reasons for adopting a respectful attitude to the medical side and you may have heard of the Bio-dynamic method in agriculture which is based on strictly Goethean principles.

The importance of the place you assign to Goethe in the history of western thought depends inevitably on the view you take of the true relation between man and nature. The place I claim for him is a very very high one for the following reasons. I believe that human consciousness, as we know it, has gradually evolved from a much older condition of what I can only call unity with nature into a more recent phase of detachment and sharp self-awareness. By nature, I mean in effect, the whole of what we perceive through our senses (including of course our own bodies), though I have been obliged to limit myself to organic nature. I believe moreover that we stand now on the threshold either of a great disaster or else of a first step forward to a third phase. This third phase must involve a reunion with nature, without loss of the self-awareness. So I hold;

and I see in Goethe's whole life and work one long struggle to take the step, on behalf of himself in the first place and incidentally on behalf of mankind.

There is always something a little sensational in pointing to particular moments in history; but perhaps you will meet me half way, if I say that, ideally, the dualism of man and nature on which our civilisation has been resting (if you can call it resting) began when the Hebrews were forbidden to make graven images and were enjoined to worship only the invisible God who named himself I AM; and that it closed when the communes all over France dethroned Him and set up a goddess of Reason in His stead. The older type of consciousness, wherein man felt an inner unity between himself and nature, and a kind of coming and going between them, remains mirrored for us in the mythologies; and in the Greek myths especially we find this sense of inner unity with nature associated with a ready faculty for grasping in images the startling business of changing from one form into another. It is no accident that the richest storehouse of these myths which has survived to us is a poem by Ovid called the *Metamorphoses*. Notice, too, that it was during his stay in Italy, when he was dividing his time between the study of classical antiquities and observation of nature, that Goethe himself first fully realised the implications of his own view. Something of this will be found in the essay on "Winckelmann".

Just as it was an event of immense importance when, in the eastern Mediterranean, before and after the birth of Christ, there occurred a certain fusion of the Greek and Hebrew worlds of thought, so I venture to see in Goethe the herald of a new and equally intimate fusion of modern thought with — no, not with Greek mythology, but with what lay beneath it. I mean a unitary consciousness older and more living than anything that still lingered in the Greek mind and the Greek language of New Testament days. For by that time Greece in her philosophy had herself long felt the impact of the dualism. And just as at that time the Jew, who was directed to look, and did look, for the law of God inside himself, instead of without as formerly, found there something very different from Ten Commandments inscribed on two Stone Tables; so I believe that Goethe's message to us is this: that if, instead of looking at nature only outwardly, only through the senses, as formerly, we begin to look for her at the same time within ourselves, then we shall find something very different from a couple of laws of thermodynamics and a struggle for existence. And yet as in the one case, so in the other, what we shall find will not be a denial of the laws of nature as we know them, but their fulfilment.

RUDOLF STEINER'S CONCEPT OF MIND

THE TRUE NATURE of human thought is a matter of concern to everyone, whether he knows it or not. Everyone is concerned, therefore, with Rudolf Steiner's concept of mind; but not everyone will wish to acquaint himself with the framework on which the exposition of that concept was first stretched and displayed, for not everyone is interested in the history of philosophy in the nineteenth century. Here, then, in the short space available, the attempt will be made to say what it was that Steiner thought about thinking, so far as the writer understands it, and without much reference to the framework within which it was originally presented.

It is founded on two axioms. Steiner himself does not call them axioms, or place them at the beginning of his exposition. He does, however, draw very special attention to them, pointing out that, though both are commonly overlooked, both are self-evident to reflection.

In the first place, *a concept as such is not one of a series of perfect replicas*; *it is numerically identical in all the individual minds that think it*. This proposition is not really even open to argument, because on it depends the very possibility of arguing. Yet, as Steiner himself points out in his major philosophical work, *Die Philosophie der Freiheit*,* it

> conflicts with a common prejudice which is very hard to overcome. The victims of this prejudice are unable to see that the concept of a triangle which my head grasps is the same as the concept which my neighbour's head grasps...

* Translated into English under the title: *The Philosophy of Freedom* (Rudolf Steiner Press, London, 1949)

It is easy to see how this prejudice comes about. The naïve man believes himself — with some excuse, as we shall see when we come to the second axiom — to be the creator of his thoughts and he is led by this to assume that each person has his detached private concepts. Nevertheless, hard as it may be,

> It is a fundamental demand of philosophic thinking to overcome this prejudice. The one uniform concept of 'triangle' does not split up into a multiplicity because it is thought by many persons. For the thinking of the many is itself a unity.

Or, as Steiner put it elsewhere metaphorically: "The mind is related to thought as the eye is to light."

The second axiom is this: that *thinking is our own activity.* This, again, is a matter of direct experience. Our thoughts cannot be thrust on us, as our sensations are, from without. They demand our co-operation, our own activity before we can be said to have thought them — before they can *be* our thoughts. Opinions, confessions, etc., brought about by modern techniques of persuasion, whether physiological or otherwise, are at most the exception which proves this rule. They are felt to be monstrous, precisely because they seek to *compel* that which bears upon it the very signature of the victim's own free act.

For the same reason — because the thought-process is so intimately and entirely *our own act* — it is impossible to observe it in its actual occurrence. We do not notice it, because we cannot contemplate what we ourselves effect while we are in the act of effecting it. This is Alexander's distinction between 'enjoyment' and 'contemplation'.* Steiner puts it as follows:

* See the opening pages of S. W. Alexander's well-known 1916–18 Gifford Lectures, published as the book, *Space, Time and Deity* (Macmillan, 1920).

> There are two things which are incompatible with one another: productive activity and the contemplation of that activity. This is recognised even in the First Book of Moses. It represents God as creating the world in the first six days, and only after its completion is any contemplation of the world possible: "And God saw everything that he had made and, behold, it was very good." The same applies to our thinking. It must be there first, if we would observe it.

But although we do not, and cannot, both think and observe ourselves thinking in the same moment, we never (while we remain sane) have any doubt that the thoughts in our minds are in fact 'ours'. So much so that, as already pointed out, we commonly — though erroneously — regard them as a sort of private world lodged within us. There is thus an important distinction to be made between *thinking* as an act, albeit an unnoticed act, and thought as the *concept*, which results from the act, and which we both notice and appropriate. Steiner emphasised that he made *thinking* his starting-point and not concepts and ideas, which are first gained by means of thinking:

> My remarks regarding the self-dependent, self-sufficient character of thinking cannot, therefore, be simply transferred to concepts. (I make special mention of this, because it is here that I differ from Hegel, who regards the concept as something primary and absolute.)

It is this, indeed, which distinguishes Steiner's Objective Idealism from the Subjective Idealism which, in one form or another, was predominant both in Germany and in England at the time when he was writing.

It was Rudolf Steiner's view that many philosophical errors have arisen from the fact that philosophers have been too ready to enquire what we can know and what we cannot know, without first enquiring what we mean by 'knowing'. This was, above all, the omission which he sought to rectify and it may be said that his own philosophy is primarily an epistemology, a theory of knowledge. Why is it so important that we should grasp the true nature of thinking? Because thinking is the "instrument of knowledge". A philosopher starting out to construct a true theory of knowledge must start, if he is faithful to his calling, from the very beginning. If we start from any assumptions at all — astronomical or historical assumptions, for instance, or assumptions about the part played by the brain and the nerves or sense-organs in the process of knowledge — we are clearly not starting from zero. We are starting from something on which cognitive activity has already been expended. The same remark applies if we start from the 'ego', or 'consciousness', or 'the mind', or by raising the question whether there is such an entity as the mind, or from the experience of a 'normal observer'. Only if we start from thinking itself, no such objection can be made. For thinking is the very first possible move we can make in the direction from ignorance towards knowledge. We cannot think about the world, or about anything at all, without thinking.

Thus, by way of example, it follows from the former of the two axioms that thinking is anterior even to the elementary distinction between subject and object. Thinking

> produces these two concepts just as it produces all others. When, therefore, I, as thinking subject, refer a concept to an object, we must not regard this reference as something purely subjective. It is not the subject, but thinking, which makes the reference. The subject does not think because it is a subject, rather it conceives itself to be a subject because it can think.

> The activity performed by man as a thinking being is thus not merely subjective. Rather it is neither subjective nor objective; it transcends both these concepts. I ought never to say that I, as an individual subject, think, but rather that I, as subject, exist myself by the grace of thinking. Thinking is thus an element which leads me beyond myself and relates me to objects. At the same time it separates me from them, inasmuch as it sets me, as subject, over against them.
>
> It is just this which constitutes the double nature of man. His thinking embraces himself and the rest of the world. But by this same act of thinking he determines himself also as an individual, in contrast with the objective world.

If, however, I owe my separate existence, as subject, to "the grace of thinking", yet something else besides thinking is required to bring this separate existence about. This brings us to the other primary element with which any theory of knowledge must deal, namely perception. Unlike my thoughts, my perceptions are private and personal to me, inasmuch as they depend on my point of observation and my separate physical organism. It is the perceptual element in the totality of my experience which thinking makes use of, as the means, to bring about my subjectivity — that is, my separate existence apart from nature and apart from my fellow human beings.

This important, and from one point of view startling, proposition requires a little further consideration. It is startling because we are accustomed to accept precisely the *perceptual* element in our experience — the evidence, as we say, of our senses — as constituting the 'public' world that is common to all mankind; while we contrast with this the 'private', inner world of our thoughts. This is justifiable enough in the ordinary loose use of language, but how carefully we must distinguish under the strict discipline of an epistemological enquiry! It is just here that the difference between 'thought' (as the product of the act) and 'thinking', the act itself, is relevant. For if it is *pure* thinking, disentangled from all perception, to which we are directing our attention, then, as we have seen, it is precisely this which *is not* private and personal to ourselves. And again, if it is pure perception, disentangled from all thinking, to which we are directing our attention, then it is precisely this which *is* private and personal to ourselves. Thus, it is not perception alone which can ever put us in touch with the solid, public, objective world, but only the percept mixed with thinking.

"Disentangled from all thinking", "pure perception" — we are of course going too fast; and it is impossible to avoid doing so in the brief space at our disposal. Concepts and percepts are, for Steiner, the bricks out of which the whole edifice of human knowledge is constructed; and the *pure* concept and the *pure* percept are accordingly the only elements on which an adequate *theory* of knowledge can be based.

> The moment a percept appears in my field of observation, thinking, too, becomes active through me. A member of my thought-system, a definite intuition, a concept, connects itself with the percept.

The terminology which Steiner employs to denote this important act of union between percept and corresponding concept may profitably be compared with the "presentational symbolism" of Susanne Langer.* It is

* Professor Langer's books, *Feeling and Form* (Routledge and Kegan Paul, 1953) and *Problems of Art* (Routledge and Kegan Paul, 1957), are gaining increasing recognition on this side of the Atlantic among those who are interested in symbols and symbolism. Her most intensive treatment of the aspect here considered will be found in the earlier *Philosophy in a New Key* (Routledge and Kegan Paul, 1951).

these conceptually determined percepts (he calls them *Vorstellungen* — representations) which make up the public world of our actual, everyday experience.

A good deal has been said already of the nature of the concept. We must now ask what Steiner meant by 'percept'. But let it first be made clear (in view of what has just been said on the topic of 'subjectivity') what he did *not* mean. He did not mean anything in the nature of a subjective representation; he did not mean the same thing as perception. *Esse est percipi*[1] was no part of his doctrine. "It is not", he writes, "the process of perception, but the object of this process, which I call the 'percept'." And again: "'objective' means that which, for perception, presents itself as external to the perceiving subject." What *are* subjective, on the other hand, are the after-images of those determined percepts, which remain in the mind when actual perception has ceased. These he called *Ideen* — ideas; and it is these which are the principal source of error and illusion, and the cause why the 'public' world-picture is by no means necessarily also an 'objective' one. The pure concept of a triangle is one and the same in your mind and mine — not so the perceptual trappings, which may have stuck, as it were, to the concept, left there by particular representations of triangles on particular blackboards.

Just as the concept unavoidably presents itself to us as the product of our own activity, so the percept unavoidably presents itself as *not* the product of our own activity. Indeed, that is almost its definition. The percept is all *that* in the totality of our experience which is *not* the product of our activity. It may, for that reason and to that extent, be properly described as 'given':

> What then is a percept? This question, asked in this general way, is absurd. A percept occurs always as a perfectly determinate, concrete content. This content is immediately given and is completely contained in the given. The only question we can ask concerning the given content is, what it is apart from perception, that is, what it is for thinking. The question concerning the 'what' of a percept can, therefore, only refer to the conceptual intuition which corresponds to the percept.

Here it will be necessary to say something of Steiner's concept of 'the Given', which plays such an important part in his epistemology. We find that he uses the word in two different ways. William James, writing on man's experience of time, adopted from E. R. Clay that useful term "the specious present".[2] By analogy with this use — once more introducing a piece of terminology not employed by Steiner himself — we will call his 'given', in the first sense, 'the specious Given'.* It is simply what we actually find, of any description whatever, when we look around us in the world. What we find, that is, at the point in our lives when we first decide to tackle the problem of knowledge (not, therefore, at the breast or in the cradle). We have made up our minds about the true nature of the instrument called thought. The next step is to apply our thinking for the general purpose of acquiring knowledge. And clearly we must start where we actually find ourselves. We have no right to start with assumptions of any sort. We have certainly no right to pretend that we start from some imaginary state of mind, such as a man might have who had perceptions but as yet no thoughts — the "blooming, buzzing

* The initial capital is intended merely to indicate that the adjective is used substantively.

confusion" of which William James also wrote. Whatever preceded the starting-point must, *to begin with*, be taken for granted. What we are actually surrounded by is a world of phenomena, both outer and inner — trees, houses, books, theories, pains, pleasures, dreams, hallucinations and what you will — some parts of which present themselves as connected or related wholes, while others are as yet unconnected and unrelated.

How, asked Steiner in his doctoral thesis *Wahrheit und Wissenschaft*, do we start upon the business of *knowing* about all this? We have to discover a bridge that leads from the picture of the world as given to the picture of it which our cognitive activity unfolds:

> Somewhere in the Given, we must discover the spot where we can get to work, where something homogeneous to cognition meets us... If there is to be knowledge, everything depends on there being, somewhere within the Given, a field in which our cognitive activity does not merely presuppose the Given, but is at work in the very heart of the Given itself.

This spot, or field, is the activity of thinking. At all points and at every moment it keeps inserting us, as it were, into the very texture of the Given. Out for a walk, we hear a sudden whirring noise, which "means" nothing to us; a moment later a partridge rises from the hedge near at hand. The concept of cause and effect arises in us to unite the two percepts and at once becomes part of the Given. Next time we heard the whirring noise, it carries its meaning within it.

And now, what proved such a disadvantage when our problem was to *notice* the act of thinking, to be *aware* of it — namely, the fact that we 'enjoy' thinking and do not 'contemplate' it, *because thinking is so much our own activity* (*so much our own very self in action*) — now this becomes the very stamp upon its passport to utility. For the problem of knowledge is always how to relate the knower to the known. What has the phenomenal world got to *do* with me, the observing outsider? Why should there, and how can there, be a link between them called truth, or knowledge? Well, it seems there is one point where the two incompatibles coalesce; one point where "the object of observation is qualitatively identical with the activity directed upon it". And that point is, precisely, the activity of thinking.

Now if we reason back a little from the example of the whirring noise and the partridge, we at once have it brought home to us that the specious Given is positively full of such conceptual determinations. This applies even to that part of the specious Given which we call 'sense-data'. We owe it to our concepts that we perceive a world of shapes, forms, 'things' at all. "The picture of the world with which we begin philosophical reflection", wrote Steiner in *Truth and Science*,

> is already qualified by predicates which are the results solely of the act of knowing. We have no right to accept these predicates without question. On the contrary, we must carefully extract them from out of the world-picture, in order that it may appear in its purity without any admixture due to the process of cognition.

This brings us to his other use of the term 'given' — according to which it coincides with the pure percept, prior to all conceptual determinations whatsoever — to that element in experience which is *wholly* perceptual. Let us call it here the 'net Given'. It is important to be clear that the Given is never actually experienced 'net'.

Thus, the net Given is something which a philosopher is concerned with, not as knower, but as epistemologist. This is a distinction Positivism fails to observe. Certainly we are not entitled to build up a picture of the world by starting from James's "blooming, buzzing confusion" — a thing we never experience. But that is not to say that we *are* entitled to treat the specious Given (i.e. the world as normally experienced) as though it were the same as the net Given. We arrive at the concept of the net Given, not empirically, but by analysis. We may say of it (as James said of what he called the 'real', in contrast to the 'specious', present): "Reflection leads us to the conclusion that it must exist, but that it *does* exist can never be a part of our immediate experience."

To seek to limit the *theory* of knowledge by applying to it, for instance, the principle of verification is like seeking to use a well-cooked meal, not for eating, but as material for making pots and pans; or like hunting for your spectacles with the help of those very spectacles which are already (you have forgotten) lodged on your nose.

Steiner declared at the beginning of the introduction to the original edition of *Truth and Science*, that his aim was "to reduce the act of cognition, by analysis, to its ultimate elements". He showed that, if we analyse it, the sense-experience from which we take our start, discloses itself to be no such ultimate element. It may be a 'public', but it is nevertheless a highly subjective, picture of the world and one which is overcome in the process of knowledge itself. Positivism (and — in so far as it is based on an uncritical acceptance of positivist doctrine — this is true of modern science also) treats this initial experience — the specious Given — as constituting also the *ultimately* given starting-point for all reliable knowledge. This was where Steiner differed from them both.

We start, he said — as we must — from the Given; but in the course of the adventure our epistemological analysis itself establishes that that starting-point was not, after all, 'given' in the absolute sense we had supposed. On the contrary, it is and was saturated at all points with the activity of thinking, past and present. Only unfortunately we cannot *experience* separately — the one divided from the other — either the thinking activity or the net Given which is independent of it. Two courses are therefore open to us. We can reject the analysis — on the ground perhaps that it raises questions which "cannot be asked" — and go on pretending to ourselves that the specious Given is as independent of thinking as the net Given. We shall then conclude that the only thing to do is to learn all we can 'about' the specious Given, with the help of precision instruments and mathematical generalisation, on the footing that our observing minds are mere onlookers, quite detached from it. Or we can, as Steiner did, deem illegitimate the refusal to distinguish because we cannot divide. In that case we shall conclude, with him, that an edifice of knowledge or science erected on the specious Given is incomplete and unreliable — for we know that the latter already includes the results of thinking — and may well, therefore, be tainted with subjectivity and error. We shall then be obliged to abandon the common assumption that all thinking and knowing is thinking 'about' and knowing 'about', and that truth is an ideal reproduction of some given object. We shall conclude, instead, with Gabriel Marcel, that "all knowledge is contingent on a participation in being, for which it cannot account because it continually presupposes it".

With this we really reach the end of our exposition of Steiner's concept of mind and are already beginning to survey its consequences and application. These are the province of the other contributors to this volume.[3] But the following should perhaps be added before we close.

If we are determined to eliminate all subjectivity and to be uncompromisingly empirical, if we insist on verifying from experience at all points, from the very start onwards, our only course is to find some way of penetrating with full consciousness into that unconscious no-man's-land (or should one say 'every-man's-land'?) which lies between the net Given and the specious Given. This is the realm where thinking performs the function of Coleridge's "primary imagination", or what Susanne Langer calls "formulation". It is, incidentally, the realm where language is born.*

It is obvious that this penetration cannot be effected with only the techniques and disciplines which science has so far developed. Instrument after instrument of ever greater precision and power is invented and applied, but, for our purpose, *the mind itself* must be treated as an instrument and *its* precision and power systematically augmented.† It follows from all that has been said of the

* In this connection it is interesting to consider the work of the late Ernst Cassirer, whose *Philosophy of Symbolic Forms* (*Philosophie der Symbolischen Formen*, tr. R. Mannheim, Yale and Oxford University Presses, 1953) appeared two or three years before Steiner's death and was first translated into English during the 1950s. For it is on the basis of an historical approach to language, looked at in this way, that Cassirer builds up his own theory of knowledge as mental activity.

† The impotence of ordinary, unstrengthened thinking to deal effectively with any subject-matter *except* the specious Given has been more than sufficiently elaborated by the linguistic variants of positivist doctrine which have been developed in the West since Steiner's death.

relation between thinking and perceiving that the strengthened thinking to which the discipline inculcated by Steiner is directed, must also result in widening the field of *perception* or *observation* themselves (as those words are ordinarily understood). This aspect he deals with in his Introduction to Goethe's scientific writings and in his short treatise *Grundlinien einer Erkenntnistheorie der Goetheschen Weltanschauung* which, together with the two books previously referred to in this article, contain the fundamental principles underlying Rudolf Steiner's concept of mind.

Moreover, since thinking is at one and the same time the activity of man himself *and* his only guarantee of objectivity, we have no right to assume that sense-perception is the indispensable witness to reality. Thinking is — and strengthened thinking will be aware of itself as being — that factor in man "through which he inserts himself spiritually into reality". It will make direct contact with reality somewhat in the manner we normally attribute to perception and if, on the one hand, it is "an active process taking place in the human mind", on the other hand it will be "a perception mediated by no sense-organ… a perception in which the percipient is himself active, and a self-activity which is at the same time perceived".

It is with the detailed results, both of that enhanced faculty of observation and of these purely spiritual perceptions, that so large a part of Steiner's books and lectures are concerned. But long before he began to bring them before the public, he had laid, in purely philosophical form, the epistemological foundation on which his investigations were based, and it is this foundation we have briefly tried to sketch here.

THE MANY AND THE ONE

As I see it, this conference[1] is going to involve an exchange of information between the participants concerning what each of them thinks and feels about the world, or the nature of reality — or whatever other name you may have for the topic that includes all other topics — at a rather deeper, perhaps even franker, level than is common on such occasions. That involves, again as I see it, that it is probably desirable for me to begin with some account of how I arrived at the position I myself shall be outlining. I will therefore tell you as briefly as possible that I was brought up without *any* particular view of the nature of reality, certainly without any religious convictions. The metaphysic implicit in my mental outlook (there is always an *implicit* metaphysic) was the one implicit in, for example, H. G. Wells' *Outline of History*; that is, broadly speaking, materialism plus a vague belief in something called "progress". At some time in the '20s (both my own and the century's) I discovered that a certain experience that came to me from reading poetry, and especially from the metaphorical use of language which poetry commonly involves, were themselves something to which it was difficult to deny the label of reality. In a book called *Poetic Diction* which I wrote as the result of that experience, I called that experience a "felt change of consciousness". Essential to the argument was a second experience which had followed on the first, namely, that the change of consciousness could be brought about, not only by metaphor deliberately created by beings called poets, but also by almost any use of language which revealed an immediate outlook on the world that was sharply different from the one habitual to myself and my contemporaries — almost any language, but especially by language stemming from *the past*. For instance, meanings which in the course of time had come to be conveyed by separate words were still present in one word in those days, and it seemed that one of the outstanding functions of modern poetic metaphors and similes was to restore that ancient unity in the consciousness of a reader. It was particularly noticeable that, in those metaphors and similes, material meanings are very commonly used to convey immaterial ones.

Thus, although the book was called *Poetic Diction*, it was really an account of the evolution of consciousness, as I was beginning to see it, and the burden of the book was, that that evolution was much more like an evolution of human *perception* than it was like a history of changing ideas about unchanging percepts. There was a time, it seemed, when perception of the surrounding world did not yet involve that detachment from the world perceived, the *monde vécu*,[2] that it necessarily does today: necessarily, because such a detachment is a *sine qua non* of our self-consciousness.

In another book, *Saving the Appearances*, which I wrote much later, I called that earlier perception "original participation". The later book attempts a much fuller account of the evolution of consciousness than the earlier one, presenting it as an irregular progress from *original* participation, through our present phase of *non*-participation — or, more strictly speaking, *unawareness* of participation — towards a "*final*" participation, the achievement of which in a remote future must depend on the creative mental activity of fully self-conscious human beings.

Looking back now, it seems to me that this outlook, or *Weltanschauung*, or metaphysic, has two unmistakeable features. In the first place the central status in it of evolution dissevers it crucially from what may broadly be characterised as orientalism. I mean by that the view which sees the predicament of each individual human soul as one of exile rather than of travel; so that the goal is to return rather than advance, and the wise man will aim at shedding rather than enhancing his individual identity. This is of some importance because at the time I am speaking of an increasing number of dissatisfied Western souls were beginning to turn away from their own cultural inheritance and to welcome with open arms the kind of transcendentalism which I have called orientalism, though I realise that my loose definition is not fully applicable to *all* the teaching that comes from the East.

The second feature is, that this doctrine, if I may now call it so, of an evolution of consciousness is quite incompatible with evolution, as it was understood by my contemporaries, and still is understood by the general mind of the West: in a word, with Darwinian evolution. The Darwinian picture of an exclusively biological evolution (which is of course older than Darwin, though it was Darwin who succeeded in riveting it so firmly on the Western mind) sees human consciousness as having begun from a condition of poverty amounting to non-existence and having gradually advanced in the course of ages to its present degree of sophistication. Somehow or other, although the human being was, to begin with, a purely natural object, in the course of that advance he had become capable of conceiving the immaterial, the subjective. Whereas the history of language and of meaning disclosed, as I was beginning to see it, a picture of evolution that was the very opposite of this — a "progress", which was at the same time a regress, a regress from an initial richness of immaterial content to the kind of poverty we know so well today, which can perceive only the material as real.

I cannot recall precisely when it was, but it was certainly after I began, and certainly before I finished, the first of the two books I have mentioned, that I became aware of the significance of Rudolf Steiner. For reasons which I hope will become clearer as I proceed, the subsequent development of my own ideas on the evolution of consciousness is so intricately connected with what I learned from his work that it will not be possible to keep them separate. The name of Rudolf Steiner is only rarely referred to in books on the kind of subject matter we are concerned with. I find that surprising in view of his actual stature, as I see it, and I suspect it must be due to a fundamental difference between his approach and that of all those others. Very briefly stated that difference is the difference between mysticism and occultism. Intellectual rebels against the kind of reductionism that has descended on the Western mind, whether they move towards some sort of revived Neo-Platonism or towards a more definitely oriental conclusion, such as we see in Fritjof Capra's *The Tao of Physics*, all seem to end up in a position which I would include under the general heading of mysticism. What then is the difference between mysticism and occultism? And I mean of course by occultism, not abracadabra and hocus pocus, but simply an epistemology that takes in the immaterial, the supersensible, as well as the material or phenomenal cosmos; one which does not simply reject, but endeavours to cognize the forces and qualities that were rejected as "occult qualities" by the pioneers of the scientific revolution.

At one point in his dialogue *Philebus* Plato delivers a significant warning to would-be philosophers. He warns them against trying to pass *too quickly* from the Many to the One. I sometimes wonder whether, in that remark, he was not prophetically distinguishing the future psychology and philosophy of the West from the past (and much of the present) philosophy of the East. At all events I suggest that, in that maxim, you have the nub of the difference between mysticism and occultism. For mysticism one step out of imprisonment in the phenomenal world takes you into an undifferentiated noumenal ocean, into some kind of Mystical Vision or Nirvana, or, as Theodore Roszak preferred to call it, "Rapture", to which the experience we call *knowledge* is irrelevant, if not impossible. For occultism, by contrast, after you have taken that first step beyond the senses, there is still a vast territory between the Many and the One, as richly or more richly differentiated than the phenomenal world of mineral, plant and animal, of earth and water and air and fire; and as human beings we are called on to make its acquaintance as best we can, not only for the sake of our own souls but also for the sake of the phenomenal world itself, since that world does not remain unaffected by our reductionism.

It soon became evident to me that, if evolution of consciousness is the truth of the matter, then this kind of knowledge is highly relevant to it, because it follows from it (as I tried to demonstrate in the second of the two books I mentioned, and elsewhere) that the immaterial, the supersensible, is not a something totally dissevered from the material, but rather is the pole of consciousness as against the opposite pole of that which is in itself unconscious, that is to say the phenomenal world as such. But at this point I must pause to outline two aspects of Steiner's metaphysic which are especially relevant to the rest of what I have to say. Speaking out of the kind of occult knowledge I have so far only defined, and of which I will say more in a moment, he put forward a detailed account both of terrestrial evolution from the beginning and of the historical development of humanity which characterises its later stages. I shall refer only to the latter, the historical development, dating from around the seventh millennium BC. In this he distinguishes five periods, each of about 2000 years length, and each of them characterised by a diminished degree of participative consciousness: an ancient Indian period, an ancient Persian period, an Egypto-Chaldean period, the Graeco-Roman period beginning in the 8th century BC and finally our own period, which dates from the 15th century AD and may be expected to continue into the 4th millennium. For the earlier periods, failing the kind of knowledge of which I shall be speaking in a moment, the shape of the consciousness they enjoyed is lost in the mists of antiquity. It is only as we approach nearer to the present day that verification or illustration by what I will call external research — myth, tradition, archaeology, surviving art and literature — becomes more and more possible; till with the Graeco-Roman age (or one may think of it as the Aristotelian age) we have a stage of consciousness which is pretty fully documented.

By contrast, the earlier periods, and of course all that went before them, can only be recovered — or perhaps, if we are willing to think of Humanity not only as an aggregate but also as a single Being, we may say "remembered" — by supersensible knowledge. That is to say a cognitive process not based on inference from the phenomenal world, not merely on imaginative extrapolation from it, but on direct perception of the noumenal or pre-phenomenal world. (Obviously the use of the word "perception" in such a context requires to be met more than half way, but for various reasons it is more satisfactory than "intuition", the meaning of which has been pre-empted by abstract philosophy in something the same way that the meaning of "perception" has been pre-empted by our empirical psychology.) I will just add that it is because Steiner claimed, and I have long been convinced that the claim was justified, that *all* his findings, whether borne out by external research or not, were based on this kind of knowledge — and also of course because of the limitations on my time — that I forbear all comment on the extent to which those findings are coincident with, or anticipated by, those of other thinkers, Madame Blavatsky for example, or the Hermetic or alchemical writers of an earlier age, in the West, or the Vedantic literature of India.

Before going any further I must say something of the steps by which this "higher knowledge", or brain-free thinking, brain-free cognition, is arrived at. They involve a training, not merely of the intellect or of the imagination but of the whole personality. I shall make no further reference to the training, none also to Steiner's earlier philosophical writings, in which he justifies on ordinary logical grounds the possibility of this kind of cognition. Here I am concerned only with the steps themselves, as he outlines them in what is perhaps the most fundamental text-book of Anthroposophy (the name he adopted to cover both the method and its results), *Occult Science: an Outline*. He names the steps Imagination, Inspiration and Intuition, and they are normally, though not invariably, to be reached in that order. It is the first two steps and the relation between them that are the heart of my matter.

Writing of course in German, Steiner does not use the more familiar *Phantasie* or *Einbildungskraft* for the first stage, labelling it instead *Imagination* — presumably because he wishes to emphasise what it can lead to in the future rather than its past linguistic provenance. I believe however that his concept of Imagination as a step on a path leading to knowledge is very relevant to the history and to the proper place of that concept in the evolution of consciousness. It is of that that I particularly wish to speak.

The notion that imagination may be potentially a cognitive as well as an inventive faculty is at least as old as Paracelsus, but it only began to be at all widely canvassed during the Romantic period. Coleridge's well-known distinction between imagination and fancy, and again between a secondary and a primary imagination, may be seen as a sort of landmark in that process, for example in the 12th chapter of his *Biographia Literaria*, where he speaks of a "philosophical imagination", and in doing so observes that

> all the organs of sense are framed for a corresponding world of sense; and we have it. All the organs of spirit are framed for a correspondent world of spirit: though the latter organs are not developed in all alike.

Coleridge himself had little more to say about those "organs of spirit", though to my mind it is apparent from some of his later observations and speculations in the domain of chemistry and physics, which are mainly to be found in his *Notebooks*, that he himself had to a certain extent developed and made use of them before he died. I have little doubt that the same could be said of more than one of the German *Naturphilosophen* but my acquaintance with their writings is not detailed enough to justify more than the suggestion.

The case of Goethe is different. He was intensively concerned with natural scientific investigation and even regarded his own contribution to it as more important than his literary triumphs. He advocated a new *method* of penetration into the mysteries of the natural world, and himself applied that method in such domains as botany, zoology and optics. The "perceptive judgment", as it has been translated, the German *anschauende Urteilskraft*, with which he proposed to supplement the accepted method of passive empirical observation followed by hypotheses based exclusively on the law of cause and effect, amounted, I believe, to a still rather rudimentary development and application of those spiritual organs whose latent presence in the human psyche was divined by Coleridge. It may fairly be seen as another step forward in the development of imagination as a means to cognition. Incidentally it is interesting that, when Coleridge heard of Goethe's work on the *Metamorphosis of Plants*, he was not very deeply impressed by what he heard; and this, not because he found it outlandish or unconvincing, but because he saw it as labouring the obvious.

The first substantial contribution made by Steiner to the world of letters was his editing of all Goethe's scientific writings, in the course of which he produced a little book, *Goethe's Theory of Knowledge*, which is as good an introduction to anthroposophy as I know. His own epistemology is closely allied to it, and it may be said that he used Goethe's work, and indeed his genius, as a kind of springboard from which to take off in developing and then applying, his own.

What then is the difference between Goethe's concept of imagination and Steiner's? Imagination is almost by definition the faculty of apprehending and of creating *images*. *Image*, *symbol*, *phenomenon* (that is to say, appearance to the senses) and even *word* (if we think of the relation between a word and its meaning) all signify, from one point of view, very much the same thing; and Henri Corbin's definition of "phenomena" applies to all of them: "things which can reveal themselves only by remaining concealed". Or, to quote the definition in full from his *The Concept of Comparative Philosophy*: "The phenomenon is that which shows itself, that which is apparent and which in its appearance shows forth something which can reveal itself therein only by remaining concealed beneath the appearance." Goethe was content, indeed determined, to remain within the limitation which that definition entails. He criticized contemporary science for going outside it by substituting intellectual theories and hypotheses for direct observation of phenomena. It was not that he was incapable of philosophical reflection. His introductions to sections of his scientific writings alone make that clear. It is rather that his theory of natural science deliberately eschewed it. He would not allow his attention to be drawn away from the phenomena themselves. His *genau auschauende Phantasie*, "exact percipient fancy", as it has been translated, enabled him to propound the *Urpflanze*, the "archetypal plant", the immaterial substructure which underlies and brings forth the forms of all actual plants.

But Goethe would not allow his mind to speculate on the archetypal plant *in itself* and apart from its function of producing phenomenal plants, for example on its history or its relation with other archetypes. One may perhaps put it that Goethe's imagination stopped short *at* imagination. It was not an end in itself, as it became much later for C. S. Lewis for instance; it was a means to an end, and that end was knowledge. But he did not, as far as I know, ever suggest that *the means itself*, the faculty of imagination, was itself capable of further development.

In Steiner's epistemology, on the other hand, as I have already indicated, imaginative cognition is only the preliminary step leading to a further and different kind of cognitive faculty, or rather experience, which he named Inspiration. (I shall not attempt to say anything concerning the further stage of Intuition.) In imaginative cognition the image-creating faculty of the knower allies itself with, merges with, and thus penetrates, the phenomenon-creating inner life of nature, as a means to understanding it. But, inasmuch as it is based on phenomena and remembered phenomena, it is still subjective. Although terming it imaginative "cognition", Steiner is at pains to emphasize that at this stage the knower is surrounded, as with a kind of membrane, by images dependent on his own mental activity. In order to reach the further stage of Inspiration, the knower must learn to apply the mental *activity* he had developed by enhancing his imagination in a different direction. He must use it to *obliterate* those very images. It is only then that he will come into direct contact with, will *know*, the spiritual in its own right so to speak, by direct experience; an experience for which, as I have suggested, the least inappropriate term seems to be "perception", though it is a perception more akin to hearing than to seeing.

All that is of course a very inadequate account of Steiner's theory, and practice, of knowledge.[3] Some rudimentary delineation of it was however necessary to a consideration of the difference between Goethe and Steiner. Whereas Goethe's field is limited to the phenomenal world, Steiner's extends far into the whole complex of the non-phenomenal, the noumenal, the supersensible cosmos. Let me give one example only, an example taken from that part of the vast field which is nearest to Goetheanism, and indeed to *Naturphilosophie* in general. Coleridge's insight penetrated to the *natura naturans*[4] as a whole that lies behind the *natura naturata*,[5] behind the finished product which we perceive as the phenomenal world. Goethe's insight distinguished within that complex individual archetypes. But they both have little or nothing to say about those things — except *as they become* phenomenal, that is, producing but "remaining concealed behind" what is apparent to the senses. But anyone who puts together all that Steiner teaches about what he terms the realm of "formative forces", or more often the "etheric" realm, including the etheric bodies of plants, animals and man (and I cannot myself claim to have gone so far) will find himself exploring, not simply a new way of knowing, but also a new *field* of knowledge altogether, differing from any field with which he is familiar, as Botany and Psychology differ from each other as from Physics. That is to say, he will not merely be engaged in satisfying himself that there *is* such a thing, that there *is* a realm of immaterial formative forces; he will be in the business of discovering more and more about its constituent parts, and their relation to one another. He will, for instance, begin to distinguish within the general category of the etheric a Fire or Warmth Ether, a Light Ether, a Sound or Chemical Ether and a Life Ether — the four ethers[6] distinct from but interpenetrating each other, which Steiner himself disclosed, and of which he and his followers are able to make some practical uses, and to suggest others. No doubt, if he knows anything of the history of science, the four ethers will remind him of an older Aristotelian and alchemical science based on the four elements, which has been lost sight of with the forward march of the scientific revolution and its determined rejection of all so-called "occult qualities". He will not object if it is said that Anthroposophy seeks to resuscitate an older wisdom which has been lost sight of, but he will also know that it is not mere retrogression. The point is that in Steiner the four elements are being cognised by the European mind *after* it has lived through the scientific revolution and in consequence is now able to maintain that sharp Cartesian distinction between mind and matter, between the supersensible and the sensible, in which that particular step in the evolution of consciousness has trained it so vigorously.

This really brings me back to the proper definition of a phenomenon, which I have suggested is the same as the proper definition of a symbol or a word. Why is it "proper"? *Is* it proper? Why does it say that the immaterial pre-phenomenon can only reveal itself by remaining *concealed* behind the phenomenon? It does so because it is determined to maintain that very Cartesian distinction between mind and matter, and to maintain it, not as a distinction but as a divorce. It says in effect that we can never speak, or never speak discursively, about the supersensible; we can only suggest it. This, I think, is where Steiner differs from all others whom I have encountered, who are aware of, and speak wisely about the necessity of overcoming our contemporary reductionism. He does speak, discursively and in detail, about the supersensible. In doing so, he has to use words; and words, as we have seen, are subject to the same limitation as phenomena. As Tennyson put it, in *In Memoriam*: "– words, like Nature, half reveal / And half conceal the soul within". How then are we to receive the words of a researcher who claims not merely to *half* reveal, or to suggest, the supersensible but to expound its nature and workings in sober detail? It is a very real difficulty. If the potentially phenomenal, the pre-phenomena, must remain concealed behind the phenomena, and if the same is true of any names with which we seek to denote the pre-phenomenal, how can we speak of it at all? Let me again give a single example. The four ethers are not the only garb in which the four elements reappear in Steiner's spiritual science. He also speaks of the supersensible Beings in whom their ultimate reality resides. And in doing so, he uses traditional terminology, the traditional names found in Paracelsus and no doubt elsewhere: gnomes, undines, sylphs and salamanders or fire-beings. Fantastic, fairy-story stuff! is our immediate reaction. How are we to take it seriously? Or, if we are interested in myth and symbol or in a general way in the Evolution of Consciousness we may say: No, of course it's not nonsense. But it's a pathetic attempt to put the clock back. And we shall still say: How are we to take it seriously?

I believe it is very important that we should come to do so. The answer, for me, is that we can easily do so if we never forget, first, the point I have been stressing throughout: that, as well as phenomena, all words, or at least all *nouns*, are not labels but are symbols concealing what they were born to reveal. We can, after all, if we choose, determine to fix our attention on the concealed part of a phenomenon, for although it is concealed, we know it is there. In the same way we can fix our attention on the concealed part, the supersensible part, of a word or name, in other words on its inner *meaning*, as distinct from any phenomenal associations we have with it. (This is incidentally a principle of interpretation of which I fear some of Steiner's enthusiastic followers are insufficiently aware.) But if the inner meaning is concealed, how can we ever become acquainted with it? How can we ever become discursive about it, think about it in detail? Well, in the same way that we became acquainted, as we grew up from children, with the phenomenal world — by learning to think about its causal and other relations with other meanings. Even for empirical thinking phenomena in themselves are impenetrable, and are only to be apprehended in terms of their relations with each other. The same is true, I believe, of supersensible phenomena, or noumena. A bare answer to the bare question, What is it? can only be answered be its name; and the name remains a symbol, concealing rather than revealing. But a fuller answer can be developed gradually in terms of the intricate relations of x to y and z, and so forth, and these relations are to a large extent apprehensible immediately and not only symbolically.

Instead of attempting to labour this point any further, I want before I conclude to say something of the position and status, as I see it, of Rudolf Steiner's intellectual contribution within the general evolution of consciousness in its later stages. Human beings do not talk or think about what they experience while they are still experiencing it. A certain *distancing* is necessary between ourselves and any element in our consciousness of which we are mentally aware. And that appears to be true not only of individual human beings but also of the general mind. In the history of Christianity, for instance, it was only as the sacrament of the Mass ceased to be a simple matter of immediate experience that Christians began to conceptualize and to reflect and dispute with one another on such matters as trans-substantiation and the Real Presence. If we see the evolution of consciousness in terms of a gradual fading away of the older participative consciousness, then we find that the same is true of the history of natural philosophy and natural science. It was precisely as an older immediate awareness of nature as a living being, of a *natura naturans*, as well as a *natura naturata*, was growing dim that it began in the Greco-Roman age to be conceptualized as philosophy. We can trace its increasing conceptualization from the pre-Socratics through Plato and Aristotle and their followers to a sort of summation in the Stoic doctrine of the Logos, Virgil's *mens agitat molem*,[7] the *logoi spermatikoi* of Philo Judaeus and others.[8] And I see the astrology, and especially the alchemy, of the late Middle Ages rather as a valiant attempt to arrest it by preserving something of the old participation, while availing itself of the new impulse to think empirically and discover experimentally. We know how all that virtually disappeared with the progress of a scientific revolution based firmly on the non-participating consciousness which had found its fullest philosophical expression in Descartes. Then, in the thinking of the Nature-philosophers of the 18th and 19th centuries, and especially of Goethe, we have, as I see it, the beginnings of an attempt to re-ascend from the nadir of non-participation, of total alienation from *natura naturans*, towards a renewed participation. This renewed, or modern, participation would be compatible with the full *self*-consciousness which the older original participation, and even the relics of it that disappeared only with the scientific revolution, had kept unattainable. I have come to see the contribution of Rudolf Steiner as something more than a further step, nay rather a giant stride forward in that re-ascent, and I have tried to outline some of my reasons for doing so.

If I am right about that, then we are faced with a big question, and with two great difficulties. The question is, will the intellectual and scientific world bring itself to recognize the fact of that giant step and its significance? The two difficulties in the way of an affirmative answer — and they really resolve themselves into one — arise from the nature of the step, that is to say, the fact that it has been made by one individual. There is in my mind no doubt that Steiner himself had advanced very far on the path of supersensible *knowledge* to which he pointed. There is also no doubt that up to now no-one else who has so far appeared has taken more than a few relatively short steps on the same path. How are the rest of us to handle, to work with, so extensive a body of information that is, by its nature, not empirically verifiable — information offered by one individual mind? Or, to put it bluntly, why should we? It is no doubt mainly, though not exclusively, because of these two difficulties that Steiner has so far been largely ignored. I come across book after book dealing, in some depth, with the sort of problem we are considering, but which makes no reference whatever to him, though a lifetime's study of his writings assures me that he knew far more about and saw more deeply into the subject-matter than any of the authors referred to in its index. It boils down to the question: can it possibly be a fact that one individual should be born into the world as far in advance of his contemporaries as I am suggesting is the case here?

To that question I find I am able to answer, Yes. Even in the realm of biology there are such things as abrupt mutations and the concept, increasingly accepted today, of a 'punctuated' evolution. But that is no more than a rather pitiful analogy on which I rest little or no weight. Rather I seem to find plenty of evidence that, if we knew more of the past than the *fable convenue*[9] of history tells us, we should find several examples of great Initiates whose supereminence, and whose significance for the age that followed them, was of the kind of I am suggesting. But we need not go as far back as that. The more you study the intellectual history of the Greco-Roman age, the more you are forced to recognize the startling extent to which the mind of one man brought together, and brought order into its fruits and enabled them to become the seed of the age that was to follow.

The age of Alexandrian and Roman philosophy was the age of Syncretism — of bits from one philosophy being fitted in with bits from another like a sort of jig-saw puzzle. It was not without its merits, but it had no future and it must, I believe, have disappeared like water into sand if there had been no Aristotle. He was the conduit through which the old age passed on into the new, and he became the trunk of the whole wide-spreading tree. He is there throughout, not only in Scholastic philosophy, where it is most overtly apparent, but in the very way we think, whether scientifically or otherwise. The scientific revolution, which rejected him as an authority, could no more have occurred without him as an abiding influence than the Copernican astronomy could have come into being without the preceding Ptolemaic one.

The syncretism of the Alexandrian age was at least limited to the academic community, or to a philosophical elite. It is otherwise today. When I look around at the immensely varied output of the 'human potentials' movement, or the Aquarian Revolution, or whatever you like to call the ferment, I seem to see a sort of super-syncretism, with everyone nibbling bits of religion and philosophy and science from everywhere. Symptoms — perhaps healthy symptoms — of the death of one age, and of the need for the birth of another. But I do not see any sign of their growing together to form the nucleus around which such a new age could, first, come to life and then increase in form and structure.

The fact is that, if the general picture of an evolution of consciousness, of a descent into individuation followed by a re-ascent towards participation in the universal, is the case, then it is not startling, it is even inevitable, that individual consciousnesses, individual minds, should appear from time to time with a wider and wider fullness of real content. I am not a prophet, but for what it may be worth the dim vision I have, when I peer into the future, strongly suggests that the redemption of civilization will depend in a very great degree on whether its intellectual structure comes to centre round the contribution of Rudolf Steiner to much the same extent as that of the Aristotelian age centred round Aristotle. To the same extent, not of course in the same way. Not in the pious acceptance of authority, with endless quotation, dissection and analysis of texts, and so forth. If you should ask me: in *what* way then? I can suggest no answer beyond the vague one, that it will be more like a nucleus than a blueprint.

With this I conclude the account which I have given as best I could of my own perspective, reached at the end of a rather long life, on the general area which I believe this conference is minded to survey. I remain aware that there are other perspectives differing, some more and some less widely, from my own; and one of the motives that has brought me here is the desire to hear more of them. At the same time I have thought that I could best comply with the underlying intention, not by spending a lot of time on showing awareness of, and respect for, those other perspectives but by setting forth my own as clearly and unequivocally as possible.

ISRAEL AND THE MICHAEL IMPULSE

THE DATE WHEN the present rulership of Michael[1] began was placed by Rudolf Steiner at the end of the 1870s — to be precise, in the year 1879.[2] We are now sufficiently removed from that moment in history to be able to perceive that it was about that time, also, that a certain kind of thinking reached its culmination. That was the kind of thinking that followed that great change of mind which has been called "the Scientific Revolution". It is true that, in many ways, Western civilisation is even more materialistic now than it was in 1879, but the vogue of materialism, as an all-embracing, self-confident world-outlook, has since then on the whole declined.

The coincidence of these two historical landmarks was no accident, and we understand neither the distinguishing feature of Anthroposophy, compared with other traditions of occultism, nor Rudolf Steiner's teaching of the mission of Michael, if we are unable to see that it was actually the coming of materialism, or at all events of the way of thinking and perceiving that underlies materialism, which made that mission possible.

How then does the human being of the age of materialism differ from the human being of previous ages? Is it simply that he has different theories — materialistic theories — about the world? No. It is more than that. The way in which men think about the outer world determines, in the long run, the way in which they *perceive* it also. Indeed it very largely determines *what* they perceive. And the world which men perceive today, as the result of the age of materialism, is a world which consists, essentially, of a multitudinous collection of detached objects; of objects detached alike from each other and from man himself. Today man feels himself to be related to nature *only* through what, in the East, they call "the contacts of the senses".

It was not always so. In earlier times it came naturally to human consciousness to see the objects — and often also the events — of the outer world, not as objects only, but as *images*. The visible world, in particular, was apprehended (not "believed to be", but apprehended immediately in the moment of perception) as an image, a representation, a copy of the invisible.

We can still hear a faint echo of this in our use of the world *phenomenon*. When a natural scientist speaks of a *phenomenon*, he normally means, today, simply an object or an event, and he thinks of the object or event as existing entirely in its own right and quite independently of men's consciousness of it — he thinks of it as "objective", in fact. (At all events, he *did* think so at the end of the nineteenth century. Nowadays the physicists, or some of them, think differently; but the other scientists go on thinking the same.) But the meaning of the Greek word *phaenomena* is, of course — "appearings" or "appearances"; and it was so that they were still, in some measure, experienced throughout the Graeco-Roman age.

We can best approach the difference, if we conceive that formerly it was really unavoidable, it was the normal thing, to experience the phenomena of nature in a way which *we* only achieve by a special effort, and with the help of the faculty we call "imagination". In a moment of vision, and of heightened consciousness, with the help of a poet or a painter, we may perhaps say to ourselves

Alles Vergängliche ist nur ein Gleichnis
All the world that passes away, is only a similitude

but the moment fades; and we find ourselves once more in the old familiar world of inexpressive objects and events. But once upon a time that vision was the normal thing. Visible nature was, without any effort at all, apprehended as *representational*, as expressive of an underlying invisible soul-spiritual substance; just as today the pictures, let us say, on a television screen are experienced in their very nature as representations and not simply as electrical phenomena in which we are interested for their own sakes. People just cannot look at them without being aware that representation is their whole *raison d'être*.

What does it signify to behold nature in this way — *imaginally?* It signifies, necessarily, that the consciousness of the beholder has another link with nature besides the link through "the contacts of the senses". If I apprehend the visible as an image, or copy, of an invisible, soul-spiritual substance, then I feel a relation between that soul-spiritual substance and my own soul and spirit; just as I feel myself related, not only to the visible body, but also to the invisible soul and spirit of another human being. It signifies an extra-sensory link between man and the phenomena. From the subjective point of view, this extra-sensory link which gives awareness not only of the object perceived but also of the invisible substance whereof that object is an image, or copy, is the "atavistic clairvoyance" of which Rudolf Steiner so often spoke. From another point of view — if we take our standpoint outside both man and nature, and contemplate their changing relation to each other — we can say that the human soul once shared or *participated* in the soul-life of nature. It is really this which distinguishes the ages of atavistic clairvoyance from our own age of mere sense-perception. The experience of nature as image, or representation, was the last relic of an even fuller participation.

This instinctive, effortless participation was still present vestigially at least, in the experience of ordinary men right down to the close of the Middle Ages. It is indeed impossible really to understand the Middle Ages, their art and their thought, unless we have begun by grasping the fact that medieval man lived in a slightly different world of ours. We experience that difference in the first place as a kind of crudity or quaintness. But this is mere parochialism on our part. The parochial man feels that everything unlike what he finds in his own parish is quaint and laughable; and there is a parochialism of time as well as of space. When we look on a medieval fresco, with its haloes and its absence of perspective, we should rather recall that in those days men still actually experienced nature, not so much as a collection of objects occupying positions in a receding space, but (compared with ourselves) more as a *picture* or tapestry — a picture of which they themselves were a part.

It came naturally to them to look upon whatever was presented to their senses as an *image*, rather than as a meaningless object; and it was for this reason that they were so satisfied with simple imagery in the world of art. The sculptor, bidden to represent in stone Elijah's ascent to heaven in a fiery chariot, was content to put him in a sort of farm-cart. For the chariot could be no more than an image; and a farm-cart itself was (like everything else in the phenomenal world) no less.

I have said that this way of experiencing the world of the senses was a relic of "participation"; and there are plenty of other indications that the men of the Middle Ages were in fact aware of themselves as participating in the soul-life of the earth and of the cosmos, in a way which has become quite foreign to us. Study, for instance, their conception of the four elements, their astrology, their alchemy, their theories of knowledge, and you will soon realise that they did indeed live in "a different world".

It was this world which was brought to an end by the Scientific Revolution. Yet the elimination of the old, participating consciousness, which was finally accomplished by the Scientific Revolution, had by no means begun with it. Elimination culminated in the Scientific Revolution, but it had begun long before. It had begun when the ancient Greeks first began to think speculatively and analytically about the world. It had begun in the preceding Michael Age, which lasted from about the 6th to the 3rd century B.C.

As soon as we begin to think *about* something, we become more detached from it. This is the case, for instance, with a strong feeling. As long as we do not start thinking about the feeling, we are one with it — possessed by it. But if we *attend to* the feeling, if we begin speculating about it, analysing it, we at once begin to be less united with it. It becomes, to some extent, an object outside of us, and our innermost selves are set over against it as subject. We may sometimes even *wrestle* with a feeling in precisely this way. We strive then, by thinking about the feeling, to free ourselves from its dominion. And if we are in some degree successful, then, although we still *have* the feeling, we are also aware of a part of our self, which is free from it — and may ultimately gain control of it.

It was something the same when man first began to think about nature. Hitherto he had been wholly possessed by her; his thoughts and impulses had been, so to speak, *her* dreams. But as the habit of thinking about nature gained strength, man ceased progressively to be aware of himself as part of the cosmic life, of the Cosmic Intelligence which creates and informs nature, and became aware, instead, of his critical intelligence operating on objects distinct from him. And this critical intelligence he could feel to be truly *his own*, *his* "Intellectual Soul".[3]

According to Rudolf Steiner, this gradual emergence of man from the old participation in nature, or in the Cosmic Intelligence which is the spirit of nature, has been the deep concern of Michael. Indeed one way of presenting the history of the Michael impulse — we might call it the Graeco-European way — is to trace the final coming into being of the Intellectual Soul in the Middle Ages, as it is reflected, for instance, in Christian and Arabian scholastic philosophy. We can watch Aristotle's two great cosmic principles — the *Nous Poieticus* and *Nous Patheticus* — changing into the *Intellectus Agens* and *Intellectus Possibilis*[4] of scholastic philosophy and, in doing so, we can grasp something of the nature and magnitude of Michael's hope. For it is Michael's hope that the Cosmic Intelligence shall gradually become embodied in the human personal intelligence — giving man an intellectual soul at once detached and not detached from its cosmic origin.

If this process of embodiment had taken place too smoothly, and with no break, it could not have ended by leaving man a completely free being. He had first — before the Cosmic Intelligence could become embodied in his intellectual soul — to lose all awareness of *any* concrete link at all with the Cosmic Intelligence. This was finally and conclusively effected by the Scientific Revolution. At the close of the Scientific Revolution men had certainly become more aware of themselves as free critical intelligences than they had ever been before. But the price of this freedom was the loss of all connection with, all realisation of, even all belief in a Cosmic Intelligence. Man looked within him and, instead of the Cosmic Intelligence, reborn there as his personal intelligence, he found — emptiness.

*

Now we have seen that it is easy and natural for the participating consciousness, that is, for the consciousness which *experiences* nature as imagery, also to *make* artificial images. And so, at the end of the Third Post-Atlantean epoch,[5] before the emergence of Greek philosophy and before the beginning of the Michael Age which preceded our own, the prevailing civilisation was an image-making one. Throughout Babylonia and Egypt the daily life of man was directed from religious centres, and the religion which they cultivated centred much round man-made images.

Then, several centuries before the end of that epoch — to be exact, during the reign of Rameses II., in the 13th century B.C. — a very surprising thing happened. In the very heart of the ancient Egyptian civilisation a man was born through whom the command went forth to his own particular nation to give up altogether this making of images. It is important to realise that, in the Second Commandment declared by Moses, the Jews were forbidden, not only to *worship* images, but also to *make* them. Indeed, the prohibition to make comes first, and is only followed, in a separate verse of the Bible, by the prohibition to worship. Moreover, they were not only forbidden to make or worship images; they were enjoined to destroy them.

> Thou shalt utterly overthrow them, and quite break down their images...
> Ye shall destroy their images, break their altars and cut down their groves.

Looking at the history of the Jews in the light of the history which preceded and followed the events recorded in the Old Testament, it is true to say that one of the impulses which they brought into humanity was the impulse to destroy imag-ination, and in doing so to eliminate the old participation of man in nature. The Jews felt this old participating consciousness, which centred round the pagan cults and was focussed in their images, as a kind of incontinence. They called it *idolatry*, and the images themselves, idols; and often enough the idolatry of the Gentiles was in fact closely associated with incontinence in the narrow sense.

Rudolf Steiner, in his lectures on St. Mark's Gospel, has drawn attention to the moment of crisis which occurred when even Moses had somehow lost control. He had lost the power to stay the sudden relapse of the Children of Israel into idolatry. It was at this moment that Phinehas — who, as the previous incarnation of Elijah, in a sense embodied the ego of the entire Jewish nation — stopped the rot by seizing a spear and transfixing one of his compatriots in the arms of a Midianitish woman.[6]

In the end, as we know, the Jewish effort to cast out idolatry succeeded. And this involved casting out the old participation. Read the beautiful hymn to nature contained in the 104th Psalm and contrast it with a Greek chorus or Plato's *Timaeus*. In the latter, nature is the garment or the body of the gods; the gods are immanent in nature. In the former, nature does indeed exist to declare the glory of God and to fulfil his law; but there is no suggestion that God is, in any sense, *in* nature.

Greek poetry and the philosophy of Plato still preserved the old participating consciousness of the East. It was only very gradually, in the course of centuries, that the analytical element in the Greek way of thought operated to exclude participation. Then this age-long process was hastened rudely to its inevitable conclusion by the Scientific Revolution. And, as we have seen, the destruction of imagination which it involved was here brought about, as it were, incidentally by the very nature of logical thought. But meanwhile the Jews had produced the same result *purposely*; with them the destruction of imagination had been an act of will.

When men eliminate from their consciousness all awareness of the human soul's participation in the soul and spirit of nature, they eliminate the divine from their perceptions. They extricate themselves from the bosom of the divine Logos which works creatively in nature. We may say that they *wrestle* themselves free. In the case of the Aristotelian-Christian stream this wrestling was a more or less instinctive process, incidental to intellectual development, whereas for the Jews it had involved something much more like an actual wrestling — an actual violence. For it had taken the form of their long, long struggle with idolatry.

I think this wrestling is prophetically foreshadowed in the account of Jacob's contest with the angel. If we read the story in Genesis xxxii., we notice, first of all, that the angel came to Jacob *by night*, that is, at the time when man's participation in his divine origin has always been at its maximum — and is even today maintained. At last the angel bids Jacob, "Let me go, for the day breaketh." And Jacob replies: "I will not let thee go except thou bless me." But before they part, there is a discussion about names. The angel asks Jacob what his name is, and is told: *Jacob*. Thereupon he tells Jacob that henceforth Jacob's name is to be *Israel*; and this is the first appearance of the name *Israel* in the Bible. Now the name *Israel* means "wrestler with God" (a strange patronymic, we may well think, for His chosen race!). It was therefore not merely an angel, with whom Jacob wrestled, but a representative of the Divine principle itself, of the Divine out of whom Jacob and all men had originated.

Then Jacob asks the angel for *his* name; and the answer is significant. The angel replies: "Wherefore is it that thou dost ask after my name?" And, instead of disclosing his name to Jacob, the angel goes on to fulfil the condition which Jacob had stipulated for letting him go. The next sentence in the text is: "And he blessed him there."

In asking the name of the angel with whom he wrestled, Israel had really been asking for the name of God. He was not vouchsafed the name, but he *was* given the 'blessing' he had asked for. I find it hard not to associate this blessing with that through which the

Children of Israel were ultimately to receive the Divine Name itself. I mean the Hebrew language. It is the peculiar quality of the Hebrew language that it contains the spirit in the *sound* and *shape* of its words. "The Hebrew tongue," said Rudolf Steiner in the first lecture of the Course, *Genesis — Secrets of the Bible Story of Creation*,[7]

> or better said the language of the first chapters of the Bible, was a medium by means of which imaginative ideas were called forth in the soul, approximating to the vision which the seer has when he is able, freed from the body, to look into the supersensible realms of existence.

And again, in the same lecture: "… at one time when one letter of it sounded in the soul, a picture was awakened within…" And there is more, in the second lecture, to the same purpose.

There is, then, in the Hebrew language a quality of imagination; but of an imagination not dependent on phenomenal imagery — a kind of supersensible imagination.

Other languages also have a quality of imagination in them, but it reaches us much more through the *meanings* of their words. For if we consider the *meanings* of words, as apart from their sounds, there too we shall find a wealth of imagery embedded in language — but it is all imagery in terms of the phenomenal world. (This is elemental Aryan etymology.) Thus, the *meanings* of words can only continue to contain the spirit, for man, so long as man himself retains his participating, imaginal consciousness of the phenomenal world. But it was just this imaginal consciousness which the Children of Israel, as we have seen, were called upon to renounce. And it was their 'blessing' that they were permitted to retain in the sounds and shapes of their language the participation which they had to eliminate from their experience of nature.

The more one studies the history of Jewish religious thought, both before and after the Mystery of Golgotha, the more one comes to feel that this spiritual quality, this non-representational but creatively imaginative spirituality of the Hebrew language, is in a manner summed up, concentrated, focussed in the Name of God, the Divine Name, or — as their learned men frequently called it simply — *the Name* (*ha Shem*).

The angel of God would not, as yet, reveal this to Jacob. But at a later stage Moses himself revealed it to Israel, the nation, when Israel had advanced farther in the task of wrestling itself free from the old pagan, clairvoyant participation in the Divine soul and spirit behind the phenomena of nature. We read in Exodus iii., how Moses asked what name he was to use in speaking of God to the Children of Israel, and how he was told: "Thou shalt say unto the Children of Israel, I AM hath sent me unto you."

The Hebrew verb "I am" is in fact a very slight variant of the usual form of the Name itself — incorrectly written *Jehovah* or *Jahve*. The actual Name — the so-called Tetragrammaton — consists (as written) of four consonants, to which the nearest English equivalent would be Y-H-W-H. Written — in common with all other words — in the sacred text, without vowels, it lies there on the page like a breath, like a whisper, like a holy breath whispering up out of itself the central mystery of Being.

The history of the Tetragrammaton is a subject in itself. In Old Testament times, and for long afterwards, it was shrouded in mystery, holiness and silence. When the scriptures were read aloud, other names of God, such as *Adonai* or *Elohim* were substituted for it by the reader. Or if it had to be spoken, the vowels from these names were inserted between its consonants instead of its own vowels. The Name itself was uttered only by the priests in the Temple when blessing the people, later only by the High Priest on the Day of Atonement. In Christian times the Cabbalists enquired whether it was really a name at all — as other nouns are — that is, by representation, or whether it was the Divine substance itself. Those who held that it differed in this way from all other nouns and names, called it *Shem Hammephoras* — *Nomen separatum* — the "Name Apart". Christians discussed whether it was the name of the Father only — or of the Trinity. And the more irresponsibly occult investigated its uses for the purpose of magic.

Meanwhile the Gentiles were building up their own, Platonic and Neo-Platonic, philosophy of names; a philosophy which was to blossom and fruit in Dionysus the Areopagite, in Scotus Erigena, in Albertus, Aquinas and others; a philosophy which disappeared altogether with the Scientific Revolution. We have seen that, down to the close of the Middle Ages, the objects or phenomena of nature were still experienced as images — representations of something other than themselves. By the same token the distinction between the *word*, or name, and the *thing*, was much less sharply felt. For, after all, both were representations — images (hence the extreme preoccupation of the Middle Ages with words — "mere" words, as they are for us today). The visible world was the body or garment of the invisible; and another way of putting this was to say that their names were also names of God. This can be studied in, for example, Dionysus's noble treatise on *The Divine Names*.

We have seen that the Jews were not interested in names; not in this way, as representations. For the Jews denied that nature was in any sense a representation of the Divine. They almost existed for the purpose of that denial. They were interested in one Name only, precisely because it was *not* a name, as other names are. Because it was not a representation. It was rather that which produces the representations — that which *does* the naming. And did they but know it — or had they not forgotten it — this Name that was more than a name, this Name apart, for ever whispering from the depths, "I AM", spoke, and could by virtue of its very meaning *only* speak, from *within* them.

*

Let us now revert to the present moment — nearly eighty years after the beginning of this present Michael epoch. We are feeling to the full the effect of the Scientific Revolution, inasmuch as we experience nature, as a system of multitudinous objects and events, independent of, and wholly detached from us and from each other. It is a system in which we have no participation, except through the contacts of the senses. This is the *effect* of the Scientific Revolution. It is however not what science now teaches. At least it is certainly not what physics teaches. The science of physics teaches (rightly or wrongly, but the teaching is *accepted*) that there is a world of nature entirely independent of man — but that this is not the familiar world which man perceives. It is an entirely unfamiliar, normally unperceivable world consisting exclusively of waves or particles, or something else not yet clearly envisaged. This is the only reality independent of man. The inescapable inference is, that the familiar world — things like Hampstead Heath and apple-dumplings — depends for its existence on our perceiving senses and minds. We hear a good deal about a 'collective unconscious'; but no-one seems to have realised that the culmination of materialism simply forces the conclusion that the familiar world we all agree that we see and hear around us is — apart from its foundation in the mysterious 'particles' — a 'collective conscious'. In other words, that we *do* still participate in the very structure of the world of nature; but we have lost the old awareness of our participation.

Yet, if this conclusion is ever acknowledged, it is instantly forgotten again. The other sciences, for instance, ignore it. They go on dealing with the familiar world as though it were independent of our consciousness as the 'particles' — and only the particles — are in fact presumed to be. If they really took the findings of physics seriously, they would have to say: "That which creates all that is familiar and recognisable in the visible universe creates it through the eyes of man; that which creates all that is familiar and recognisable in the audible universe creates it through the ears of man." And if they said this, then, when they looked within man, they would divine behind the mystery of his consciousness the infinite riches of the spiritual world which also created the universe. Instead, they forget. There is a time-lag between the progress of science and the habit of materialism which the Scientific Revolution in its earlier stages engendered. They go on treating nature as though it existed independently of man and without his participation. And so, when they look within man himself, they find, instead of riches — emptiness.

This forgetfulness of the creator spirit that underlies man's consciousness, and the inner emptiness which results from it, are parallel in many ways with the state of affairs which had come about in Israel by the time of the birth of Christ. The Divine Name, which was to speak the I AM from within, was then no longer being uttered by man. The Pharisees had removed it to the status of a detached Power ruling over man from without. And in the inner emptiness which resulted — the desert, or 'wilderness', as it is called in the New Testament — that human spirit which had once lived on earth as Phinehas and then again as Elijah, arose once more in Israel in the body of John the Baptist, to prepare the way and bear witness to the Christ. And Christ, when He came, strove to refill the emptiness by awakening in men the realisation that the Divine Father, by whom all things were made, spoke now from *within* them. When the Representative of Humanity proclaimed, "The Kingdom of God is within you", when he spoke of "The Father in me and I in you", he was exemplifying and making plain the truth already foreshadowed by Moses beneath Mount Sinai. The Aramaic tongue which Jesus spoke is very close to Hebrew, and to those who encountered him on earth and heard the great "I am" sayings which are recorded in St John's Gospel, it must indeed have seemed that the Divine Name was at last openly uttering itself forth from the lips of humanity.

He came to fill the emptiness within. And if we ask how we, too, with His Help are to fill the inner emptiness which afflicts mankind today, that is tantamount to asking how we are to let the Divine Name speak from within us, speak in our thinking, speak in our perceiving, and speak in our willing.

The old emptiness was the wilderness wherein the voice of John the Baptist was heard crying: *Prepare ye the way of the Lord!* It made possible, through the coming of Christ, a new, more fully realised indwelling in man's inmost being of the Father-Spirit present in all creation. In the same way our modern emptiness can only be filled by the indwelling of Christ, and through Him, of the Father, in our thinking, perceiving and willing.

We may recall how, between Jacob and the angel with whom he wrestled, the question of names arose. The angel did not tell Jacob his name; and it was suggested here that there may have been a link between that name and the Divine Name itself. Later, in Exodus xxiii., 20 and 21, we are told of another angel; or it could, for all we know, be the same one. And here the link is definite.

> Behold I send an Angel before thee, to keep thee in thy way
> and to bring thee into the place which I have prepared.
> Beware of him, and obey his voice: for he will not pardon
> your transgression: for my name is in him.

For my name is in him – much has been written about this mysterious "angel in whom God's name resides". He has been called by commentators "the lesser Y-H-W-H"; and his name according to tradition is "Metatron". In his book, *The History of Jewish Mysticism*, the late Ernst Müller, the Jewish anthroposophist who died not long ago, tells of scholars who have identified Metatron with the Archangel Michael.

In the 35th and 54th of Rudolf Steiner's Leading Thoughts, he speaks of human consciousness descending on the ladder of unfolding thought, of will coming to life in like manner as the spirit, soul and life in human Thought recedes, and of "the gulf of Non-being in relation to the Cosmos", across which man is called upon to leap, "through Michael's activity and the Christ Impulse". If we think of Michael as the angel in whom God's name resides; and if we recall that God's name is the Divine Name, the I AM, which seeks to whisper its way up and out from beneath the deepest depths of our inmost Being, then we shall be in no danger of forgetting what distinguishes Anthroposophy from so many other occult traditions, or of misunderstanding the mission of Michael.

What are those "transgressions" which the particular Angel, "in whom God's name resides", will not pardon? It might perhaps be maintained that there is room in Anthroposophy as a whole for a different approach, but (if I have understood Rudolf Steiner rightly) the Being whom he names *Michael* is not interested in any kind of pantheism; in any pagan veneration of, or participation in, nature; in any incontinent going forth into nature; in any direct astral or etheric participation in a nature, whose life and being are conceived as existing independently of man; in any participation of which the Ego is not total master.

The participation which Michael wills for man, is an ultimate participation in the phenomena of nature as, and because, the Ego itself participates the Divine Hierarchies who are the substance of nature. We have seen that the subjective aspect of the old pagan participation was an "atavistic" or instinctive clairvoyance. There is also a subjective aspect of the ultimate participation to which Michael beckons us. And this is the higher knowledge, which begins with Initiation. It is indeed principally this subjective aspect of which we hear but Rudolf Steiner also not infrequently emphasised that initiation — for example, the initiation of Johannes Thomasius in his Mystery Plays[8] — is not simply an epistemological event. It is a cosmic event. For higher knowledge is not *only* knowledge. It is participation; it is a becoming one with the things known; and it is therefore important for the "things known" as well as for the knower.

Steiner also declares that it was always the mission of the Jews to prepare the Ego, and in particular to prepare it against the coming of our own, *non-clairvoyant*, age. They had begun preparing it already, far back in the time before man was capable of perceiving any 'outer' world at all. Therefore it is, that we feel the breath of the Divine Logos, not so much in the *meanings* of the words in their language (for meanings come to us *via* perceptions of the outer world), but rather in the *shape* and *sound* of them.

Conversely, it was just through this increasingly non-clairvoyant perceiving of multitudinous, detached objects in an outer world that the Aryan nations *found* the Ego. Instead of this, the Jews had their language — and the Divine Name. They brought to the development of Ego-consciousness, not only, as Rudolf Steiner has pointed out, "all that could be given to the natural being of man through the organisation of the blood", but also the 'blessing', the mystery of their Hebrew speech and of the Divine Name in which it seems to centre — the persistent inkling that, behind and beyond the physical unifying influence of the blood, there stands that other mysterious Hierarchical Unity, which Rudolf Steiner also speaks of in *Genesis — Secrets of the Bible Story of Creation*. For there he tells us that the Elohim themselves first achieved a new unity in the act of creating man. It is, in fact, only *after* the first creation of etheric, bi-sexual man that the Tetragrammaton appears in the Book of Genesis, and the Elohim are for the first time referred to as *Yhwh-Elohim*. It is in this direction that, with the deepest reverence and awe, we must look for the true Ego of every man.

Ha Shem! The Name! Shem — or Sem — it is the same root that we find in the name given to the *Semitic* race. We call them the Semites; but we could equally well call them the 'Name-ites'. Now just as Shem (*name*) was the symbolical ancestor of the Semitic race, so another of Noah's three sons, *Japeth*, was the symbolical ancestor of the Aryan nations. (*Iapetos* is the 'Noah' of Greek mythology, who survived the great flood, which ushered in the Post-Atlantean or Aryan epoch). In the ixth Chapter of Genesis it is recorded that Noah uttered the following prophecy concerning these two sons:

> Blessed be YHWH, the God of Shem...
> God enlarge Japeth,
> And he shall dwell in the tents of Shem.

Many meanings have been attached to this prophecy, and there is one obvious historical sense, in which it has already been fulfilled. But the depth of inspiration from which such archetypal pictures are drawn is such that they often have different meanings at different levels of reality. I feel this prophecy has another and a deeper significance than the destruction of the Temple or the occupation of Jerusalem.

Just as the names *Israel* and *Shem* (in common with many other Hebrew names) have meanings, so has the name Japeth. It is in fact the same word as the verb "enlarge" which occurs immediately before it, and which can also mean: "to cause to be multiplied or divided". When we read of God causing Japeth (that is, the whole Aryan stream) to be multiplied and divided, and of Japeth "dwelling in the tents of Shem" — the people of the name — I think we are justified in looking ahead to a time which still lies far in the future; to a time when the extended multiplicity of nature, created by the Divine Logos and further multiplied and divided into an infinity of detached "objects" by Aryan thinking, and by the type of perceptions which that begets, will be gathered into the unity of the Divine Name, uttering itself forth from the depths beneath the depths within man's own soul. We may look forward, whither Michael beckons, to a time which will bring with it, not just a *restoration* of the soul and spirit in nature but a veritable rebirth thereof out of the place wherein they have been entombed.

Perhaps it is at no shallower level that we must seek, if we would find healing for that old sore, the ancient antagonism between Jew and Gentile which, for centuries past and in our own time most of all, has brought such untold miseries, such unspeakable agonies to this our Aryan age.

THE NATURE OF MEANING

It has often been pointed out that, if I say "All cats are quadrupeds", I have not said very much. It is not inaccurate, so the argument runs, but it is only not inaccurate, because quadrupedality is already implicit in the meaning of the word *cat*. It purports to be an assertion, but, since by its nature it is not either verifiable or "falsifiable", it is not really an assertion at all. It has no meaning.

I am inclined, as will appear, to feel that there is much truth in this contention and, for that reason, I wish to consider a different kind of statement altogether. How if I deliberately tell a lie? Suppose I boldly affirm that all cats are bipeds! The proposition must be falsifiable, because it is actually false; and therefore it may be allowed by all at least the possibility of meaning something. Untrue propositions appear to possess one very comfortable advantage. Whatever other vices they may possess, nobody can call them tautologies. And it seems to follow from the tautology argument that this extremely inaccurate statement is nevertheless meaningful precisely because it is an attempt, however ill-advised, to alter or add to the meaning of the word *cat*. In other words, the rule, if it be a rule, that tautologies are meaningless, involves three corollaries: (1) that propositions are only meaningful when they purport to modify the meaning of one of their terms; (2) that this happens when they are untrue; and (3) that there is some kind of conflict between meaning and accuracy.

I suppose the number of possible untrue statements is infinite. Are all of them meaningful, and, if not, how do we decide which? It would be pleasant to be able to say that untrue statements are meaningful, only when they would also be meaningful, if true. But we have seen that this is not the case, since they would then be tautologies. Must we then concede the virtue of meaning to any mortal thing we say, provided only that it is inaccurate? Suppose, for instance, I say "The dawn is subject to income-tax at 50 pence in the £"; or "Income-tax has rosy fingers". Perhaps there is a reply along the lines that "income-tax is not the sort of word that can be used in that sort of sentence". It is an argument that always sounds to me suspiciously like begging the question; and I do not propose to adopt it. Fortunately I am not much interested in laying down rules applicable to all inaccurate statements. What I am interested in, is the effect which some inaccurate statements do in fact have on the meaning of their terms — and on many other things.

I will therefore drop income-tax and begin, instead, with another thumping lie about the dawn. Suppose I say "The dawn has rosy fingers". Can that picturesque or poetical proposition be said to possess a something which the others lack? There is some very strong evidence that it can and does, and indeed it is just that something, which the one inaccurate statement possesses and the other three do not, that I am concerned with. The nature of the evidence will, I hope, appear as I go along.

I personally think, and I have tried to show why, that the proper name for the something in question is "meaning". But all that does not matter very much. Above all, I do not want to get involved in a dispute about terms, and if anyone thinks this is an improper use of the word "meaning" and prefers to call it "Murgatroyd" or some other name, that will not cause me any pain. It is the something I am interested in, not the name for it.

Now it is obvious that the special kind of untrue statement I am talking of occurs in many concealed forms. I chose the obvious one of metaphor. But it is not always as overt as that. For instance, in answer to the question "Watchman, will the night soon pass?" the Watchman might reply, without actually mentioning the dawn, but perhaps with a slightly arch intonation in his voice: "Cheer up! I expect that lady with the rosy fingers will be along very soon now!" Or, even more coolly, I may beg the whole question by merely using the epithet "rosy-fingered" and talking, as Homer does, of "rosy-fingered dawn", as if all the world knew it. The norm, or underlying model, so to speak, is an untrue statement which asserts or implies something other than its own untrue content. But even that untruthful element may be concealed. If I write a poem about a road "winding uphill all the way" or "the wounded surgeon plying the steel that questions the distempered part", it is only untrue, in the sense that I am not speaking of a geographical road or a historical surgeon. In other words it is a fiction. The important thing is that, in talking about roads and surgeons, I *also* mean something about invisibles like *perseverance* and *guilt*.

In fact the "something" appears whenever, to put it crudely, a man says one thing and means, or also means, another. I do not know a very good word for this mode of assertion or utterance. "Allegory" and "Symbolism" are both rather too specialised. "Parabolic" has been used, but to me it always suggests, not so much "parables" as *carbolic* and *parabola.* I toyed with *allolaly*, but I got wet and gave it up. I propose to call it simply "other-saying". And, of course, from the symbolic or allegorical sort of poetry to which I have just referred you are led straight on into the whole vast realm of myth and fairy-story and symbolical fiction — all of them instances of "other-saying". All of them, from a sentence like "Agnes, you're the guiding-star of my existence" at the one end of the scale to the *Pilgrim's Progress* or the *Odyssey* at the other, have this in common, that — as far as factual content — truth or untruth — is concerned, the primary meaning is felt as subservient to the secondary. The primary meaning may be either reasonably probable, as in the case of Rex Warner's book *The Aerodrome*, or wildly improbable, as in the case of the story of the *Twelve Dancing Princesses*. That is largely irrelevant. However probable the primary meaning — indeed even if it consisted entirely of historical facts — it would have to be experienced *as* we experience fictions, in order that the secondary meaning should transpire.

I realise that by dragging in historical facts I expand rather suddenly, and perhaps seems to confuse, the subject. For, having first presented the element of untruth or fiction as necessary, I now seem to suggest that not only words, but fact itself, actions, history may have the quality of other-saying. The point at the moment is, that even if that is so (as I believe it is), still, in order to 'read' the other-saying through the facts, we should have to contemplate them as we have first learned to contemplate some fictions. When Keats wrote that "a man's life is a perpetual allegory and very few eyes can see the meaning of it", he showed by his choice of the word "allegory" that he felt this to be the case. "Typology" is the name usually given to this way of contemplating history. To begin with, however, it will be safer to stick to fictions.

All this is of course a long way from cats and bipeds; and I suspect a complaint that all this talk of truth and untruth, and what is meant by saying that the dawn has rosy fingers, is a lot of rather solemn fuss about precious little. To say that the dawn is rosy-fingered, it will be objected, is obviously no more than poetic shorthand. What is really meant is, that the dawn is *like* a hand, or a person, with rosy fingers. I agree that a metaphor displayed is a simile, and that the *form* of the assertion which underlies all "other-saying" is simile, and that the form of the assertion which underlies all "other-saying" is an assertion that "A is like B". But if you are going to analyse, you must do it thoroughly. The question is, what does the word "like" mean? If you say "A is like B", you are really making an assertion which, if displayed in the same way, would run: — "A is the same as B in some respects, and other than B in other respects". (Whether it is true to say that you "really mean" that; or that *I* "really mean", when I say the dawn has rosy fingers, that it is *like* a person with rosy fingers, is another question. It is generally rather rash to allege that somebody really means something he doesn't think he means. I am inclined to think that, in this instance, it depends on whether we are thinking only about the object or thinking at the same time about our own thinking.) But I have no wish to linger in this metaphysical region. All I am doing is, to issue a sort of warning, that, if you insist on resolving my untrue but meaningful statement into a humdrum assertion that "A is like B", you will oblige me to resolve your assertion that "A is like B" into a not so humdrum one, that "A is identical with B in some respects, and other than B in others". You cannot shuffle off the mystery of predication merely by inserting the word "like" after the copula; nor of course by substituting a quasi-transitive verb, to "resemble", for both.

I do not think, therefore, that it will do to distinguish sharply between *meaning* on the one hand and *truth* on the other — even if we seek to add that meaning is the raw material of truth. I do not think we can say that meaning, in itself, is either true or untrue. All we can safely say is, that that quality which makes some people say: "That is self-evident" or "that is obviously true", and which makes others say: "That is a tautology", is precisely the quality which meaning *hasn't* got; and that the absence of that quality is a *sine qua non* of its presence.

And now to get back to those rosy fingers. I am going to ask you to imagine something rather unlikely. I want you to imagine that, as time goes on, everyone starts using the expression "the rosy-fingered one" instead of saying "the dawn". A time will come, when people will say "rosy-fingered", without thinking or imagining actual fingers at all — just as, when we have a certain sort of suspicion, we say "I smell a rat", but no longer usually think of real rats, or what they smell like. A few more centuries, or millennia, and the syllables themselves will perhaps have been eroded, passing through something like "rosy-fingered 'un" into the single word *roffingdon*, and by that time no-one but a few scholars will be aware that the word has, or ever had, any connection with rosy fingers at all. Homer's ϱόδοδάκτνλος ήώς will of course be translated "the rosy-fingered roffingdon" and if a contemporary poet writes "I saw the rosy fingers in the

East", it will be carefully explained to the boys and girls in the poetic appreciation class that this is a metaphor, and that the *literal* meaning of the line is simply that "it was the hour of *roffingdon*".

You will have guessed my reason for this flight of fancy. It would be pointless enough if it were not for the fact that so many words, and quite possibly all words, have come into being in just this way. I am not going to give examples. Anyone who cares to nose about for half an hour in an etymological dictionary will at once be overwhelmed with them. I don't mean out-of-the-way poetic words, I mean quite ordinary words like *love*, *behaviour*, *multiply*, *shrewdly*, and so on. What I wish to emphasise is that there is one large class of words, of which it appears reasonably certain that they *all* came into being in this way — and that is words which express, or purport to express, invisibles and impalpables — feelings, states of mind, thoughts, relations, classes, moral qualities and so on.

To instance two extreme cases, the words *right* and *wrong* appear to go back to two words meaning respectively "stretched" and so "straight", and "wringing" or "sour". And the same thing applies to all our words for mental operations, *conceiving*, *apprehending*, *understanding*, and so on; while the provenance of such words as *soul* and *spirit* from words that originally signified "wind" and "breath" can still be felt in the original Greek of the New Testament, where the one word πνεύμα has had to be translated in different ways in different contexts, sometimes as *wind*, sometimes as *breath* and sometimes as *spirit*. Today however the meaning of the word *spirit* has, or appears to have, nothing to do with 'wind' or 'breath.' The metaphorical or other-saying element which was present, or seems to us to have been present, in the words πνεύμα or *spiritus*, has disappeared. Or if it is still there, it is somehow fossilised.

I have supposed, in my imaginary example of *roffingdon*, a word which began by imputing a sort of entity or inwardness to nature, and which, in the course of time, gradually ceased to do so. But of course the words actually coming under fire in our own day are rather that other class — the names of invisibles — words, in fact, which seem to impute inwardness to *man*. Words like *soul*, *mind*, *self*, *thought* and the rest of it. We are told, at least I think we are, that if I say "my mind was troubled on Wednesday", I am, or ought to be, using the word "mind" in the same way as I use the word "golf", when I say "my golf was appalling on Wednesday". It is all right, and not nonsense, just as long as I do not hypostatise and suppose the existence of a ghostly entity called "golf", simply because there is a word "golf" which can be used as the subject of a sentence. And although there is no danger of my making such a silly mistake over the word *golf*, there is every danger of my doing it with the word *mind* or *soul*; in fact it is just what nearly everyone has been doing for centuries. *Nomina numina.*[1] You started (they[2] tell the human race) by inventing a useful collective noun, and then you went and spoilt it all by depriving that noun of the very collectiveness which is its *raison d'être* and fancying, instead, a single spectral entity to be its meaning. And I think, but again am not quite sure, it is further suggested that the persistent tendency of philosophers and of human beings in general to impute to man an inwardness, or inner world of thoughts and feelings and so forth, arises from just this misunderstanding of these rules of language, which has led to their continually being broken.

The difficulty about this theory is, that although it is excellently adapted to explain a *possible* set of facts, it really bears no recognisable relation to the actual facts. From what has been said one might perhaps have expected these critics to say: "the word *soul* really means *wind* or *breath*, but you are so poetical or so superstitious that you have invented a sort of immaterial 'breath,' which you now think you mean, when you use the word *soul*, but you can't really mean it because we know it doesn't exist". But that is not what they do say. What they do say is: "By the rules of language the word *soul* is really a class name for a series of physical events, but you are such a slovenly thinker that you have fallen into the habit of using it as though it stood for something which is as real as a physical event and have thus managed to deceive yourself into believing in its existence". I hope that is fairly accurate. I think some of them also allege all sorts of rather shabby motives for the self-deception, but a theory ought not to be dismissed merely because it is occasionally supported by irrelevant arguments. No. The real trouble is this, that, except in a few rare cases, abstract and collective or class-names have not been *invented*; they have emerged, by other-saying, from collective names. Often their meaning passes through the three stages, first, concrete, then immaterial substance, and lastly abstract. This is what has happened to the word *spirit*, when it is used as an abstraction, as for instance when we contrast the *spirit* with the *letter* of a law.

If, then, there is indeed a rule of language that every word which is capable of undergoing this development ought to be, or "is really" without our knowing it, already at the terminus; and that this third stage is what the word always "really meant", then it is a rule which produces some very strange results.

The word *disposition*, for instance (which is of astrological origin) must always really have meant the probability that a human being will behave in some particular way, even when people thought they were talking about the arrangement of the heavenly bodies; and the Latin word *anima* can never have really meant anything more palpable than the word *golf* does today in the phrase "my golf", even when some Italian steersman, anxious about the breakers ahead, was foolish enough to fancy he was referring to the stuff that filled the sails of his ship. Or is it suggested that the rule only applies to words which have already reached the middle stage? That is, the stage which purports to signify immaterial being. But if so, what is the rule which decides whether they have reached that stage or not? Moreover, whatever the rules are, I do not know what evidence there is said to be, for their existence, or whether it is suggested that they have ever in fact been observed by any community of speakers. Indeed, I doubt if this problem has yet been seriously considered. This whole approach to the problem of language and meaning shows a curiously total detachment from history. And yet I doubt whether it would be readily conceded that the postulated "rules" are like the rules of the games I used to play with grown-ups when I was a very small child — and which they told me (unfairly, I felt) I was making up as I went along.

In plain words I am suggesting that it is rather rash to try and analyse meaning or lay down rules for the proper use of words without first taking a good look at their history. That of course is not the same as saying that the meaning of a word and its derivation are the same thing. Or that ambiguities and disputes can best be resolved by a resort to etymology. If a lawsuit turns on the precise meaning in a will of the word *securities*, it is not likely to help either party much, to point out that the word is derived from a Latin adjective meaning "free from care". What I do say is, that if the subject under examination is meaning *in general* or language in general, then you will get into a mess if you leave out history. After all, much the same thing happened with the science of biology. The early 18th-century biologists put up all sorts of rival theories about the variation of species and disputed them passionately, but it was all pretty amateurish until Darwin and some of his predecessors began to say: "Let us first see how the species gradually developed into what they now are". When we reflect that, in the case of meaning, language is not only the *corpus vile* under examination, but also the scalpel and microscope with which we have to do the examining — I submit that the need for patient observation, humility and caution is at least not *less* apparent than in the case of biology.

And the first thing we observe, when we look at language historically, is that nearly all words appear to consist of fossilised metaphors, or fossilised "other-saying" of some sort. This is a fact. It is not a brilliant *aperçu* of my own, nor is it an interesting theory which is disputed or even discussed among etymologists. It is the sort of thing they have for breakfast. And it does seem to me very odd that people who interest themselves in epistemology and the relation between thinking and perceiving never so much as refer to it. At all events, in the course of my own very limited studies I cannot recollect ever coming across such a reference. The one instance I know of of its being so much as mentioned in a philosophical context is C. S. Lewis's very stimulating paper called "Bluspels and Flalansferes", which was printed in the book *Rehabilitations* and to which I am much indebted. There, nevertheless, the fact is. Whatever it ought to be called, whether meaning or murgatroyd or make-believe or emotion (and it seems to me a good reason for choosing to call it "meaning"), it is precisely this, out of which the present-day meanings of practically all our words have somehow grown into what they are.

The second thing, which is a kind of corollary of the first, is, that all words which now stand, or pretend to stand, for ideas and abstractions and for the whole apparatus of human consciousness, once long ago stood for something that could be seen, heard, touched, smelt, or done with the muscles. What are we to make of it? When and how did they start meaning something else — whether that something else is a class-name or is an event in a private realm called individual consciousness? That seems to me to be the first question of all. And I do suggest, with all earnestness, to those whose business lies with the nature of meaning, that they should take a hint from the history of biology, should pause awhile from verbigerating about what *is* and begin, instead, to ask what *happened*.

How did it all come about? As in the one case, so in the other, we have a relatively short period over which changes can be observed with some certainty from vestigial records, and presumably a much longer prehistoric period at which we can only guess. As far as the period covered by etymological records is concerned, the first thing we notice about language in general is, that the further back we look, the more this element of "other-saying" increases. Words that will later signify only mental activity, still signify both bodily *and* mental activity; words that will later denote only natural phenomena, denote natural phenomena *and* sentient being. The next thing we observe is a sharp divergence in the behaviour of two broad classes of words. Of those which refer to nature, or what we now call nature, we observe that, *the further back we go*, the more they appear to connote sentience or inwardness. Of those on the other hand which refer to human consciousness, the opposite is the case, and their meaning, if I may put it so, becomes more and more outward. Nature, as expressed in words, has moved in the course of time from inwardness to outwardness; consciousness, as expressed in words, has moved from outwardness to inwardness.

So much for the recorded period. We can now, if we choose, go on to guesses about the pre-historic period. We can ask how these old meanings, out of which, whether we like it or not, our own meanings have developed, arose in the first place. One curious theory was advanced by Max Müller during the nineteenth century. He had observed how the element of "other-saying" in language appeared to increase with every step into the past and, in order to account for the existence of these words, he supposed what he called "a metaphorical period" in human history, a period during which the metaphors were invented wholesale, in much the same way as modern poets invent *their* metaphors. And the mythologies of the world, those meaning-systems which represent nature as a community of sentient beings, he described as an extension of the metaphor-making activity, calling it a "disease of language".

There are difficulties about this view, which appear, I think, if we re-examine what is implied in the concept of metaphor. In order that there may be metaphor, there must be an assertion realised as untrue or fictive on the face of it, and a meaning, other than the fiction, which transpires through such assertion. A speaker may of course intend a metaphor and, by his hearers' mistake, be mistaken literally. But, unless somebody at some stage contrasted a literal meaning with the transpiring one, there will never have been any metaphor at all. If, therefore, there was indeed a "metaphorical period". there must have been a number of people in existence in the prehistoric world who were already able to distinguish literal from metaphorical meaning. In order to introduce *Helios* and *Zeus* as metaphorical expressions for what we now mean by the *sun* and the *sky*, they must first have been *able* to think of Helios and Zeus "literally". i.e. with no reference to a round yellow thing and a wide blue thing, which nobody had yet noticed particularly enough to require a word for them! This seems unlikely and is certainly not what Max Müller meant. I believe he was really thinking of something more like "animism", and had in a confused way transposed the literal with the transpiring or emergent meaning, forgetting that, in a metaphor, it is always the literal meaning which is presented as fictitious.

The theory of "animism", according to which people first noticed a round yellow thing and a wide blue thing and then invented two gods, Helios and Zeus, to account for them, is open to a different objection. Language and thought are so clearly interconnected that it is impossible to believe that people could first think about the sun and the sky "literally" (i.e. with no reference to Helios and Zeus) without possessing words for them. To explain the former inwardness of words like *sun* and *sky* in this way, therefore, necessarily involves assuming another prehistoric language, all traces of which have disappeared. This seems otiose.

The theory of a metaphorical period is perhaps most plausible when applied to the other class of words, namely, those which now only express inwardness, but formerly expressed outwardness also. We do, I think, feel that the later meaning of the words πνεύμα or *spiritus* was at one time transpiring or emergent from their earlier meaning in a way that reminds us very much of metaphor. But we must never forget that they were not really being used as metaphor unless the literal meaning was presented as *fictitious*, and all the evidence suggests that they had already begun to connote inwardness long before they had ceased to denote outwardness. Here therefore there may have been conscious other-saying, but there was not metaphor.

It is admittedly guesswork, but it has always seemed to me more in accordance with common sense to assume that the changes in the meanings of words which were going on in the prehistoric period were changes of the same nature, and in the same direction, as those which have been going on and are still going on, in the recorded period. What then, does such an assumption involve? It involves, finally, the proposition that meaning is always an inwardness expressed as outwardness, whether that outwardness is a word or words, or some other image. And, secondly, I think the development of language reveals up to date a transition, as it were, from inwardness of nature to inwardness of man. I must pause here, to make it clear that I am not saying: the evolution of language suggests that early man *believed* that his soul was part of a sort of world-soul: I am saying something quite different; I am saying it suggests that his soul actually *was* part of a sort of world-soul. I am of course not entitled to insist on your agreeing with me about this, but I am, I think, entitled to insist — if need be, with a touch of asperity — on your agreeing that the two contentions are distinct the one from the other and that I am in fact affirming the second and not the first. I am sorry if I seem to labour this to the point of idiocy, but I have suffered more than once from a really startling inability or refusal to observe this quite simple distinction. You see, the other contention, the one I am *not* raising, is really our old friend "animism" once again, and I have tried to point out that, whatever other evidence there may be for this theory, it is not borne out by the development of language. In order to have a theory that your soul is part of a world-soul, you must first have acquired a sufficient degree of inwardness, or soul, to form theories with. Of course you can *then* form that theory among others, and it has in fact been formed before now, but only at much later stages than that which I have at present in view.

I think it also follows that there is only one inwardness and that what has been changing over is not the inwardness itself, but what I may perhaps call the centre of gravity of the inwardness. So that, for us, now, it would be truer to say, if we want to say something of the sort, that the soul of nature is part of our souls; or that nature is a system of collective representations of our own inwardness. You will perhaps say that this is a pretty tall observation. I agree that it is tall; but I am not flinging it out casually. On the contrary I find it so tall that it fills the earth and the sky and is for me the whole meaning of history and, if you like, of time itself.

"Directness", as Kierkegaard said, "is paganism". A few thousand years ago, in a world alive with fertility cults, corn goddesses, white goddesses, sun-myths, animal sacrifice and other emphatic expressions of man's direct link with the inwardness of nature, a nation appeared whose major impulse seems to have been to detach, as it were, the inwardness from Nature. Or they were made the instruments of that process. They worshipped one God, whose name was I AM or I AM THAT I AM, and to whom the most acceptable sacrifice was a broken and a contrite heart. It is clear enough from the Book of Job and the 104th Psalm that he was to them the God of Nature as well as of Man, but in no sense, I think, the God *in* Nature or Himself the inwardness of Nature. They were strictly forbidden to bridge the gulf, which resulted, between their own inwardness and the inwardness of nature by means of imagery; for they were not allowed to make any graven images. In a symbolical world they were pioneers of the quality of literalness. But in the last resort literalness is meaninglessness, and a time came when their own inwardness was afflicted with a sort of sterility and lost itself in a labyrinth of increasingly empty moral and ritual laws — rules of conduct which, as St Paul observed, nobody had any real hope of observing.[3]

It was at this point in history and in this race that the Man was born, of whom Christians believe that His inwardness was that same inwardness, which the Jews had worshipped under the name of I AM. And here a personal word. It happens that I was interested in the history of meaning before I shared that belief and that one of the reasons, perhaps the chief reason, why I do now share it, is the way in which it seems to me to accord with the shape of that history. For this reason I thought it might be interesting if I concluded by pointing out the relation I see between the two. It must not be thought that, in doing so, I claim to *demonstrate* the very very brief, almost aphoristic, remarks on history and other things, which I am now making, in the way that I do claim to have demonstrated the general principle that meaning is a process and not a hard-and-fast system of reference or attempted reference.

First, then, three observations relating to the words and deeds of Jesus. He said to other men "The Kingdom of God is within you". His teaching is often spoken of, as if he had only said "There is within you a candidate for admission to the Kingdom of God". I think he did say something like this; but he also said "The Kingdom of God is within you". Second, there is about His life itself, as recorded, a marked quality of other-saying, of emergent or transpiring meaning. He loved to teach in parables. What is recorded in one Gospel as a parable of a barren fig tree, appears in another as part of his biography. Others of his actions are presented as being themselves the emergent meaning of prophetic other-saying of the past. And his life as a whole bears such a strong resemblance to elements in the Mystery-cults that some people have even inferred that he never existed historically at all. Thirdly, on one occasion, when he was asked to give the literal meaning of a particular parable, he complied with reluctance. According to all the Synoptic Gospels he spoke on that occasion, and on that occasion only, of the "mystery of the Kingdom" and suggested with startling emphasis a mysterious connection between inability to grasp other-saying and hardness of heart or indeed reprobation.[4]

It does seem to me that our best hope of understanding these things and many others is, to think of him as bearing within him, bringing finally down to earth as it were, the centre of gravity of "inwardness", as the Bearer of meaning. If, then, his incarnation was, as I believe, the crucial point in this passing of the centre of gravity of inwardness from nature to man, consider what it implies. It implies that the future of meaning lies, with Christ, in the hands of man himself. Meaning was the Son of God and is the Son of Man. Unless you believe that, there does not seem very much point in going on saying that the Word was made flesh and dwelt among us.

We may well ask what has been occurring in the brief period since his coming. In the first place, we have continued very vigorously with the business of depriving nature of inwardness. Just as the Jews reduced their own inwardness to a labyrinth of increasingly empty moral laws, so we have reduced nature's inwardness to a labyrinth of increasingly empty natural laws. Of course, for some practical purposes, it has proved extremely useful. There is no other way in which we could have got steam-engines, motor-cars, radio and atomic piles. But it does rather look as if, in our own day, the advance-guard of empirical science is in the act of making a further discovery, which also has its parallel. For just as, according to St Paul, the only positive result of all this business of moral and ritual laws was awareness of their very opposite, namely *sin*, so the net result of all this business of natural laws appears to be turning into awareness of *their* very opposite, namely *chance*. We have tried to take nature literally. We have not remembered that all outwardness is inwardness expressed. And this seems to be the result. Literalness is, in the last result, that which is almost by definition meaninglessness masquerading as meaning. It is accuracy and nothing else. It is the nothingness to which Wittgenstein drew attention, when he said that "All propositions of logic mean the same thing, namely nothing." And because there is only one inwardness, we cannot treat nature or any kind of outwardness, in this way without reducing our own inwardness to zero. To analyse language without regard to its history is to attempt to take it literally. And to take it literally at this level is to reduce it, apparently, to a series of increasingly empty rules which there is no real hope of anyone observing; and to discover, in the process, that most of the words most people use most of the time mean precious little. It is no wonder we were warned that literalness is begotten of hardness of heart and begets hardness of heart in its turn. Hollow men become guilty men, and guilty men grow hollow.

I said it is to "discover" these things. And that is how it at first appears to us. But it follows from the nature of meaning (if I am right) that it is really to bring them about of our own volition. The rules by which all words for invisibles and impalpables really mean only abstractions and relations without substance, are man-made rules. They are *really* like the rules of a small boy playing with an adult. But words do actually mean in the end what they are used to mean. And if the rules are long enough and widely enough observed, they will become correct, and we shall have succeeded in excluding from meaning all that substance which is the

Son of Man. Words will mean what we choose they shall mean. No paper on words is complete without a reference to Humpty Dumpty, and this is where he comes into mine; but not as a comic figure.

I believe that it is time we began to reverse the process. And I am inclined to think that the impulse and ability to do so are closely connected with a grasp of, or better say a feeling for, this principle of other-saying, of which I have been speaking. For to be aware of other-saying is to be aware of our own inwardness, of our own meaning (our own, because it has been so freely entrusted to us) and that, for us today, is the only road by which we can also become aware of the meaning of nature. Conversely, we can only restrain our own meaning from evaporating into literalness by restoring it, through other-saying, to nature, the arch-symbolist. The meaning of nature is today potential only. In the act of becoming aware of it we restore to nature the inwardness of which we have gradually and, I think, unlawfully deprived her. Nature today is, so to speak, hungry for myth or its equivalent, a fact of which some of the poets have had an inkling. She is tired of being experimented with and longs to be known. But man is also hungry for myth, if some of the psychologists are to be believed. What I really wanted to suggest is, that serious consequences are likely to ensue unless, as we say in my profession,[5] in due course some arrangement is come to, which is satisfactory to both parties.

JULIAN THE APOSTATE

JULIAN, AFTERWARDS CALLED the Apostate, was born in Constantinople in the year 331 A.D. The age was one which in some respects resembled our own. Rudolf Steiner indeed compared the first four hundred years after the Mystery of Golgotha with the three or four centuries which have elapsed since the scientific revolution. There was the same gradual and increasing loss of confidence in an old order, both of life and of thought, which had hitherto held unchallenged sway. The most thoughtful and the best educated men feared the impending collapse of a way of life which their ancestors had built up with painful labour, sacrifice and heroism over a thousand and more years. Yet they were helpless to save it because of their own diminishing confidence in its spiritual foundations. Moreover the period culminated in a crisis during which the continued existence of the Roman Empire was itself in issue.

If we would seek to understand Julian, to grasp in some measure all that was at stake for him — and for the world in the tragedy of his life — we must begin with some kind of picture of the background into which he was born. I must therefore try first of all to sketch in, however crudely and imperfectly, the point in the long perspective of world-history at which the spiritual evolution of Western man had then arrived.

What chiefly concerns us in this context is the state of religion — using the term in its widest sense. From the earliest days of human civilization this had taken two contrasted forms: — On the one hand the experience of the mass of mankind in myth, cult and ritual; and, on the other, for a selected few, initiation into the Mysteries, where the spiritual world was apprehended in a more direct way and where a strenuous effort was made to transform the personality and to become, as it were, reborn.

But, from the beginning of the Graeco-Roman Age, the attempt began to be made to link these two extremes with a third way. And this is the way that the Greeks called Philosophy. In the writings of the Greek philosophers we find the myths being interpreted more and more as allegories. At the same time, from frequent and guarded allusions, we are kept aware that the content which they were seeking to transform in this way from pictures into thoughts — the very ability to distinguish the thought-content from the myths which portrayed them — was something which these philosophers owed to their own participation in the Mysteries.

Long after the death of Plato, this aspect of philosophy (and of course it is only one aspect) began to come more and more into the foreground. From about the end of the second century A.D. those of Plato's followers whom we now call Neo-Platonists — men like Plotinus, Porphyry, Proclus, Iamblichus — began to develop in a most elaborate way both the allegorical approach to mythology and what I will call for short: the "Mystery-Approach". At the same time they tried to bring the two together into some kind of harmony. Iamblichus, for example, who died about the time Julian was born, and whom Julian revered above all other philosophers, wrote a treatise on *The Mysteries*, which is still extant. The full title is *On the Mysteries of the Egyptians, Chaldeans and Assyrians*; and this draws our attention to another process, which had been going on at the same time.

With the consolidation of the Roman Empire and the ever-increasing ease of communication between East and West, other myths and cults — with their corresponding Mysteries and Mystery-teachings — had been spreading their influence in the Graeco-Roman world. Osiris, Isis, Attis, Cybele, Serapis and other Divinities, pointing back to earlier Ages than the Greek, made their appearance in the Roman Pantheon; and one of the characteristic tasks which the Neo-Platonists set themselves was to relate these with the familiar gods and goddesses of classical mythology and to demonstrate that they were the same Beings under another name.

Alongside of all this Christianity was steadily increasing the number of its adherents.

This — very crudely and onesidedly put — was the cultural background to the time of Julian the Apostate. He was born into a world in which the three modes or ways of religious experience to which I have referred were still very much in evidence, but in which all three had acquired a modified form: First, the post-classical life of myth and cult in the popular sense — but even here, more conscious of itself, now, as having a symbolic significance, and diluted, as it were, with all sorts of exotic and oriental additions. Secondly, philosophy, in its predominantly Neo-Platonic form — more of a theosophy than a philosophy in the modern sense of the term. And thirdly: — A much more widespread, more easily accessible, and for the most part a degenerate, cultivation of the Mysteries, including not only those of Delphi, of Eleusis and of Ephesus, but also Mysteries of Hecate, Isis, Cybele — and, above all perhaps, the Mysteries of Mithras, with their Persian origin, to which we shall have occasion to refer again later.

There is one further thing I want to draw attention to. Beginning, I should say, well back in pre-Christian times there is observable a gradually increasing emphasis, a growing concentration of religious attention, on one particular phenomenon of human experience — at once a very common and a very important phenomenon. It is not that this phenomenon had never played a part in religious experience before. It had, at least in one period, occupied the leading position. But now, in these particular centuries, it was coming steadily more and more into the forefront; and it had reached a kind of maximum at about the end of the third century. I am speaking of the Sun.

It is not till the revival of Hellenism under the later Roman Emperors that *Helios* — the God who actually bears the name of the shining disc which we seem to see in the sky — is heard more often on the lips of many than the name of Apollo, or even of Zeus himself. Nor was it only in realms permeated by the Greek spirit that this change was going on. Let me only instance the Jewish religious sect of the Essenes, for whom the rising Sun played an important part in their ceremonial life. The religion of Mithraism, which found such a hospitable welcome in the hearts of numberless Roman soldiers, centred very much round the *Sol Invictus* — the Unconquered Sun, whose birthday was celebrated on the 25th December in each year.

Now in the Roman world, as happened also with so many other things — for that is the nature of the Roman impulse — this movement of the human soul — if I may so call it — also found a more external, and a coarser, expression. Claudius II, Aurelian (who even assumed the title of "Lord and God" on medals) and, above all, Diocletian, linked the worship of the Sun more and more closely with the worship of the Emperor. Diocletian, indeed, made himself a *Roi Soleil*, not in the artificial manner of a Louis XIV, but with the most literal intent. He was more like an oriental despot than a Roman Emperor. His courtiers were obliged to prostrate themselves before him. His was the last persecution of the Christians by the Roman power; and it was instituted in an attempt to restore the pagan religion, or "Hellenism" as it had begun to be called, to its former splendour. When he died, in 305 A.D., he was succeeded by Constantine.

Most people know that Constantine was converted to Christianity and that, after the battle of the Milvian Bridge, he installed Christianity as the established religion of the Roman Empire. Many are aware that his moral character nevertheless left much to be desired. But few perhaps have realised the extent to which the first Christian Emperor managed to combine the new faith with this recent image of the Sun-King, or Sun-Emperor. For instance, Constantine erected in his new capital of Constantinople a huge porphyry column, 120 feet high. This column was surmounted by a statue of the God Apollo, the head surrounded by seven mystic Sun-rays. The rays were said to be made out of nails from the Cross of Christ. The countenance of the statue was however a portrait of Constantine himself. We are told that both Pagans and Christians bowed before this column when they passed it.

Perhaps this hasty summary may have given some slight idea of the religious climate prevailing in the Roman Empire, and particularly around the Imperial Court, when Julian was born, in Constantinople, in 331 A.D. — only 20 years after the battle of the Milvian Bridge.

I have called what had been happening a "movement of the soul"; but of course the history of religion — man's relation to the spiritual world — is not simply a history of the human soul. This assumption that religion is a purely subjective affair has done more than anything else to make modern history the caricature of the truth which for the most part it is. In fact, the history of religion, and indeed of the human race, includes those objective events occurring in a non-physical, supersensible realm, to which religion is rather the *response* of the human soul. And it is just here, of course, that those who have made some study of the work of Rudolf Steiner confidently accept his help.

The truth is that the changes I have been tracing cannot possibly be understood in depth without some understanding of the great historical event which formed the core of all Dr Steiner's teaching about the history and destiny of the Earth and Man. I refer to the fact that the great Being, who incarnated in a very special way in Palestine and died on Golgotha, had been, before His descent to Earth, in an equally special way the Spirit of the Sun. He ceased to be the Spirit of the Sun only in order to become the Spirit and Meaning of the Earth. But this event, although it culminated in the years of His earthly incarnation, was not a sudden one. He had been — and this was always known in the uncorrupted Mysteries — on His way down, as it were, for some thousands of years before He entered a human body and walked as a Man on Earth. It was there — on Earth — from now on, and not, as formerly, in the Aura of the Sun, that He was to be found by the questing soul of man. But this change, too, did not take effect quite abruptly.

One of the consequences which the great Event was gradually to entail was a change in the relation of man to his etheric body, and this not only during his life on Earth between birth and death, but also in the spiritual world before birth. It is particularly in this latter connection that Rudolf Steiner refers, in one of his lectures, to the period between the Mystery of Golgotha and the fourth century A.D. During these three or four hundred years, he says, man could still see the Sun-Spirit (though Christ Himself was already united with the Earth), because he still had an intimate relation with his etheric body *before birth*. Men saw the Sun in such a way that, through the etheric body, they still beheld, as it were, His after-image — as on a kind of spiritual retina. These conditions, he says in the lecture called *Man's New Need for the Christ*, continued until the year 333 A.D.; and he adds that there did not live in such people the *need* for the Christ, and instances Julian's soul as one of the last to reach the Earth with this pre-earthly experience as part of its equipment.

Perhaps some at least of the things I have been saying may have inclined us to glance with a touch of more than ordinary interest and understanding and sympathy at the baby called Flavius Claudius Julianus, a nephew of Constantine the Great, who was crawling and running about in the women's quarters of his father's house in Constantinople in the early thirties of the fourth century A.D. His mother — a Christian of patrician birth — had died before he reached an age at which he could recognise her. We imagine him growing up, a rather solemn child, wide-eyed and full of eager questions on all manner of subjects. And he had already reached the ripe age of six, when he suffered the first of the many uprooting experiences which were to punctuate his short life on earth.

On the death of Constantine, in 337, his son Constantius instituted a family massacre, in which Julian's father and several of his relations perished. When they reached Julian, the soldiers hesitated a moment before so young a victim; and in that moment a Christian priest somehow managed to snatch him away from the soldiers and hide him beneath an altar.

We catch a glimpse of him after this at Nicomedia in Bithynia, with his tutor, Mardonius, who (he tells us) was very strict with him and, for instance, made him keep his eyes on the ground as he walked through the streets to school. Mardonius was a Christian; but he loved the Greek Classics, and he knew them inside out in a schoolmasterly fashion. It was probably at this time that Julian acquired his intimate knowledge of Homer's poetry, from which he afterwards quoted so frequently in all that he wrote. Later, he spoke of Mardonius with respect and affection. Mardonius had formerly been employed by his mother to read Homer and Hesiod aloud to her; and we find it difficult not to imagine the little boy, as he trotted along to school beside the old eunuch, piping up with a good many questions about her — especially as there is plenty of evidence of his affectionate nature; and we know that, as a grown man, he treasured her jewels and named a city (Basilinopolis) after her. Perhaps it was in answer to one of these questions that he learned that Basilina, before her delivery, dreamed that she had given birth to Achilles. But I rather doubt whether old Mardonius would have told him that — it might have given him a swelled head!

Then, when he was ten years old, came the second of those abrupt changes of fortune which were characteristic of Julian's destiny. On the orders of Constantius he was sent to the gloomy fortress of Macellum in Cappadocia and there he grew up for the next six years, practically a prisoner, with little company except that of his elder half-brother, Gallus — a boy of very different character. Both boys knew that they were being strictly watched by the servants; and one imagines whispered conversations about this, and about the frightful day of the massacre — which Gallus himself had only escaped by an accidental circumstance. They were brought up in the Christian Faith, and there is little doubt that Julian, who took everything seriously, was by no means unimpressed by the Christian ritual and the Christian teaching. Later, after his apostasy, he showed how well he knew the Gospels. Nevertheless, it must have been at this time, too, that he began to have those vivid experiences of the sun and the stars of which he tells in the opening sentences of his *Hymn to King Helios*:

> from my childhood an extraordinary longing for the rays of the God penetrated deep into my soul...

Elsewhere he describes how he was once thrown into a kind of ecstasy, in which Helios revealed himself to him.

And now, at the age of sixteen, another change, equally abrupt. He was released from the fortress, and his life suddenly blossomed into that of a wealthy and popular undergraduate. He travelled, visiting a number of Greek cities, and finished up in Athens, which was the Oxford of that time and was full of Neo-Platonists. Formerly he had been obliged to procure and study their teachings by stealth; but now he assiduously attended their public meetings. Like every good undergraduate, he studied hard — and talked even harder. We have a description of him at this period from his friend, the Orator — or, as we should say, the Lecturer or Don — Libanius:

> Of medium stature, broad-shouldered, his body well knit and above all of an attractive countenance. His eyes were full of radiance, and he had that moving look of ardent youth, ready to raise itself to all that appears just and noble.

We are told that he was ready to chat on equal terms with anybody he met in the street or elsewhere. His affectionate nature inspired affection in others and he was soon surrounded by a happy circle of friends and fellow-students.

From Gregory of Nazianzus — his friend and fellow-student in Athens, who after his death wrote of him with such venom — we learn that there was another side of the picture. He was nervy. The broad shoulders were in constant motion, the radiant eyes were restless, the head for ever too violently nodding assent or shaking in disagreement. He laughed too loud and too easily and his words came tumbling out on top of each other in his eagerness to ask and answer questions.

It was at this time, too, that he developed his strong appetite for — what I will call the "Sensational Occult" — Theurgy, Mediumism, Soothsayers, Magic on the physical plane and at the level of the conjuring-trick, all shared in his rather undiscriminating enthusiasm.

We must remember that all this time — and indeed from the age of six onwards — like Hamlet towards the end of the Play — he knew he was being watched, watched, watched... watched, as also in Hamlet's case, by the secret agents of an absolute Monarch, who had murdered the father and now lived in perpetual dread alike of the ambition and the vengeance of the son. At any moment the knife of the assassin or the sword of the executioner might fall — as it did fall in the year 354 on his brother, Gallus. Meanwhile, at the age of nineteen, Julian had turned against Christianity and formed his resolution, should he ever attain power, to restore the worship of the ancient Gods; though he concealed this movement of his soul from all but his closest friends. During the same period he was initiated into more than one of those Mysteries to which I have already referred.

Then, at the age of twenty-three, another of those violent changes! He was directed to leave Athens and all his friends and report to Milan, where the Emperor, Constantius, was at that time holding his Court. He supposed that the bright day was over and he was travelling to his death. But, when he reached Milan, instead of being murdered, he was raised to the dignity of Caesar — a sort of Prince of Wales but with much greater responsibilities — and sent into Gaul, which was at that time overrun by the Germans and in danger of being lost altogether to the Empire.

How he dreaded it! He wrote a letter to the Empress, Eusebia, who had previously taken him under her protection and perhaps saved his life, begging to her to get him sent back to Athens, instead, to go on with his beloved studies. And then… he pulled himself together… and did not send the letter! It must have been a kind of climacteric of his life. He invoked the aid of Athene and of King Helios and accepted what he took to be his destiny. This included marriage with Constantius's sister Helena — an event which seems to have stood for very little in his life — and perhaps also in hers.

What followed in Gaul is wholly fascinating to read about. For consider the situation! Here was a gentle student — almost a bookworm — suddenly converted into a General; and a General with a victorious enemy in front, a corrupt and demoralised Army theoretically — but *only* theoretically under him — and behind him a mass of spies and intrigues and professional jealousy, all directed to ensure that he should have no real power whatever, and no substantial success which might render him too popular.

This was the challenge and somehow or other he met it. In the 4½ years he spent in Gaul he crossed the Rhine four times and transformed the Germans from a growing menace to the Empire into a beaten enemy, glad to sue for peace on any terms. He transformed Gaul itself from something like a waste land into a smiling and prosperous province — so that her wretched inhabitants compared him to the Sun, rising once more on the darkness of their misery. He transformed the Army from a sullen and rebellious mass into a devoted band of enthusiastic followers. And, in the course of doing all this, he transformed himself. He had to. He transformed himself from a mild and excitable student into — I will not only say, an intrepid and efficient administrator — but into something like what we should now call a Tycoon. The telephone had not been invented, so he could not use four or five at once; but you can read in the contemporary historian, Ammianus, how he wore out his secretaries by dictating to them, so that they had to take on in relays; how he could listen to one secretary reading a report, while he dictated to another, and at the same time employed himself writing on a third matter with his own hand. It is possible that, by doing all this, he saved from a premature collapse, Rome's Western Empire, and with that the whole of her pregnant influence on Western civilisation. He slept on a rug on the ground and shared the rations of the common soldier. His nights were divided into three parts, of which only the first was devoted to sleep. This part ended at midnight, when he rose and, after a prayer to the God Mercury (the divinity who leads our quickness of intellect) he gave the remaining hours till daylight, half to business, and half to the Muses, as he called it. It was in such circumstances that he wrote his fairly well-known *Hymn to the Sun* and the less known, but hardly less striking, *Hymn to the Mother of the Gods*.

But the Emperor, Constantius, had had enough of his cousin's growing popularity, and made up his mind to get rid of him. He sent orders from Constantinople that Julian's best troops were to be withdrawn and transferred to the East, while Julian himself was to return home. The troops mutinied. They clamoured to declare Julian Emperor. Again he hesitated. His wife was laying ill, and at the point of death. On his way to her apartment he passed an open window. He looked through it and implored a sign from Zeus. That night the Genius of the Roman Empire appeared to him in a dream, rebuked him for his previous delay and threatened to desert him for ever if this opportunity were let slip. Julian allowed himself to be crowned Emperor.

I find the bare chronicle of these events, which occurred in Paris in the Winter of 359, more exciting than the dramatic version of Ibsen, or the novel of Merejkowski.[1]

There followed some months of long-distance and abortive negotiations with Constantius. They failed; and it was war to the knife between the two Emperors. One of the things which Julian had learned, in his capacity of "Tycoon", was always to be a move ahead of the other fellow; and he now made and carried out brilliant plans for a lightning march on Constantinople. The troops were happy enough to march East with *him*. One last picture of him, on his way to the Danube, this time from Mamertinus: —

> beneath the weight of his armour, leading the march at a breathless pace, his shoulders running with sweat, his hair and beard thick with dust, but his eyes shining like the fire of the stars, which know naught of fatigue.

But, before he reached Constantinople, news was brought of the death of Constantius, and he found himself, without a struggle, Master of the civilised world — except for the Persian Empire.

There followed his twenty brief months on the Imperial Throne. He might have been expected to relax a trifle. Instead, he instantly began to devote the same unflagging energy, which he had formerly applied in Gaul, to the reformation of the Empire, including not only the system of taxation and the administration of justice, but also the system of public transport — all of which were in a pretty bad way. Including also — and above all, for him — the restoration of the pagan sacrifices and the pagan religion. Everybody knows of the difficulties he encountered here: on the one hand, the deep-rootedness of the Christian religion, which he never seems to have understood; on the other, the growing apathy of the Pagans and their loss of any real faith in, or enthusiasm for, their own religion. You may read of it in his own Letters, in his short satirical essay called *Misopogon* and in what has been recovered of his Polemic *Against the Galileans*.

He did not actively persecute the Christians, but he grew more and more embittered, both by the obstinacy of the Christians and by the apathy and frivolity of the Pagans. One thing that is remarkable is that the "new Look" which he endeavoured to give to Paganism bore a striking resemblance to the habits that were growing up among the Christians themselves. So that it has been said that, if he had had his way, he would have ended by establishing, not Polytheism, as it formerly existed, but "a polytheist Church". Not only did he exhort the Pagan 'congregations' to live in charity with one another; he advised the priests to introduce into the temple ritual an address, which in a Christian church would be called a sermon. He was even fascinated by the organ — then newly invented — and so much so that he wrote a poem on it, which is still extant.

What would have happened, if there had not been good reasons for his conducting a campaign against Persia, we cannot say. In fact, he left Constantinople at the head of his Army in the Spring of 363 and on the 26th June of that year, somewhere near the banks of the lower Tigris, hastening up without his armour to restore the morale of his soldiers during a temporary reverse, he was wounded by a spear — probably thrown by one of his own Christian followers. He tried to pull out the spear in order to return to the battle, but he cut his hands on it so severely that he had to abandon the attempt. The following day, in his tent, surrounded by a group of devoted military and philosophical friends, he died of the wound. He was 32 years old.

I have purposely concentrated attention on his life rather than on anything he thought, or wrote. There is great spiritual depth in the *Hymn to King Helios*, and the ardour and sincerity which breathe through it can make a deep impression. But it does bear the marks of the haste with which it was composed (he tells us it took him three nights) and the words and ideas tumble out in bewildering disorder. Of actual content there is probably not much that could not be extracted from the works of other Neo-Platonic philosophers. It was because of what he *was* that Rudolf Steiner could refer to Julian as "one of the really great figures in the history of the world". It was by virtue of what he *did* and *suffered* that he was indeed a Leader of Human Experience.

Of what he did, I have said a good deal. He transformed himself so completely, that by the time he died, the Ego that once had slept so mysteriously in the little boy trotting along beside Mardonius was wide awake and in absolute control of almost every movement of every muscle of his body. I think no-one but the wilfully blind can fail to connect this with the fact that, before he went into Gaul, Julian was initiated into more than one of those Mysteries to which I have referred — and, in particular, the Mysteries of Mithras, to which he himself attached the most importance.

These Mysteries were specially calculated to develop physical endurance and physical courage. But this, of course, was not all. One of the highest stages of Initiation in them was that of the "Sun-Hero". Probably very few genuinely attained this grade. And it may well be that, of that few, Julian was the only one who has left a recorded mark on the history of the world.

And yet, perhaps most of all it is in what I have said *less* about — because it is probably already in the thoughts of many here — it is in what he *suffered*, at a crucial moment of the spiritual conflict between the Old and the New in the evolution of human consciousness, that Julian takes his place as a Leader of Human Experience.

There is an abiding tragedy in that evolution, and it is this: — That, on the one hand, the Old must, it seems, be utterly rooted out, destroyed, obliterated, to make way for the New; and yet, on the other hand, it is wrong, and even disastrous that it should be so. It is disastrous, because it is precisely the old Wisdom that is best adapted to comprehend the New. Everywhere there is that tragedy. If only the Old could be *aware* of its need for the New — while there is still time! In Julian's day, it was just those whose hearts most needed the Christ, whose *minds* were the least prepared to understand Him in depth. On the other hand it was the minds that were still basking in the spiritual sunlight lingering on from the past, which were best equipped to comprehend the light that was coming into the world. It was those souls, which had had the pre-natal experience of the Sun in their etheric bodies, who might have grasped the fact that the Christian Mystery is also the Mystery of the Spiritual Sun; but they did not feel the need.

And so, instead of harmony, the two extremes clashed. The pagan philosophers saw nothing in Christianity but ignorant and vulgar iconoclasm. The Christians had no eyes for Julian's sublime Mystery of the Threefold Sun. They could only see the coarse idolatry implicit in the external Sun-Cult of Constantine and his predecessors, and this they rightly abhorred.

Thus, after Julian's death, the battle continued to rage — and Christianity won. But it was, in many respects — certainly not in all — an external, superficial Christianity, a Christianity of the Extremists, a Constantinian

Christianity. One interpretation of Julian's last words — *Vicisti, Galilaee!* — is that he really said: "The Galilean has conquered — not the Christ."

Julian was not in a position to understand the inevitable tragedy. He did something else. He *lived* it. And he lived it in a way, and to a degree, which has perhaps never been done before or since. He lived it, as his own intimate, personal experience, in effort and frustration, in bitterness and sorrow, in anger and resentment, in broken friendships and wounded affections. He lived it on his deathbed — when there seems no doubt that he did exclaim, at one point: "Helios, thou hast destroyed me!" He lived it in the hopes and joys and the moments of glad insight, of which he also had some share.

But though he did not understand it, it may well be that the subconscious pressure of the immemorial tragedy was one of the motives that lay behind his expedition to Persia. There were good enough political reasons for it; but Rudolf Steiner has affirmed — what others also have suggested — that one of his motives was to seek in Persia for the original Mysteries of Zarathustra, from which Mithraism had sprung. There perhaps — who knows? — he would have found at last the true secret of the Sun-Spirit, which the original Zarathustra was the first to teach, and which itself pointed back to a time past, when the Sun was still united with the Earth — before the seeds of the tragedy were sown — and forward to a time future, when the tragedy might be transcended. It was this very secret, which Julian really longed to bring to mankind.

Nor is that longing of his merely an interesting historical event which is past and done with. In that new perspective of history which we are slowly learning to master, it can become quite obvious to us that such a longing as this, energised with a lifetime of self-transformation in selfless activity — works on. That, not only in subsequent incarnations on Earth but also from the spiritual world between death and re-birth, it has worked further, will work further, and is now working further towards its ultimate fulfilment.

Today, also, we live in the shadow of a great misunderstanding. Now, the question is, whether East and West will clash in violent conflict, one seeking to obliterate the other — or whether a wisdom which penetrates to the depths from which they both spring, will harmonise and unite the two conflicting impulses. The tragedy is, as I have said, that this is the thing which, we must feel, ought to happen; and this is the thing which never does happen. Always the two extremes clash and one of them is destroyed. Must, then, the old tragedy by played out again — and this time on a scale which may destroy the world? On past form, the prospect is not hopeful.

And yet... there is one thing, which modern historians who look down vast perspectives and infer the future with scientific accuracy from the past, always (or is Teilhard de Chardin an exception here?) leave out of account. And that is *the very fact that they have that perspective*, whereas those at whom they are looking did not; that those on whom their backward gaze is fixed, had not themselves a backward gaze. *We* are not only involved in the tragedy; we can also be aware of it. With the advent of world-history — and it is really quite recent — the secret of the evolution of human consciousness has begun to emerge from the Mysteries and to penetrate into the minds of an increasing number of men. It is just of this emergence and of this penetration that Rudolf Steiner was a pioneer of pioneers. *We* cannot go out and find — at least I do not think we should find — in the heart of Persia, or of the East, the Mystery of the Threefold Sun; but we can seek the Christ everywhere on Earth and indeed in the heart of the West. And, if we were successful — because of this emergence into the light of day of the secret of our evolution — we should in fact also find the Threefold mystery of the Sun-Spirit — of the Cosmic Christ, Who is as relevant to man's knowledge of the material universe as He is to those social and moral values which the West has built up so painfully and laboriously and now refers to so vaguely as its "Way of Life".

If I am right in my suggestion, and this vast perspective of the past, that is opening up to us, really does give us a peculiar advantage over all the generations that have gone before, it would seem we cannot avoid the conclusion that we bear a correspondingly heavier burden of responsibility for the future than ever they did. Let me only add, therefore, that, if anyone were minded — or perhaps only half-minded as yet — to acknowledge a formidable responsibility, or nerve himself to cope with what bears all the marks of a desperate situation, I cannot at present think of any historical figure, whom he would do better to set before himself in contemplation than that of Julian the Apostate.

EQUITY

Students of Rudolf Steiner's *World Economy*[1] are not likely to forget the difficult lecture[2] in which he attributes many of the morbid symptoms displayed by the economic life of the world today to the tendency of capital to accumulate in the form of land-values. He speaks of the way in which the economic process of the production and consumption of commodities subsists between two poles: Nature and Spirit. In the first place human labour operates upon Nature (that is, essentially, on land); in the second place the creating and organising spirit works upon human labour, "saving" it and making it more and more productive; and in this way the thing which we call *capital* is built up.

Steiner goes on to point out how it is not merely morally but also economically necessary that — as a third stage — the capital so accumulated should be placed at the service of the *spirit* and thus allowed *indirectly* (that is *via* its disbursement on educative and other spiritual activities) to flow back into the land and into further production. Instead of this the spirit is omitted, and as a result huge masses of capital, vainly attempting to complete the circuit and return to the land, but without dissipating themselves, pile up in mortgages and land-values and produce a terrible congestion.

The whole course makes us more sensible of the true nature of capital. Most people today suffer from the incorrigible illusion that capital is "wealth" — an illusion easily explained by the fact that the individual who is placed in control of some capital may, in a civilised state of society, very conveniently change it into wealth at any moment. This does not, however, make it wealth, any more than the fact that a salesman earns his family's bread and butter by his labours makes salesmanship a productive activity.

Capital is rather (to use an electrical metaphor) a "difference of potential". It is a state of disequilibrium, of unequal pressure, and, as such, is the pre-requisite of all economic *activity*. If the economic process were complete, these pressures, after doing their work, would discharge to earth again, that is to the land. But the conductor is wanting. Instead, therefore, they pile up *above* the earth, *over* it. This creates a static charge of steadily increasing intensity; and a static charge is, for the people living in it, the atmosphere before a thunderstorm.

*

If we ask, what is the *practical* arrangement which makes possible the accumulation of capital, which makes possible its conversion into personal wealth and, above all, its congestion in the form of land-values and upon the security of land, the answer is short and simple. It is the fact that there is a law of property. It is the fact that men have certain rights as against each other, rights which the law guarantees and will if necessary enforce. The history of the law of property is the history of these rights. And one of the first things which the study of this history teaches us is the fact that these rights tend to vary widely with the different kinds of property concerned.

What are these different kinds of property? The basic distinction is, of course, the distinction between land on the one side and all other kinds of property on the other. English law calls these two classes Real Property and

Personal Property, and there is possibly no better illustration of the typical differences, and of the typical relation, between the varying rights to which they may give rise, than the English law of property. At any rate, an historical view of this part of the law illuminates this relation in a peculiarly interesting way.

To understand the law of real property, it is necessary to be able to think with a certain amount of sympathy of the feudal system. In a feudal society, we have, to begin with, a social organism in which the land is everything and the human being (except possibly for a few exalted nobles) is attached to it almost after the fashion of a vegetable. If he is a serf, he is *adscriptus glebæ* — "annexed to the soil" — and is not allowed to leave the place of his birth. The notion that the word 'law' involves a separate, abstract system of personal rights, rights independent of topography and attaching equally to all men simply because they are men, is as yet hardly existent. The very rights themselves spring, as it were, from the soil. Thus, just as today land may be sold with certain rights (of drainage, light, etc.) over adjacent land attaching to it, so in the time of the feudal tenures rights of quite a different kind would pass with a given piece of land — rights which *we* cannot think of as concerning the land, as such, at all, rights and obligations of a personal kind; some of them of a very personal kind indeed.

It was only gradually that there first emerged from this older conception of "real" property, and afterwards grew up side by side with it, steadily increasing in relative importance, that very different conception of "personal" property, which covers the sort of property that is easily transferable by simple delivery and in which (as far as the law is concerned) any man may acquire a good right, irrespective of his status or the place of his birth, by paying the price which its owner demands for it. The distinction between real property and personal property is, however, not quite as simple as it is apt to appear on the face of it. One is tempted by the terms themselves to think of land as having been called "real", because it is nice and solid and immovable, while "personal" property would be the kind of property (cash and so forth) which can be carried on the person. But this is not really the meaning of the terms. They arise, as has been pointed out, from the fact that the *right* involved in the ownership of real property was of a different kind from the right involved in the ownership of other kinds of property.

It is necessary to explain this difference. What is a right? How is its nature defined and determined? The lawyer answers this question by asking another. If my client's right is infringed, what sort of action can I bring and against whom? It is in the answer to this question that the origin of the difference between real and personal property is to be found. The owner's right to his land was a right which he could enforce against the whole world. It was a right *in rem* — to the thing itself — so that if he were dispossessed, he could bring an action for the recovery of the thing itself. But the law at first recognised no such right in the case of personal property. He who was deprived of this could not, at law, enforce its return. His sole remedy was an action *for damages* against the particular person who had wronged him. Such an action was called a 'personal' action.

For similar reasons a distinction arose between two different *kinds* of personal property. Just as there is real property and personal property, so personal property itself may consist either of "things-in-possession" or "things-in-action". The difference is again a question of rights. If I see my watch lying on your table, I am entitled to pick it up and carry it away without your permission. But the fact that you owe me ten pounds does not entitle me to remove from your table ten pound notes or a bearer cheque for £10. In order to recover "my" £10 against your will, I must bring an action.

These rights to acquire property by bringing an action, as distinct from property itself, are called things — or (not to shirk the Norman French) — 'choses-in-action'. My watch, on the other hand (quite apart from the question whether it is actually at the moment in its true owner's possession or not) is classified as a chose-in-possession. Thus, choses-in-possession are concrete, ascertained chattels; choses-in-action are, in essence, rights enabling me to obtain something if I choose. These rights may be contingent only, for there may be nothing to be got. The copyright of this article is a chose-in-action and, as such, forms part of the writer's personal property. So are the shares in a limited company. Thus, though choses-in-action are only 'rights' to property, they are also a form of property itself. They may be bought and sold, and a large part of the buying and selling that goes on in the world today is concerned with them.

We can now amplify a little the original distinction between real property and personal property. We have instead three categories:

Real property	(land)
Choses-in-possession Choses-in-action	} (personal property)

It is obvious that choses-in-action lie at the opposite pole to realty. On the one hand, the actual possession and enjoyment of something ascertained is guaranteed and maintained by the law; on the other hand, it is only a *right* to possess something unascertained which is supported.

The gradual recognition of this often not very clearly defined *right* to possess is, in this country, closely bound up with the history of Equity. What is Equity? How has it come about that this academic name of a universal principle of justice or equality is now used in such peculiarly technical ways, so that, for instance, a man who has signed a contract to purchase a house is said to "have the equity" in it, and the ordinary shares of the most bogus and disreputable limited company that can possibly be imagined are properly called "equity shares"?

In the same course of lectures by Dr. Steiner (*World Economy*) there is at one point a very curious sentence. The lecturer is speaking of loans. He begins to illustrate his thesis. "A lends B money", he says (or words to that effect) and then he adds: "There you have a relation between two persons." The remark seems so unnecessary that for that very reason it pulls up the reader. In any other writer one would not think twice about it, but the more experienced one becomes in the study of Anthroposophy, the more one is inclined to adopt towards Steiner's words the attitude which scientists adopt towards nature. That is to say, one assumes an underlying principle of uniformity in the light of which nothing is meaningless, if one could only learn to understand it. The history of Equity (I mean in English jurisprudence, where the development has been quite peculiar) is precisely the history of the recognition of this relation between two persons by the Courts. Equity begins as soon as the "relation between two persons" begins to be recognised as a *thing*, as an object no less 'real', in fact though not in name, than a piece of land.

*

It is too commonly assumed that the subjection of the processes of litigation to a hide-bound formalism is a disease of civilization from which primitive societies were immune. This is far from the truth; at any rate, it is far from the truth in the case of those peoples among whose customs we must look for the origin of the English common law. One has only to read one of the Icelandic Sagas to realise two things: first, that a Viking was obliged to give a far greater portion of his time and attention to the business of conducting lawsuits than, let us say, a member of the stock-exchange; secondly, that the operation of law, even at its most primitive stage, when nearly every dispute ended in personal combat, was bound hand and foot by the necessity for correctness of form. Everything depended on using the correct words in your summons. A right was enforceable only if there happened to be some established form of action (and there were none too many) which would fit the particular infringement of which you had to complain. If not, no matter how unjustly you had been treated, the courts could do nothing for you. "Where there is a remedy," ran the old maxim, "there is a right." Whereas it is quite instinctive with us to reverse the order and say: "Where there is a right, there must be a remedy."

This cramping limitation of the right of action lasted in England well into the thirteenth century, and the remedy, when it came, took a rather curious form.

People who had a genuine grievance for which, owing to formal reasons, no relief was available at law, turned to the King as the ultimate fountain of justice: and the person who had to deal with their petitions was the King's highest official, the Chancellor. Down to the Reformation this official was invariably an ecclesiastic, and he was known among other titles, as the "Keeper of the King's Conscience". The way in which the Christian Church had taken into itself and metamorphosed certain conceptions developed by the Roman lawyers is beyond the scope of this article. Here we have only to notice that the story of equity is the story of how the relief which the Chancellor gave to oppressed and remediless suitors became more and more systematic, until it eventually resulted in a whole set of courts existing parallel to and yet quite distinct from those of the common law, and known as the Courts of Equity or "courts of conscience". It is from these extraordinary courts, whose jurisdiction was both concurrent with, and superior to, that of the courts of common law, that the present Chancery Division of the High Court has descended.

The term "courts of conscience" was in many ways a singularly correct description of the courts of equity, and indeed it conceals in itself the very essence of equity. For, while on the one hand it is still necessary today for a lawyer to have some understanding of the meaning of this phrase, "courts of conscience", even for the ordinary practical purposes of his business, at the other end of the scale it carries us deep into the roots of human consciousness. What does it mean?

Equity is of course a branch of civil law, and the court would move only at the instance of a plaintiff with some grievance. But in spite of this, the principle which underlay the relief granted was *not*, as at common law, the satisfaction of the aggrieved plaintiff. On the contrary, the court was concerned *to clear the conscience of the defendant*. His conscience could be cleared only by repentance, and in order that he might repent, it was necessary that he should first of all make restitution to the person whom he had wronged. One cannot, as the King in *Hamlet* knew, "be pardoned and retain the offence".

Now the common law took no account of such personal rights and obligations as these. A man might be a notorious rogue, but nevertheless he could succeed in evicting from a piece of land (if he could show that it was technically "his") another man whose *personal* right to the land was universally admitted to be far better than his own. This was where equity stepped in. When such a situation arose, the sufferer could apply to the Chancellor, and, if satisfied of the rights of the case the Chancellor would say, in effect, to the oppressor: "It is perfectly true that you have this legal right to the land, and if you choose to go to law to enforce it, the common law will assist you. I cannot stop that. But there is something else which I both can and shall do. The moment you begin any such action, in order to prevent you going on with it, I shall imprison your person for contempt of *my* court." Thus the would-be oppressor was helpless. He had a legal 'right', but equity prevented him from enforcing it for 'personal' reasons. The maxim was: "Equity acts *in personam*."

*

There was another sense in which the courts of equity were 'courts of conscience'. The person who applied for relief must be able to show that *his own* conscience was clear. Otherwise the court would not help him. "He who seeks equity must do equity." In enforcing this principle the Chancellor would particularly take into account the degree of *knowledge* of certain significant facts which the parties could be shown to have possessed at the time when they acted. (This is the important equitable doctrine of "notice".) Thus the courts of equity were indeed concerned with a *relation* between two persons; the relation itself was felt as a reality, as something which changed its nature according as the state of mind — as the state of *knowledge* — of either party in relation to the other changed.

Now criminal law also takes account of the state of mind of the wrongdoer. An accident is not a crime. Yet the criminal courts could never be called 'courts of conscience'. With them it is simply a question of establishing that the accused did in fact *intend* the consequences of his actions. A crime is essentially an offense against the *group* of which the criminal is a member. It is a breach of the King's peace. Whereas the infringement of an equitable right is the wronging of *another individual human being*. It depends on a relation between two persons.

To understand this, it is necessary to go rather deeply into the meaning of the word 'conscience'. Like 'consciousness', of which it is philologically merely a variant form, the word conscience originally means 'knowing with'. It implies a state of knowledge either shared with, or at any rate considered in relation to, *another* being. That this 'knowing with' another (which, reduced to its lowest terms, is the bare admission that there *is* another being) is, first an act of will, and, secondly, that it is the basis of self-consciousness — these are sublime truths, which may be demonstrated philosophically, as they were by Hegel and by Samuel Taylor Coleridge. But they are also truths which may be won from purely moral experience by persons of the most limited intelligence. By watching ourselves, by watching the harm that we keep doing in some of the most intimate experiences of life, we may come to grasp this truth.

Let us suppose, for instance, that in the midst of some argument we pull ourselves up, finding that we are becoming excessively dogmatic, excessively self-assertive. We discover that we no longer wish the other person to arrive at the truth by his own voluntary act. We are now trying to force our own thought outward at his expense, to remove him from the path, to put him to sleep. We do not want to admit his right to a separate existence. We should like his mind to be a sort of mechanical attachment to our own, registering assent at intervals, simply in order to keep us sufficiently conscious to be able to enjoy the act of thinking and the accompanying sense of power. But this is not a true increase of self-consciousness. Such an increase will come only if we are willing to accept the pain of his otherness, to acknowledge his full and equal right to be other than ourselves. It is only this pain and contrast which can shock us into a real awareness of ourselves.

This is only an example. The point is that out of quite ordinary everyday experiences (between two persons) one may come to perceive the profound truth that is contained, for instance, in Coleridge's *Essay on Faith*, where he shows the necessary relation between consciousness and conscience. Self-consciousness is made possible only by the voluntary recognition of *another* self-consciousness. It becomes possible when, by an act of free will, we resist the impulse to regard other human beings as mere phenomena, as mere points on the circumference of a circle; and it is developed in us at any moment only to the extent that we are able to acknowledge with our whole heart that these others too are centres, centres of equal status with ourselves. In Coleridge's words, we must "negative their sameness in order to establish their equality". Self-consciousness has its rise in the recognition by one being of the *equality* of another being. It is a gift which men can receive only at the hands of one another.

*

It may be objected that too much importance is attached to self-consciousness. Why is it so desirable that we should become aware of what we are? The answer is, of course, that only by doing so can we become aware of the Spirit *in* which we are. It has been common ground for the great religions of the world that self-consciousness, when deeply realised in self-knowledge, involves God-consciousness. But it is just here that an important distinction may be made. Religion has always possessed as its heart the truth that God is to be sought for in the Ego of man, and Moses so far made this doctrine exoteric to the ancient Hebrews when he preached the I AM. But here the Ego is always emphatically the Ego of the seeker. Only one religion has ever taught that God is to be sought in the Ego of *another* man, and that religion is Christianity.

The central discovery wrought in a man by the ancient mystery religions was the discovery "I am divine". The crucial discovery wrought in a man by Christianity is the experience "thou art divine". It is only reflected in another that we can see the eternal Self which we are, but not yet. Christ can only make his home in a "relation between two persons". For a relation between more than two implies the relation between each two — where two or three are gathered together.

If the incarnation of Christ be indeed at the centre of the evolution of the Earth, then, as only 2000 years have elapsed since it occurred, we can hardly in our time have touched the threshold of the age of Christianity. For contrast this paltry 2000 years with the æons that have preceded it and the æons that are still to follow! Such is in fact the view of Spiritual Science. We also realise, when we begin to get that firmer grasp of the evolution of consciousness which it assures, that the fourth post-Atlantean Age (beginning with the year of the foundation of Rome and ending in 1413 A.D.),[3] while it was in some few respects the best, was in many others the worst adapted of all for *understanding* the great Event which it brought to Earth. It was, for example, an age in which the institution of slavery was widespread and acknowledged. The word "equity" (Latin *æquus*) is closely bound up with the notion of equality. If we recollect all these things and if we also carry in our minds a sense of the great spiritual significance of this recognition of an *equality* of status as between two persons (a feeble attempt has just been made to put this before the reader), then it becomes a simpler matter to comprehend the really very strange and distinctive quality of this equity — this 'roguish thing' as one of the old common lawyers called it — which springs rather suddenly into prominence in England at the dawn of the fifth post-Atlantean Age.[4] Then too (and there is much more that could be said, were there space) in spite of all the nonsense which no doubt has been talked, in spite of all the base uses which the growth of technical equity has served, and of which something is shortly to be said, it is impossible not to abandon prejudice and admit that the true body of equity has a certain breath of fragrance about it and that that fragrance is the fragrance of Christianity itself.

*

One of the most remarkable things in Rudolf Steiner's book, *The Threefold Commonwealth*,[5] is the way in which he identifies with the three members or systems of the modern State the triple ideal of the French Revolution — Liberty, Equality and Fraternity. He points out that the ideal of the equality of all men is indeed capable of realisation, but that it will be realised only if it is understood to what sphere of the whole social organism, and thus to what aspect of the individual human being, it applies. To be an expression of the equality of all men is characteristic of the politico-legal structure of the State, of that life of reciprocal rights which corresponds in man himself to the life of feeling, out of which his private social relations with other men are built up. In other respects men are not equal.[6]

Now the phenomenon of equity and the way in which, originating in the sphere of rights, it has gradually spread outward and incorporated itself in a metamorphosed form into the economic life, throws much light on this conception. It is characteristic of the three members or systems of the modern State to interpenetrate in this way, just as it is characteristic of the threefold man.[7]

The important thing is that they should be able to be separated in our thinking about them. And the history of Equity assists us to do this. We trace its progress from the rights sphere, through a changing conception of property, into the economic sphere. But its nature is such that in doing so we do not easily lose sight of its essentially juristic origin. Thus, equity enables us to feel how equality, not the abstract uniformity of the bureaucratic foot-rule, not 'standardisation' but equality in a truly inward and truly human sense, is at the very heart of the life of rights.

So far it is only the first stage of this progress from the rights sphere into the economic sphere at which we have looked. We have seen how the emergence of social and economic life from feudalism has been very closely connected in this country with the solvent influence exerted by the doctrines of equity on the conception of property. A man's land might at law be tied up in all sorts of complicated ways connected with his family status, so that, for example, he could not sell it, even though he might wish to go and live somewhere else, nor could he dispose of it as he desired in his will. Or again he might wish to sell without going through the elaborate public ceremony which the law required in the case of real property. In such circumstances he could escape many of his difficulties by providing that A should "own" the land, but that A should hold it *for the benefit* of B (who might possibly be himself).

The result was that, as far as the ordinary courts of law were concerned, A (the 'trustee' as we should now call him) was the owner. Theoretically he could, if he chose to ignore the trust reposed in him, confine the whole enjoyment to himself. The common law courts would not recognise B's right at all. But the courts of equity would prevent A from doing anything of the sort. By putting his trust in A, B had created a certain relation between two persons, a relation which bound A's conscience; and equity would see (such was the theory) that A's conscience was preserved from the damage which it must suffer by ignoring that obligation. B's personal right to enjoy the land was thus something so secure, so concrete, that he could sell it, and the purchaser would obtain something which for practical purposes was as good as the land itself.

Thus the ancient feudal attachment of man to the land was allowed to fade away into the background. It did not wholly disappear; but there came into existence, hovering as it were above it, a quite separate system of ownership, in which the theory was that, not the land itself was owned, but the personal *right* to enjoy it. Under the feudal system it had been in some respects almost as true to say that the land owned the man as that the man owned the land. But now these personal rights had come to be felt as *things* no less actual and concrete than the land itself. They could be left in a will, bought and sold, dealt in. The conception of property had thus become a much freer one. It no longer involved a kind of physical oneness with the object owned. It was a personal right.

The characteristic of this kind of property was the ease with which it could be transferred from one person to another. Thus in a sense the equitable doctrines of ownership underlay the whole phenomenon of the growth of commerce and the rise of the free cities. In commerce, the relations of human beings to one another are based not on the land but on cash. This is not necessarily an evil. It is rendered evil by the egoism of human beings, but that makes other things evil also. A commercial 'bargain' is not essentially a transaction by means of which one human being 'does' another and gains something at his expense. Essentially it is a transaction from which both are the gainers, and as such is a material reflection of the spiritual significance of men's coexistence on the Earth: how great that significance may be, we have just seen. It was precisely in connection with the commercial loan of money that Steiner pointed to a "relation between two persons".

But the development of that conception of property which equity fosters did not stop here. We have traced it, in the case of land, from the old feudal conception to that of a mere right, albeit a right which could be bought and sold for cash. There remains the question of the nature of property in cash itself.

*

In the same course of lectures on *World Economy*, Dr. Steiner, speaking of the history of the *loan*, points out that the loan in its pristine form was a gift for which the consideration was not a defined contract to repay the exact amount with or without interest, but rather a tacit understanding that the present borrower would be willing to become a lender in his turn, should occasion arise. Again one sees that he thought it characteristic of the loan that it creates a peculiarly personal relation. Now it is just this whole sphere of personal relations, relations which are based on some kind of confidence, some 'trust' or 'credit' that is so peculiarly the sphere of equity. Trust is the soul of equity. So strong is its sense of the concreteness of the situation which is created as soon as one man places confidence in another and acts accordingly, that it will, up to the limits of possibility, presume that the confidence is justified. Equity, it has been said (and the doctrine is of practical importance — for instance, in the construction of Wills), "imputes to a man the intention to fulfil his obligations". It does much more. As a judge on the Queen's Bench asserted in 1885, "Equity looks upon that as done which ought to be done".

This does not, of course, mean that in the ordinary course of litigation a man who has made a promise will be excused from fulfilling it. But there is one sense in which it almost amounts to this. The influence which such conceptions have had on the development of *money*, and of those numerous substitutes, such as cheques, which are its virtual equivalent in many of the transactions of modern social life, can hardly be exaggerated. It is one thing for a freemasonry of merchants and bankers to have acquired the habit of exchanging one another's promises to pay in settlement of their debts. It is another when such customs become incorporated into the law of the land, so that some of the sharpest and most subtle brains are occupied in defining the situations which result and endeavouring to make them of universal application.

The economic process deals with physical things. When rights begin to be bought and sold and used for the payment of debts, we see them trying to turn into physical things. They become abstracted from the personal relation which is their essence, and the result is confusion. For instance, it is apparent enough to common sense that there must be some difference between "paying" and "promising to pay". But today, if the Bank of England has promised to pay me £5, it will fulfil that promise by handing me either one or five or ten pieces of paper having printed on them the words, "Bank of England promise to pay the Bearer on demand the sum of £5" (or £1 or 10/- as the case may be). Must a "promise to pay" be a promise to pay something, or may it be a promise to pay nothing? Are these promises "money"? What is money? Does it exist before it is issued, and, if so, to whom does it belong?

These are some of the questions upon which an absolutely hopeless confusion reigns today, not only in the minds of persons in the humbler walks of life but also among those whom destiny has called to the task of governing the central banks of the great nations of the world. It is only necessary to look at the evidence given before the recent Macmillan Committee on Finance and Industry (1931) to see how total is the darkness out of which decisions are fetched which determine the material welfare of the world.

*

We have glanced at the emergence, in the past, of a system of ownership based on cash from a system of ownership based on land and the family. Today we appear to be in the midst of another process — the emergence of a system based on credit from a system based on cash. The principles of equity are influential in both cases, but there is this difference. In the former process the personal element which underlies equity was never quite lost sight of. Personal relations and the rights based on them were indeed felt to be realities, *things* — they were freely bought and sold — but they were never actually confused with *physical* things. The physical thing with which they might have been confused — the land — was there in the background of men's consciousness, in pointed contrast to them, and the equities hovered above it, as it were, in a different sphere. Such is the essential nature of the Trust Settlement.

This transition from cash-finance to credit-finance is inevitable and beneficial; what is disastrous is the application to the latter of forms of thought proper only to the former — through lack of the ability to create fresh forms of thought. The obligation which is produced by a "promise to pay", and the corresponding right called "credit" — these things have become actually confused in men's minds with physical objects. They are indistinguishable from "money", and money is still thought of by most people as an aggregation of physical objects.

Money in its earliest form was in fact a commodity among other commodities, and it has always been so treated by the common law. It is not regarded as evidence of a right to demand goods; it is itself goods. It is not a chose-in-action, but a chose-in-possession. Yet bank-notes, when they are also currency notes or when they are legal tender and inconvertible, are indistinguishable from money. On the other hand, bank-notes are merely "promises to pay!"*

* In the last century, when all English bank-notes were as a matter of course freely convertible into gold, it was settled that they are negotiable instruments and thus choses-in-action. I do not know if the modern bank-note has yet been classified. But, since this article was written, the courts have decided that not only banknotes and bank deposits, but such typical choses-in-action as stocks and shares, are now "money", at all events for the purpose of determining the meaning of the expression "all my money" used in a Will.

No better evidence could be required of the heights which doubt and confusion on the subject of currency have now reached than the decision come to in April of this year (1932) by the Appeal Committee of the House of Lords in the case of *Banco de Portugal v. Waterlows*. This is the highest tribunal in the kingdom and from it there is no further appeal. It had to decide (inter alia) the question whether a bank (with a right of note issue similar to that of the Bank of England), when it issues its own inconvertible notes in exchange for forged ones, is the poorer by the face value of the notes or whether it has lost merely the cost of printing them. It had to decide whether the Bank of Portugal was correct in claiming that the replacement of the forged notes "cost" it half a million sterling, or whether Messrs. Waterlow were correct in claiming that it had cost only a few thousands. This would appear to be a pretty fundamental question. *The House of Lords does not know the answer to it!* Of the five Lords Justices of Appeal, three decided for the half million and two for the few thousands. It is perhaps worthy of remark that the first three are men who have gained their experience in common law advocacy, while the two dissentients come from the Chancery, or, as it is often called, the Equity Bar.

*

Such confusion on such a subject is unfortunately of more than theoretical importance. For what effect does it have when the essentially inter-personal nature of promises and "credit" is forgotten, when rights are metamorphosed in men's minds into the semblances of physical things, so that the attempt is made to compel them to obey physical laws? The result is that the world is caught within a network of unreal ghosts of personal obligations. A situation arises in which the whole world is in theory (but the theory is acted on) head over ears in debt to — itself. Huge sums of money are owed to nobody and are withdrawn from circulation to liquidate that spectral debt. But without money the world cannot get at the goods which it produces, and, as a result, it soon ceases even to produce. We therefore have a world starving to death in the midst of material plenty. The latest (1932) unemployment figure from America alone is 8,000,000.

The failure of the whole system of financial credit built up by the Western world, with which we are now threatened, will not be due to a lack of personal confidence between human beings. This has probably never been greater than it is now, as is proved by the very abuses to which it is exposed. Confidence could not be abused on the scale practised by the late Ivar Kreuger, if there were not plenty of it there to abuse. No. The failure will be due to ignorance of the nature of credit and the position it has come to occupy in the economic life of the world. It will be due, and so far as it has already happened, it is due, to inability to realise that confidence is an immaterial substance, and not a material one. The failure of credit reacts on the land itself. The substitute for genuine credit, for personal trust, is collateral "security", and people quickly come to feel that the safest of all securities is land. For it alone is indestructible. Thus the land becomes pledged deeper and deeper, as attempts grow more and more desperate to postpone the meeting of the enormous debts, the ghostly obligations, the obligations to nobody, which in fact will never be met because it is mathematically impossible that they should be. Laws are passed which make it easier to alienate land, easier to chop it up into small separately-owned pieces, easier to pledge it. Such was the tendency of the 1925 legislation, which is associated with the name of the late Lord Birkenhead.[8]

The picture is indeed nearly as dark as it could be. Pestilence and famine have come upon men before, but they have come as the result of the natural forces of the earth. Or — over smaller areas — they have been brought about by certain easily identifiable personal crimes. Never before have they been caused, as they are being caused today, by something between the two, by the natural or at any rate impersonal, forces of a sort of second earth, an earth which is not the physical earth at all, but is compacted of the personal relations of men with one another and of the uneasy ghosts and decaying relics of such relations.

Perhaps it is for this very reason that more and more people seem to be drawn to the study of money-problems. In the last decade it has been by no means uncommon for souls impelled rather by a vague spiritual unrest than by any instinctive interest in economics to apply themselves to the study of such things as credit and currency. Is this because behind the thick darkness in which money, the "root of all evil",* is shrouded, a darkness which has now extended itself from the moral over the intellectual sphere, they divine the mysterious presence of the root of all good? Really to understand a perverted and morbid growth involves understanding

* I fear this is misleading. The allusion is to a remark by Dr Johnson, but what he actually said was: "The *love of* money is the root of all evil." [Editor's note: this footnote accompanied a 1960 reprinting of the article.]

the healthy body of which it is the perversion. Really to understand money involves understanding that above the decaying, increasingly mechanised physical body of the earth, whose future even science predicts to be increasing cold and darkness, there is coming into being another earth, an earth which is literally composed of the relations of human beings with one another, an earth whose destiny it is to become increasingly one of light.

This at any rate was the teaching of Rudolf Steiner, and it is this picture of the two earths, the "real" and the personal, of which the old-fashioned "trust" of settled land appears to me to be a sort of clumsy but honest caricature. Or rather it is more than this. For what is contained in this most characteristic of all the creations of the old courts of equity? Apart from all other considerations, there is contained in it a certain striking and impressive *form of thought*; and anyone who has ever attempted to inculcate an idea with even modest pretensions to being *new*, will understand what an important part of the task is this establishment of a suitable form of thought.

At the end of his *Republic*, Plato makes Socrates reply to someone who objects that the city which he has been describing exists nowhere on earth. "But perhaps there is a pattern laid up in heaven for him who wishes to see it and seeking to dwell therein himself. Nor does it matter at all whether the city is or ever will be in any particular place." This has often been interpreted in the sense that philosophers ought to go on dreaming and not to trouble whether or no their dreams come true. The city is called the "ideal" city, and ideal today means non-existent. This is not what Plato meant at all. He intended to say that his city *is already there* as a spiritual reality, and as one whose very nature it is to seek material expression on earth.

Those who become aware of such spiritual realities, allowing their minds to be filled with such (in this sense) ideal pictures are really in a position to say from one point of view that it "does not matter" whether or no the spiritual reality is "realised" in the earthly sense at some particular time and place. But this does not mean that they will be indifferent and inactive — like a lazy politician for whom the ideal is the conveniently unattainable. On the contrary, those whose grasp of the eternal is strongest, and for whom therefore at a certain level no earthly event matters, will be precisely the ones to act most as if the destiny of the earth mattered to them. For they will have the strength which such action demands.

1960 POSTSCRIPT

In 1932, when this article was written, the economic and social climate in this country, and in the West generally, was very different from today. In the late twenties great misery had been created here by extensive and lasting unemployment, while in America the storm of the 1931 economic crisis had only recently burst. Raw materials, labour and the necessary skills appeared to be available in plenty, but they could not be brought together and set working because of a shortage of "money". The paradox of "poverty in the midst of plenty" was the all-pervasive and startling phenomenon which had led to monetary theories such as that of Professor Soddy, and to the small but growing Social Credit movement inaugurated by Major C. H. Douglas.

The production of goods cannot be financed unless there is a reasonable prospect of selling them later on and so recovering the cost. They will not be able to be sold unless a sufficiency of purchasing-power is, *at the time when they come on the market*, being distributed to the consuming public in the form of wages. These are the (largely false) assumptions of orthodox finance. In a highly organised industrial society, however, a large and ever-increasing proportion of the wages so distributed is paid out in respect of current production (of tools, machinery, etc.) which will only bring further *consumable* goods on to the market in a relatively remote future — long after the wages so distributed have been spent. Meanwhile, in order to absorb the money *now* being distributed, the prices of the goods now on the market tend to rise. The circle, or spiral, thus being created, is arrested whenever production ceases to *expand*, or whenever it is feared that production will cease to expand; and there comes about what is called a "slump". This is the disease which results from the false assumptions.

I must be content with this very lame epitome of the arguments of the credit-reformers of the twenties and thirties. Now on one interpretation of the Portuguese Bank Case (and it is the one I accept, though it did not find favour with the majority of the Law Lords) in such a highly organised society, when the gold standard has ceased to operate, "money" is the same thing as "credit" and "credit" is daily created by banks in the form of loans, even when they have not, as in the case of the Bank of Portugal, any right to issue their own notes. Whether I own the particular "chose-in-action" called a banknote, or enjoy the other kind called a bank loan (resulting in a credit-balance on which I can draw cheques), makes no difference.

Thus, the fact that "banks create credit" and only banks create it (and, by calling in their loans, destroy it) was another plank in the platform of the credit-reformers and was adduced as one of the prime causes of poverty in the midst of plenty. Nor were they by any means alone in this view of credit-creation. During the years 1920 to 1927 the Chairman of the Midland Bank, The Right Hon. Reginald McKenna, had been regularly utilising his annual speech to its shareholders to educate the public in the same view. "I am afraid", he said in January 1925, "the ordinary citizen will not like to be told that the banks or the Bank of England can create or destroy money." (In some of his own speeches to his own shareholders, the Chairman of the Westminster Bank made it clear that he did not like it either.)

Briefly, in the thirties a large number of people were becoming convinced that there was an artificial shortage of purchasing-power, and of these a not inconsiderable number held that the uncontrolled power of creating and withdrawing credit, which lay in the hands of the banking system, was at least one of its causes. For the people who run the system *did not even understand it themselves*, the ideas in their heads being applicable only to a state of affairs which had ceased to exist. Everyone knew that reckless inflation of the currency, of the kind that had occurred in Germany soon after the last World War, was disastrous and must be avoided at all costs, but the real bugbear of the thirties was *deflation* – the wholesale restriction of credit by the calling in of existing bank-loans and the refusal to issue fresh ones except on onerous terms. For it was this that produced unemployment.

Today the climate is very different. We rarely if ever hear the cry of "poverty in the midst of plenty". There is virtually no unemployment problem, and on the whole it is inflation rather than deflation that we fear. Nobody seems to bother very much whether banks create credit or not, or at all events the number of those who do would appear to be decreasing rather than increasing.

A number of causes have contributed to bringing this about. In the first place, Douglas himself had always said that the alternative remedy to his own was a large-scale war. During war, production is undertaken and maintained on an enormous scale (with the resultant liberal distribution of purchasing-power) and there can be no slump, because no one dares stop to consider whether the loans which provide the expanded purchasing-power will ever be repaid. Moreover, this production is of the kind that does not bring further consumable goods on to the market. You do not produce a torpedo or a rocket in order to sell it. Not only has there in fact been such a war, but ever since it ended a high level of expenditure on the development and maintenance of war-potential has continued. Under war and post-war conditions the shortage of actual goods is more apparent in most parts of the world than a shortage of money to buy them with.

Secondly, the world's ideas on the subject of land-finance have undergone a considerable loosening, largely under the influence of Keynes and his disciples, here and abroad. Those who heard President Roosevelt's broadcast inaugural speech on assuming office will remember his beginning the assault. If financial rectitude, according to banking ideas, meant the starving of millions, financial rectitude could wait. The mental picture of large-scale, and particularly international, "loans" as temporary advances to be repaid in due course, as when one man borrows half-a-crown from another, has ceded somewhat to the mental picture of them as a mere machinery for financing production and distribution. Moreover, since the war, under the name of "Economic Aid", the highly unorthodox principle that some of the product of industry must be *given away*, if the wheels of industry are to be kept turning, has by force of circumstance been widely, if reluctantly, accepted in the United States.

Again, the notion that plenty was to be had for the asking, once the economics of distribution could be solved, was based on views of man and nature which are less widely accepted than they were. Non-economic motives have been proved to play a much larger part in the behaviour of the masses than was assumed by the credit-reformers, many of whom proclaimed, during the early stages of Hitler's rise to power, that he was a mere tool of controlling financial interests, and would be discarded when he had served their purpose!

Again, soil-erosion and other disasters and warnings have brought home to many that nature herself is not an inexhaustible mine of plenty available for crass scientific exploitation, and populations are increasing rapidly. Finally, there is the spectre of nuclear warfare. All things considered, the shadow under which we live today is not predominantly a financial one.

It was otherwise in the early thirties, and I think this needs to be remembered in reading the foregoing article, if some of its emphases are to be understood. On the other hand, I doubt if there is any less confusion of *thought* on the issues which it raises towards its conclusion than there was then. I doubt also whether the moneylending fraternity is much less powerful than it was then, though it has learnt willy-nilly how to fiddle the worst effects of the system under which it operates.

The whole structure of investment, loan-finance and credit-creation cries aloud for the application of those clear concepts of "loan-money" and "gift-money" which Rudolf Steiner developed in his *World Economy*. But where is the will towards this to be found? It is, one fears, symptomatic of the absence of any such will in responsible quarters that the question raised by the Portuguese Bank case should have been buried by common consent, instead of being squarely faced. It may have done no harm therefore to call it to memory now.

WHY REINCARNATION?

YOU MAY HAVE found the title of this address rather sensationally interrogative. It has the advantage however that it can be taken in two different ways. It can be taken as meaning: Why should any sensible person interest himself in anything so fantastic and unprovable as reincarnation? It can also signify: Why would it be a good thing if a good many sensible people did so? I propose to deal with both these questions, and to deal with them separately.

If one tries to take a sort of bird's-eye view of the mind of humanity as a whole, one does find that a conviction to the broad effect that one individual has more than one life on earth is a very persistent ingredient in it. I think this is true, whether the bird in question is surveying humanity as a spatially distributed whole at the present moment — or as a historical whole in time. In our own time, the anthropologists seem to turn it up in almost every part of the globe that has remained unaffected by Western civilisation. As one or the other variant of Hinduism or Buddhism, it pervades the whole of the densely populated Far East.

Historically, even in the West, when the human mind first became self-conscious as doctrine and philosophy, the notion of reincarnation was very strong in it. One thinks for example of the *Egyptian Book of the Dead*, of the teaching of Pythagoras and its development by Plato. It is there in Zoroastrianism. Systems such as Taoism and Confucianism, which do not emphasise it, nevertheless allow of it. But I am not here to tabulate. What I do suggest as fairly obvious is, that if the bird already referred to were to combine his spatial and his temporal perspectives and, from somewhere outside it, to survey the inhabited earth (the 'oecumeme', as the Greeks called it) as a sort of tapestry of beliefs about the invisible world (let us suppose him doing it in the future, say 1000 years from now) he would see it as woven in a very large measure out of a belief in reincarnation. True, he would see one large hole in the tapestry — the hole being 2000 years or so of that part of the oecumene which is covered by one of four widespread systems of belief — either Judaism or Christianity or Islam or Materialism. It is a large hole, and a very important one. It raises for instance the question of the supposed incompatibility between belief in reincarnation and belief in Christianity — which I shall not have time to go into this evening. A large hole in itself, but by comparison with the size of the whole tapestry, not so very large. Everywhere else — you cannot quite say *Quod semper, quod ubique, quod ab omnibus*;[1] but everywhere else — this tenacious conviction concerning *some* form or other of reincarnation.

Some form or other. Much turns on that, and I will return to it in a moment. Meanwhile I hope I have shown good reason why a sensible man who is interested in the world around him, and behind him, and its relation to reality, and who is not minded to hide his head in a bag, can really hardly avoid being at least *interested* in the subject.

If he does begin to interest himself in it, and to enquire a little into details, I suppose the first thing he discovers is the extraordinary number of different forms it has taken and still takes, this belief in reincarnation — forms so widely divergent from each other that he may well begin to doubt whether there is really any justification for grouping them together under a single label at all. It is a far cry, for example, from the system that characterises one variant of Buddhism — which is often referred to as reincarnation — a better name is probably 'Karma' — and which is really no more than an application of the principle of causality to the relation between one particular earlier human life and one particular later one — to the notion of a so-called Transmigration of Souls, or Metempsychosis, that takes in not only human beings but animals — and even plants. In some communities there is a fixed belief that the soul returns to earth always in the body of one of its physical descendants. Some suppose a long interval of time between one earthly birth and another; others imagine the soul transferred to a new body at the instant of death. And so on. You have in fact a vast array of beliefs, some of them very fantastic, at all events in our eyes, some of them less so, and many of them quite incompatible with each other. Nevertheless the term 'Reincarnation' *can*, I think, justly be used as a category label; inasmuch as they all have that one element in common: for one person, or at all events for one psychic entity, more than one life as a physical body on earth.

Confronted with this historical and social phenomenon, it seems to me that a sensible man who is at the same time open-minded — and, after all, if he is not open-minded he is not really very sensible — is bound to ask himself this question: leaving aside the intricate variety of its manifestations, how do we account for this one kernel of conviction which they all have in common? How did it *originate?* Is it just an aberration that has gone on repeating itself in different times and places, and in some places has persisted through thousands of years? Something for which there is *no* reason? There is tradition of course, but tradition can only preserve, it cannot originate. Does it originate as a mere invention of the human fancy or do its persistence and its ubiquity betoken a deeper source altogether, call it what you will, a sub-conscious intuition, an instinctive wisdom, a non-scientific knowledge, innate in the structure of the human spirit?

One thing is clear. If it was some kind of knowledge that it came from in the first instance, it must have been a very inaccurate kind of knowledge. The incompatibility between the different forms in which it has found expression makes that clear. If there is a kernel of truth behind them, there is obviously also any amount of superstition and error among them. Is it by any chance possible to winnow the truths from the errors?

I have just used the expression "inaccurate knowledge", and you may think that was a contradiction in terms. I shall not be surprised if you do; because — and here you must allow me a fairly lengthy digression — it is an outstanding characteristic of our age that we demand accuracy as an absolute condition of knowledge — if not indeed as the very substance of it. What is not known accurately, we feel, is not knowledge at all; it is mere *speculation*. It is from that conviction that the word 'Science' gets its contemporary meaning, and on which modern science rests its reputation. We may think it is a well-deserved reputation, and we shall be right. But we are not obliged to forget that it is a very *recent* conviction among men — one that dates from about the 17th or at earliest the 16th century of our Era. Putting it loosely: one that dates from the Scientific Revolution, or a little before it. Moreover, anyone interested in the history of ideas will have noticed that this increasing emphasis on accuracy went hand in hand with another change in the general attitude towards what constitutes knowledge. I mean a more and more exclusive concentration on the evidence of the senses, as being the only possible *source* of knowledge — of any knowledge that is not mere speculation: in other words a more and more conscious limitation of the field available to knowledge to all *that* in the universe for which the generic term is 'matter'.

Previously it had not been so, for the simple reason that this sharp distinction we make between Material and Immaterial, between Matter on the one hand and Mind or Spirit on the other, was not clearly perceived and felt, as we today perceive and feel it. No doubt it was already being felt more and more clearly before his time, but it was the philosopher Descartes who first formulated that distinction in his famous dichotomy between Extended Substance on the one hand and Thinking Substance on the other. On that dichotomy the whole of modern science — if we exclude a few advanced philosophical Physicists — is firmly based. Meticulous observation of any data presented to the senses, the formation of hypotheses to account for them, the verification or falsification of those hypotheses by prediction and experiment, statistical organising of any data for which the hypotheses fail to account — such is broadly speaking the method of cognition, which has developed since the Scientific Revolution; and it is a method in which accuracy has become all in all. Avoidance of an error takes undisputed precedence of any inaccurate divination of a truth.

Its advantages are obvious enough; and it is really only during my own lifetime that certain concomitant disadvantages have begun to be at all heavily stressed. One of these is, that, if you think it through, you will find this method involves in the end the reduction of all Qualities to Quantities. Everything in our experience that comes under the heading of quality — light, sound, colour, beauty, ugliness and so forth, and indeed pretty well everything that we actually experience, as distinct from merely inferring it — must be reduced, and thus transformed, into quantitatively measurable (or ponderable or numerable) material, before we can be said to *know* about it. It is a growing realisation of this particular disadvantage, I think, which has produced a tendency I have noticed in the vocabulary of those who are interested in these matters to substitute the word 'Reductionism' for the older term 'Materialism'.

This is proving, as I warned you, a long digression from my principal topic. But it is really a very necessary one. Why am I here at all, speaking to you under these particular auspices? I am here because Rudolf Steiner is, as far as I have ever discovered, the only thinker who has made a certain very important observation concerning the Scientific Revolution and its place in history. Its major significance, he said, for the future of mankind lay, not in the contribution it has made up to now to the general sum of knowledge of ourselves and the world about us, though it certainly has made a very important contribution to that (since knowledge of quantities *is* certainly knowledge); but precisely in its novel emphasis on accuracy. And the real importance of this determined pursuit of accuracy lay, not in the results it was to achieve — and has since achieved — but rather in itself; in itself as a habit of thinking, or rather as a new kind of *activity* in thinking, a new kind of self-consciousness in thinking.

What we call the Scientific Revolution, then, was characterised by those two outstanding features: on the one hand, exclusive attention to the material realm; on the other, a new self-consciousness in accuracy. The second was correlative to the first and could not have come about without it. But now that it is there, this faculty of accurate attention — well, it is *there*. And there is no reason (Steiner insisted) why it should go on for ever being confined to the material realm. Moreover, if it should go on being so confined, the only real contribution it can offer to humanity will be an increasing precision and ingenuity in technology. And this does seem to be what is happening. Scientist and Engineer have already become less and less distinct from one another — at least in the domain of Rocketry — and already there are not wanting those who maintain that there *is* no real distinction between technology and knowledge itself.

If on the other hand the same self-consciously accurate mental activity — not, you understand, the restricted methodology that has so far been based on it, but the psychological *core* of the method — should now be brought to bear, not only on the material realm, but also on the immaterial, it will be a different matter. As far as knowledge is concerned, the immaterial realm is the domain of inaccuracy. Or it has been up to now. We have known it only as the domain of myth, mystery-teaching, revelation, tradition, wisdom — and also of superstition, fancy and fiction — all of which played into the method of pre-Cartesian science, to confuse it. Yet if it is knowledge we have in mind, and not merely technology, we must concede that they also enlighten it. They at least preserved its field from growing ever narrower and narrower. Above all, pre-Cartesian science, by contrast with modern science, was a Science of Qualities as well as Quantities. Science could continue to include qualities in its field, precisely because that sharp distinction between material and immaterial had *not* yet been apprehended. For quality *is* both material and immaterial. It is at the same time objective Fact and subjective Experience. Nevertheless it can be not only experienced but known, and (as Goethe pointed out long ago) *accurately* known. Only it requires a different kind of accuracy from the kind that can only be applied to quantities — something that could perhaps be called 'perceptual accuracy' — the kind of accuracy that poets and artists still have to develop for their own ends. And this kind of accuracy (if men succeed in developing it) can be applied not only to the material realm — for instance in the cognition of qualities — but also to that wholly immaterial realm which Cartesian science itself has trained us to discriminate so antiseptically from anything material.

There are really three aspects of Steiner's life work, which can be considered separately. In his early publications he sought to establish, on purely philosophical grounds, the bare possibility of such an accurate cognition not only of qualitative nature, but also of the immaterial reality in which all quality participates. Any accurate cognition can properly be termed a science. By definition *that* kind of cognition could not be Cartesian science (which is what the word 'science' by itself has gradually come to denote), and therefore he called it 'spiritual science'. The other two aspects belong more to the later part of his life. On the one hand he expounded in much detail the kind of training and self-development that is needed by those who seek to develop the perceptual accuracy of which I have spoken. On the other hand he developed it to a very high degree in himself. I should perhaps add that all three of these aspects are connoted by the label 'Anthroposophy', but that in sheer quantity it is the third which predominates; and very much of the literature of Anthroposophy consists of a quantity of books and a vast body of transcripts of lecture-cycles, in which he endeavoured to communicate to others the facts, relating to both the material and the immaterial realm and, above all, to the relation between the two, which his own highly developed faculty had enabled him to perceive. I am simply stating all this as fact, not because I assume everyone agrees with it, but because it is not my purpose this evening to argue the validity of such a statement. I have tried to do that elsewhere on occasion, but all I am now concerned with is its bearing on the topic of reincarnation.

So now, to resume after the digression, whatever else it is or purports to be, a doctrine — any doctrine — of reincarnation is an account of transitions from the material to the immaterial realm, and vice versa. It was inevitable therefore that Steiner should have much to say about that among other things. There was, by his own account, no question of any picking and choosing from among that welter of beliefs of which I spoke at the beginning. He simply reported what he actually perceived. I believe it is just because his pronouncements on the subject were *not* the product of any eclecticism or syncretism that a slowly increasing number of people in many different parts of the world (of whom I am one) are well assured that those perceptions of his do have the effect of winnowing the truths within that welter from the falsities.

You may think it a little abrupt, but what I am now going to do is to enumerate, quite baldly and very briefly, three or four of the features that characterise Rudolf Steiner's teaching on this subject. If it is a little abrupt, there are nevertheless two good reasons for it. In the first place you are presumed to have come here at all, because you want to hear some more about Rudolf Steiner. And in the second place it will lead into the second, and shorter, part of my lecture; in which I shall attempt to answer the alternative interpretation of the brute question, *Why Reincarnation?* — according to which it signifies: why would it be a good thing if more and more people did come to believe in it?

In the first place, then, the entity which he presented as experiencing more than one life on earth, was a trans-personal one. It is not the personality familiar to himself and his friends — and which the more trendy educationalists think it so important that he should be encouraged to "express" — but the core of a man's being, of which he is normally unconscious, that passes from one life to another. Earthly personality is more like a shadow, or mirror-image, of the ultimate Self (for which Steiner used the term 'Ego'). And it is rather what the ego has *made* of that personality during one particular lifetime that will be transmitted to the new personality it will assume — or build — or grow — in a subsequent one. Putting it more briefly, it is the spirit and not the soul, that is born again.

Secondly, there are indeed relations of a causal nature between one life and another, and in this case Steiner normally used the oriental term. There is in fact a moral law of 'Karma' that obtains in the immaterial realm, just as the law of gravity does in the material one. I cannot go into the many differences which nevertheless distinguish his presentation of Karma from the characteristically oriental one. I will only mention that with him — as perhaps generally with the idea of Karma, where it has reappeared in the West — the emphasis was mainly on the future rather than the past. Not the gradual elimination of the individual spirit's apostasy and its eventual extinction in Nirvana, but the continual enhancement of that individual being from life to life.

Thirdly — and here, by contrast, his treatment of the subject departs very far from anything that I at least have found elsewhere — the experiences undergone by the spirit between one life and another — its experiences, that is, in the spiritual world — are presented as being at least *as* important as its experiences during its incarnation on earth. He often dealt with them in great detail.

More specifically — and it was his habit to be very specific indeed, both on this and on other subjects — the *normal* length of the period that elapses between one incarnation and another is of the order of 1000 years. It is a norm that is often widely departed from — as is of course the case with life on earth; where, although the norm is, say, threescore years and ten, plenty of human beings die before they are three years old, and quite a few live on to ninety or even a hundred.

Finally, it is again normal — though here again only in the qualified sense I have just emphasised — for an incarnation as a man to be followed by an incarnation as a woman.

Such a bald and abstract summary gives, I fear, no real impression of what it is like to read Rudolf Steiner on Reincarnation and Karma — of the manner, for instance, in which he illustrated their process by particular historical developments, and indeed in the lives of particular historical individuals. Anyone who wants the substance rather than the mere shadow I have sketched, would have to read for himself. I have risked it only because I want now to go on to the rest that I have to say. And, before doing so, I must make clear what I am *not* saying. I am not saying that, because it looks as if it would be a fine and healthy thing if a lot of people came to believe something, therefore it must be true. I am merely passing on a reflection which has been borne in on me more and more forcibly during the last few years. After all, thought is free, and there can be no harm in my sharing such reflections with you, supposing you are willing to listen. If the majority of people were to become convinced of reincarnation, as I have just outlined it, as a fact, what an enormous difference it must make to many of the discords that are at present threatening to tear our civilization to pieces!

Take for instance the Women's Liberation movement. Well, there is first of all the rather obvious and crude reflection that the emotions of a woman confronting a male chauvinist pig could hardly help being considerably modified by a firm conviction that the said pig will himself in all probability be born as a woman a little later on in the course of evolution. But I am not thinking of that so much as of the narrow and jaundiced view of the past history of mankind which the movement seems to engender in its more enthusiastic adherents, and of the bitterness that results from it. Historical judgements are one thing; personal bitterness is another. The judgements need not be affected. Women, let us say, have always been the oppressed sex. But the bitterness, the venom in it comes of the speaker identifying herself with her sex as a whole, both now and in the past. Whereas, if she is aware that, in the core of her being, she is as much masculine as feminine, she is free to identify herself not with an artificial class consisting of all women living and dead (which is after all a numerical abstraction) but with Humanity as a whole; which I would say is a reality and not an abstraction at all; and which is in any case not a divisive concept, like that of sex.

I am thinking of course of *conviction* and not of a half-hearted belief in reincarnation. I am thinking of a state of mind that would take its truth for granted in much the same way as most people, under the present dispensation, take for granted the Lyell-Darwin-Freud model of the past history of the earth and humanity. Perhaps I can make more vivid the sort of difference I feel that would make with the help of an impossible analogy. Suppose a man who was well-up in all such things as geology and physics, but who for some reason or other had never heard that there is such a thing as sculpture. And now suppose that, in the course of some digging operation or other, he unearths a marble statue. He wonders about its peculiar shape and about the whole nature and origin of the object before him, and he starts to form theories about them. But owing to the defect in his knowledge which we have supposed, these theories can only take the form of more and more elaborate hypotheses about the geological adventures of marble in the remote past, and perhaps the operation of climatic changes on it in the more recent past and in the present. And now, if you will imagine the difference it must make to such a man to learn that, in addition to the substance marble, there is such a thing as sculpture, and that in addition to the history of marble, there is a separate history of the art of sculpture, it may help you to see what I am driving at. You have only to substitute for the statue the idea of *homo sapiens* that prevails in the minds and imaginations of most sociologists — and indeed in the minds of most men and women in the West in our time.

I believe that it would affect profoundly the relation of every man jack (or woman jill) both to himself (or herself) and to his fellow human beings. I see it operating as a kind of disinfectant, inasmuch as it would tend to substitute the right kind of identification for the wrong. Especially when that is extrapolated into history. A good example of what I mean by the wrong kind of identification would be what is called 'class-consciousness'. There is nothing more abstract than a *class*. In fact, it is almost *the* abstract word. 'Class' and 'member of a class' are the terms employed by modern logicians, in preference to the older terms 'genus' and 'species', precisely because they do not admit any immaterial unity underlying a collection of similar individuals. The collective noun *Lion* means simply the numerical sum of all the individual lions that have been, are, or will be. Now there *is* no doubt a real underlying unity there, when a man emotionally identifies himself with his ancestors — inferior, if you like, but real. But there is no underlying reality, only a fancied and artificial unity, when a poor and despised man, or a rich and honoured one, in the twentieth century identifies himself emotionally with "his" class in, let us say, the fourteenth century — a fancied and artificial unity, which has no real significance beyond the part it can play in superheating animosity. I do not see why the pricking of that bubble should discourage anyone from struggling just as hard as before to reform the evils and injustices that oppress the present; but I do feel it would take much of the personal venom out of the struggle, if it became habitual to think of history and our relation to it as embodying not only the development of groups and movements and their relation to each other, but also our own previous lives on earth; if we identified with the thought of *them*, as least *as well as* with the groups and movements.

Whatever group or association a person may feel identified with — or choose to identify himself with — there can be no identity more real than his identity with his own existential kernel — a kernel which transcends divergences of race and nation and sex as absolutely as it must obviously close the so-called "generation gap". In the case of race — and in a different way of nationality — there is of course a real underlying unity between the individual and his community, including the past history of that community. And it is most unfortunate that well-meant attempts to legislate it away, with the persistent emphasis on the topic which that entails, tend rather to enhance than to diminish the awareness of that unity and a consequent relapse into it.

People today — and maybe this applies especially to the young — do seem in a peculiar way — obscurely and half-consciously — to be groping after the roots from which they spring. The growing appeal of Archaeology, far outside professional circles is, I would say, one symptom of it, and I suspect that the startling success of Alex Haley's book *Roots*, and of the film based on it, may be another. For that, and those other reasons I have tried to adumbrate, I can see almost no bounds to the healthful changes in the face of society that might come about, if most of its members should acquire an abiding sense of their spiritual root — of a spiritual heredity alongside of, or rather permeating, their physical heredity and their cultural inheritance — an awareness, let us say, of the sculpture as well as of the marble.

In conclusion I feel disposed to modify a little the disclaimer with which I began this second and more speculative part of my address. You may remember I emphasised that I was not arguing that, because a belief would be beneficial, it must be true. Nor am I. But that is not to say that the two propositions have *no* bearing at all on each other. Quite apart from Jamesian pragmatism, at this sort of metaphysical depth I feel they *are* related. Either the universal process in which we are caught up is a mere fortuitous concourse of atoms, or it is in some way meaningful, morally as well as physically. And if the latter, then a hypothesis which it would be morally healthful for humanity to accept must, I think, be judged, more likely to be true than its contradictory.

THE CONCEPT OF REVELATION

SIXTY OR SO years ago, when I was engaged in the awkward operation of turning from a boy into a man, the world of weekly, monthly and quarterly journalism was a much richer one in England than it is today. The peculiar literary form called the 'essay' was still in full flower, and the periodical literature of the day was begetting them in regular profusion. It was a characteristic of the essay as such that, while it certainly might be an essay *on* some particular topic, it need not necessarily be so. To secure a public it might just be a good essay. In practice it tended very often, because the writers were themselves literary men, to be concerned, whether topically or allusively, with literature past or present, but it need not necessarily be so. I think of such names as J. C. Squire, Robert Lynd, Desmond McCarthy, J. B. Priestley in his younger days before he became a novelist. It was the climate in which Hilaire Belloc could publish from time to time little collected volumes of his own essays with such titles as *On Everything*, *On Nothing*, and finally just *On*.

I suppose Charles Lamb was the father of the genre. He was still being read with appreciation by the literary-minded in my generation, when their contemporaries over here were perhaps still pasturing on James Russell Lowell and Oliver Wendell Holmes. *Belles-Lettres*, the weekly or monthly *Causerie* — it was this phenomenon the compilers of the Oxford Dictionary must surely have had very much in mind when they included in their definition of the term *literature* the words: "now applied to writing which has claim to consideration on the ground of beauty of form or emotional effect".

Of course one can trace its origin farther back. What are Addison's *Spectator* and Johnson's *Rambler* but collections of essays? But on closer inspection there turns out to be a difference, almost of kind, between the typical eighteenth-century essay and the kind of essay that characterized the late nineteenth and early twentieth centuries. The former were avowedly aimed not simply at entertainment or emotional effect, but also at *improvement*. Jane Austen's characters, for instance, take this requirement for granted. And parallel with this difference there was another. The eighteenth-century essay was allowed, although not obliged, to "bring in" religion. Whatever the causes (and the rapid growth of doubt, or in eighteenth-century language "infidelity", during the nineteenth century is an obvious one), it is just a fact that this is exactly what the twentieth century was *not* allowed to do. Not on any account. Not only was all overt reference to religion, and particularly any that assumed the possibility of religious faith in the reader, ruled out by contemporary canons of taste, but the veto also applied to anything on which religious belief might have a *bearing*, whether positive or negative. First principles of any sort in fact were in bad taste. If you saw them looming uncomfortably ahead in the direction your argument was taking, the red light came on, and you veered off into some vague remark about the subject being "touched to finer issues", or something of that sort.

The genre had many merits. A genial and well-informed mind could do much with it. I at least owe a heavy debt to a long line of belletristic essays, from Charles Lamb onwards, for the development in myself of an affectionate taste for literature in general. Yet I cannot see much of a public today for essays of the sort

I have been trying to describe. For the next thing that happened, if my historical survey is correct, was a rather swift falling-out-of-love with the whole image of literature that underlay them, and of which they were symptomatic. Nonconformists began to appear on the literary scene. Little magazines with aggressive titles were printed and talked of. Two of them, I remember, were entitled respectively *Wheels* and *Blast*. It was the time when, on a soberer level, T. S. Eliot and Ezra Pound were busily undermining the ascendancy of the Georgian poets, who had continued to rely for nourishment on what remained of the Romantic tradition. What the nonconformists had come to feel, though they did not always succeed in preaching it very clearly, was that this whole literary tradition was somehow sterile. There was too much inbreeding. And here I think they were confronting a fundamental problem that is inherent in the very concept of 'literature' as a thing in itself. It is this. When people write, they have to be writing *about* something. Yet, as soon as we become really interested in the something they are writing about, literature has ceased to be a thing in itself — unless of course they confine themselves to writing about — literature! Hence no doubt the swelling spate of books about books, and books about books about books.

Literature as such is felt to be an important category. Yet literature, almost by definition, must refer outside itself. But what could it legitimately refer to without ceasing to be literature as such? It was a problem which a little earlier had confronted Matthew Arnold, and his solution was to say that serious literature is a "criticism of life" ('criticism' having a convenient literary connotation). Now, I think it is true to say that, by the time I am speaking of, this notion "criticism of life" had developed in two different directions. On the one hand there was the "commitment" school — much in evidence in the Thirties during and after the Spanish Civil War. Literature must have a practical aim. It must, broadly speaking, be directed to bringing about social reform. On the other hand, and by a very different class of writers, criticism, rather than participation, did indeed become accepted as the true function of literature, provided always that the criticism was implied rather than argued, provided it was limited to *irony.*

Irony for many was the perfect answer. Nearly perfect for I. A. Richards; quite perfect for Cleanth Brooks. Not only was the unavoidable element of reference to life outside literature disinfected, so to speak, by a simultaneous detachment from it, but a pervasive tone of irony — unrelated, unparticularized irony rather than irony *about* anything — had the protective advantage of making no claims. It was almost synonymous with literature's awareness of its own limitations.

But I do not think these two developments of a "criticism of life" approach exhaust between them what was happening to the concept of literature. The early twentieth century was marked by another phenomenon, not less symptomatic and, I would say, a good deal more significant for the future than either of them. I am thinking of the discovery of the Russian writers, notably Dostoievsky, and the enthusiastic acclaim with which they had just been welcomed by the literary élite in the West. I suspect that the warmth of that welcome sprang from an uneasy feeling that there must be rather more to humanity than was dreamed of by the good-natured 'humanism' which characterised not only essay writing but Western literature as a whole at the time of their appearance. The Russian writers went deeper. *Their* literary aim seemed to be not so much observation or criticism or detached valuation, as the disclosure of hitherto unsuspected sources: sources of valuation, sources of behaviour, sources of human consciousness itself. Insofar as it had any *practical* aim, it aimed at altering that consciousness by increasing its knowledge of itself, rather than at any persuaded improvement either of the individual or of society. I cannot attempt to trace its influence in any detail, but without it I doubt if there could ever have been a D. H. Lawrence or even an F. R. Leavis; perhaps not a Thomas Mann, perhaps not even (in spite of his avowed distaste for the Russians) a Joseph Conrad.

My suggestion is that the startling warmth of that response betokened a groping endeavour towards a concept of literature, not as a means of improvement, not as a vehicle of criticism of any sort, and not simply as entertainment, but as a revelation of hitherto unsuspected depths in the inner being of humanity. Revelation is related to criticism as discovery is to observation and judgment. It may be an unfamiliar term in the vocabulary of literary criticism, but it is not an entirely new thing in literature. Poetry, for instance, as a revelation of nature had already been well developed by the Romantics, notably Wordsworth. But I do not know that it has ever been explicitly characterised as such; and anyone who seeks to employ an old word in a new sense is under some obligation to justify his audacity.

In an English court of law, whenever the proper definition of a word comes up for discussion, reference is sure to be made at some stage of the argument to the

Oxford Dictionary. I will go back to it myself then and mention that the first definition it gives for revelation is: "The disclosure or communication of knowledge to man by a divine or supernatural agency." I think it is a good definition and it accords with the historical fact that the word has in the past been used mainly in the context of religious thought. It is in that context then that we had better begin by looking at it. When we do so, we find that already in that context its proper meaning has been widely, even bitterly, disputed. If we look for instance at the controversy in the early nineteenth century over what was called the doctrine of 'Verbal Inspiration' of the Scriptures, we soon notice how judicious was our lexicographer's choice of words. 'Disclosure' or 'Communication'? Which? And are they the same, or are they different things? That was the issue that lay, usually unperceived, at the heart of the controversy — as Coleridge so clearly divined in his *Letters on the Inspiration of the Scriptures*. The main error of the Bibliolaters (or, as we should probably now call them, Fundamentalists) lay, he said, "in the confounding of two distinct conceptions, revelation by the Eternal Word, and actuation by the Holy Spirit". It was in consequence of this that the term 'Inspiration' had acquired a double sense. "First, the term is used in the sense of Information miraculously communicated by voice or vision; and secondly, where without any sensible addition or infusion, the writer or speaker uses and applies his existing gifts of power and knowledge under the predisposing, aiding, and directing actuation of God's Holy Spirit." Between these two concepts — information communicated through the medium of the senses, and disclosure through non-verbal, or pre-verbal, inspiration — there was, he said, "a positive difference of kind — a chasm". Or, in the terminology of our definition, two different kinds of disclosure are possible, one by communication and the other by inspiration, and we have no right to assume that only the former is made a divine or supernatural agency. Coleridge himself held that the former kind was only to be found in comparatively few places in the Bible, notably certain Dominical utterances, and certain passages in the Pentateuch. For the rest, though he did not put it in precisely that way, the Bible should properly be read as a special case (in view of its sublimity, a *very* special case) of literature. The inspiration, which is its overall substance, is not readily distinguishable in fact from Imagination, from Imagination in the sense which he himself was instrumental in imparting to that word, and which it has since become customary to signalise as 'creative'. The epithet has become almost a conventional one, really adding nothing to its noun. Coleridge himself, rarely, if ever, joined the two together. What he did call Imagination was "a *repetition* in the finite mind of the eternal act of creation in the infinite I AM".

Let me try to summarise by putting it in a slightly different way. Either we accept the real presence of a divine or supernatural agency, or we do not. If we do not, there is not much point in talking about religion, and therefore not much point in talking about the relation between religion and literature. If we do accept such an agency, and further the possibility of that agency disclosing any knowledge of itself, then there appear to be two conceivable kinds of disclosure. The one from *without*, that is through the senses, and the other from *within*. My suggestion, with support from Coleridge, is that this second kind, not less than the first, may properly be called 'revelation', whether it is found in sacred or profane literature.

The terms 'within' and 'without' make a neat antithesis. The distinction between them is surely sharp enough. But it is very important to be absolutely clear about the point where the one limb of that antithesis is divided from the other. It is not primarily a spatial antithesis. It does not contrast a source located inside the cuticle of a human organism with a source physically outside it. No. The contrast is between the immaterial and the material — between what is or could be an object for the senses, and what is not and could not be so. It is very important, because to be incapable of discriminating between these two different sorts of relation between 'within' and 'without' is, in my view, to be incapable of forming a satisfactory concept of revelation in *any* sense, and whether occurring in the present or in the past. One recalls how the failure to do just that has bedevilled anthropology, psychology, and through them theology, with the purely spatial concept of a 'projection' of the within upon the without; a concept which rapidly became the basic hypothesis for all interpretation of ancient traditions and records coming under the head of myth or religion, including of course the Jewish and Christian Bible.

The effect of this has been to exclude, if not all avowed belief, certainly all *confidence*, in the divine or supernatural origin of such traditions and records. We today are familiar with the kind of utterance, the kind of communication from one human being to another, that springs from imagination and therefore, we agree, from within. It may for instance take the form of poetry, and it may even contain an element of disclosure. We are quite unfamiliar with the phenomenon of the same kind of communication coming from a transpersonal source. Accordingly, when we are confronted with it, in past tradition, we assume that, however it purported to come from without, it must in fact have come from within. And since we have already preempted the meaning of within and without to a merely spatial parameter, we assume (again more often implicitly than explicitly) that it must have been a product, or figment, of the brain.

As I see it, this tacit assumption is the biggest lion in the path of any attempt to present literature as being, at least ideally (which is not at all the same as saying metaphorically), a form of revelation. To overcome it, we must become able to accept that the older kind of revelation could be no less actual than the new, instead of regarding it, as Freud and Jung for instance have done, as having been merely the new kind misunderstood. I know of only one way in which this can be done. And since I have already referred to Coleridge, I will add that it is a way towards which he was undoubtedly feeling *his* way towards the end of his life. I am thinking particularly of his late lecture on the *Prometheus of Aeschylus*, though there are many other indications. The apostle of creative imagination was indicating, before he died, that the old traditions and records, and in particular the myths, demand for their proper interpretation a perception that human consciousness itself — not merely human ideas and beliefs, where the changes are obvious enough — but consciousness itself — has been evolving in a direction that entailed transformation of the old kind of revelation into the new. Only on this premise is it possible for us to acknowledge that, while we must look within today for the source of revelation, the older kind of revelation was, in *fact* and not merely supposedly, from without, that is through the medium of the senses; and further that these two sources are nevertheless not two different sources, but one and the same source.

As to the validity of such a premise, I have obviously no time to contend for it here and now. For most people, the principal stumbling block in the way of accepting it is that it entails abandoning the received view of evolution as a biological process, whereby merely physical events resulted later on in mental ones. Elsewhere, and in more than one book, I have tried to dig away at that stumbling block and some others. Very briefly: The elements of attention and intention in contemporary sense perceptions makes hay of any hypothesis, for example, of natural selection as the only, or even the predominant, agent of evolutionary process in its early stages. Further, in its later stages (namely prehistory and history of humanity), there is ample evidence, for example in the development of language, of a continuing evolution of perception itself away from a pre-intentional towards an increasingly intentional experience and activity. I must confine myself to that bald synopsis. Here I am concerned only with its consequences for the concept of revelation.

It means that, looking back into the past, we look into a state of affairs where the distinction I have stressed between disclosure and communication was much less marked, that there was a time when mere perception itself contained an element of disclosure, and when the whole relation between sensation, intention, and thought, which is embodied in language, was very differently adjusted. And my suggestion is that such a perspective, clearly focused, must have important consequences in the domain of literature, whether for the historical and critical study of it — all that used to be called (and which I will continue to call) 'philology' — or for the actual production of literature in the present and future.

I must endeavour, in the time left to me, to illustrate with a few sketchy examples the sort of consequences I have in mind. I begin then with a philological one. In the study of literature the word 'source' is today extensively employed. In the domain of criticism we carefully, and rightly, distinguish 'primary' from 'secondary' sources: the text itself from books and essays about the text or in some way based on it. Now this principle is of course easily applied to modern or recent literature, where an author's identity and the genuine productions of his pen are rarely in doubt. In the case of much ancient literature, where the element of tradition is apparent, and where therefore criticism tends to merge with historical research, it has long been customary to *endeavour* to apply the same principle and to make the same sharp distinction. But in order to do so, it is first necessary to identify '*the*' text; this entails specifying some particular manuscript, whether extant or validly inferred, in which the concatenation of ideas that afterwards became traditional made its first appearance, and of which later manuscripts or books embodying the same tradition must (we assume) have been, in effect, *copies*. In this way philology becomes, sometimes almost exclusively, a hunt for 'sources' in that personal sense of the word. And, whether the hunt is disciplined and responsible, or feverish and over-ingenious, it generally seems to exclude any sympathetic entry into the substance of the tradition itself. The notion that that substance may have been antecedent to the birth of even the first individual who strove to articulate it in writing is rarely so much as entertained. The only question for the modern scholar is: Who started it all?

This, I think, is where the modern hunt for sources differs so sharply from the medieval reverence for "olde bokes" and, in general, what they called "auctorities". The oldest book that could be referred to was the most valuable to them, not because it was itself the source of what they were retailing, but because it was the nearest to the ultimate, transpersonal source, nearest in fact to the truth revealing itself. That point of view entailed a totally different attitude from our own to such issues as plagiarism, forgery, inaccurate attribution of authorship — a point of view which is, I believe, very generally overlooked by contemporary philologists. Themselves living in an age when the person of the individual author is felt to be more important, not to say more interesting, than the thought he is transmitting, they understand the concept of copyright very clearly and the concept of revelation not at all. Otherwise they would not, to give a single instance, take such immense care to go on showing that they have not been taken in, by never on any account simply referring to Dionysius the Areopagite, but always to 'pseudo-Dionysius'; this practice subtly undermines the actual substance of the *Celestial Hierarchies* and the *Divine Names*, and any value those works may have as revelation. For who would think of paying any serious attention to a 'pseudo' anybody?

I spoke just now of truth revealing itself. If we accept the reality of a "divine or supernatural agency", I think we must accept that this does occur, either from without or from within or in both ways. And if I was right in what I said about the true moment of division between without or within, then it follows that the source of that revelation may be, indeed must be, noumenal, that is, spiritual, whether or not it comes through a phenomenal medium. Furthermore, if we do not allow ourselves to be hoodwinked by the crudely extrapolating hypothesis of animistic 'projection', all the evidence there is proclaims aloud that the older modes of revelation did in fact occur from without, that is, through the phenomenal medium. And what is all important, in my view, for a fruitful study of all but comparatively recent literature, is that this should come to be fully accepted, not just admitted in the abstract, but accepted by the imagination as well as by the judgment, so that it is not forgotten as soon as the mind has left the general principle behind and is applying itself to particulars — accepted in fact by whatever part of us it is that takes certain things for granted, or as matter of course.

That would mean our apprehending it through the mind's eye, not as an interesting fancy that was started by somebody at some time or other, but rather as a truth that is basic to our very existence, a truth which was temporarily obscured by the Age of Enlightenment, rather as the sun during an eclipse is obscured by a more solid body, which is itself undoubtedly capable, when in opposition, of shedding a light of its own, though even that pale illumination was borrowed by reflection from the ultimate source of light.

C. S. Lewis, in his little book *The Discarded Image* (1964), tried hard to put students of medieval and Renaissance literature in a position to understand and enjoy that literature by expounding and depicting in some detail the very different world in which its writers lived. And the one great difference that underlies and pervades all the rest is that they experienced the relation between the within and the without not as simply a spatial traffic between eyes and world, or brain and world, but in terms of macrocosm and microcosm, of humanity as a whole (but also of each human being) as a little world within the greater world surrounding it, which was both its source and its goal. Dig into almost any serious book written much earlier than the eighteenth century, and you will find that cosmology assumed and underlying it. What I am suggesting is that, if it is impossible really to *understand* such literature at all without being alert to this, it is no less impossible to *study* it intensively, to research it, or to speculate intelligently about its so-called 'sources' without at the same time taking that cosmology seriously. That is, without having realised that, whatever extravagances it led to here and there, it was substantially nearer the truth than our own, if indeed we can now be said to have one at all. Moreover, unless we do take it seriously, I do not really think we can take any concept of revelation seriously. For what is revelation if it is not the macrocosm, in one way or another, imparting knowledge of itself to the microcosm? Either it is theophany, or there neither is nor ever was any such thing as revelation — and it is merely an archaic metaphor for barking a little more loudly than usual at the moon.

I could adduce plenty of examples of the kind of source-hunting research and criticism I have in mind, and one or two of a different and better kind, but for that

I should need a great deal more time than I have left to me. I must go on instead to say a word or two on that other aspect of literature, the actual production of it in the present and future. I really see no other avenue of salvation from the rising tide of triviality, often tending towards bestiality, than some such change as I have been trying to adumbrate in the prevailing notion of what constitutes 'creativity'; a general recognition of the fact that it is much nearer to revelation than it is to inventiveness or stripping. By all means call it 'self-expression', if you will, provided you know something at least of the history of selfhood and something of where the true self of everyman resides. By all means go on speaking of man's 'creative imagination', provided you are aware that imagination is the true successor of inspiration and not merely the parading and parading of superficial idiosyncrasy and fleeting impulse. But then you will also be aware that both of them are in fact modes of revelation, pre-personal in the first case and metapersonal in the second. To speak of 'metapersonal revelation' is perhaps coming rather near — as near, I hope, as I have yet come — to jargon. St Paul put it better in the *Epistle to the Romans* when he spoke of "the Spirit itself bearing witness with our spirit".

You would be mistaken if you took this concept of literature as revelation as implying that all literature must henceforth be deadly serious and aimed straight at Heaven, that there shall be no more cakes and ale. I am thinking of great literature. But I am also persuaded that the prevalent idea of what constitutes great literature is effective in some measure at all levels, influencing its texture and determining its tone. Here, as elsewhere, the fact that the idea, or ideal, may be only realised by a few does not mean that its presence or absence is of no importance for the many. It is something the same in the domain of sexual behaviour. Very few perhaps actually realise the man/woman relation as a sacrament or even marriage as a socially responsible act, but the presence or absence of such a few and of the idea in their minds may well determine in the end whether a given society is to be civilised or Gadarene. It is a mystery no doubt, but it is also a fact, that the taste and the quality of cakes and ale themselves are very different according to whether there is, or is not, an Olivia, an Orsino, a Viola hovering in the background behind them.

No, I see plenty of room for light literature of all kinds, as also for critical discrimination and painstaking critical research, including research into historical sources. It is the ultimate Idea underlying it all, or, if you like, the soul in its complex body, that I have been trying to address myself to.

So also with religion and theology. There is no question of ruling out exegesis or the niceties of textual criticism. But here there is, I imagine, no need to argue for the importance of a right concept of revelation as their underlying Idea. The only question is: What is that right concept? It seems to me almost self-evident that normally religion begins as revelation and gradually becomes tradition. I shall only suggest in conclusion that the essential difference between the Christian and all other religions, including Judaism, is that the former did *not* begin with a revelation but with an historical event; the event namely by which the potential source of all revelation was passed from macrocosm to microcosm, and thus from without to within. That, as I see it, is why the Incarnation has also been correctly described as the Word becoming flesh. If it be objected that that event was itself a revelation, inasmuch as it was certainly a theophany, I shall, to say the least of it, raise no objection. I shall only ask leave to distinguish that particular revelation from revelation in the sense in which I have been using the word, a sense which is already wide enough in all conscience. Beyond that I cannot attempt to expatiate. After all, the principal concern of this paper has been with literature, though its object has been to suggest that a healthy future for both literature and religion depends on what I would call the Idea of literature coalescing, as it were, with the Idea of religion in an evolutionary concept of revelation.

MEANING, REVELATION AND TRADITION IN LANGUAGE AND RELIGION

Paul Ricoeur, in his book *The Symbolism of Evil*, referring to a certain sentence on which he is about to expatiate, begins: "That sentence, which enchants me..." Well, there is a sentence which enchants, and has always enchanted *me*. In his case the sentence is "The symbol gives rise to thought". In my case it is the opening verse of St. John's Gospel: "In the beginning was the Word and the Word was with God and the Word was God." I think that "enchant" is the right verb because, if the word is hopelessly inadequate to convey the significance of that sentence to me now, I remember being curiously fascinated by it long before I was really able to attach any intelligible meaning to it, and at a time when I certainly had no intention of accepting on faith anything I couldn't understand. I happened not to have been brought up that way.

Of course I was already beginning to feel the fascination of words in the ordinary sense — bits of human language — and no doubt that had much to do with it. But what connection could there possibly be between words and their history — the sort of thing that Archbishop Trench and Max Müller and M. Bréal and Logan Pearsall-Smith wrote about — and "the Word" in that fateful sentence? It is only since I started trying to arrange my thoughts on the subject of this lecture that I suddenly realized that practically all I have ever written on the subject of language and other matters connected with it could be characterized, not inaccurately, as attempts to answer that very question.

The next reflection was that my best hope of imparting any sort of coherent structure to the jumble of ideas that I should be hoping to lay before you was to string them on the thread, as it were, of that underlying question. It was borne in on me that that would be the best, perhaps the only way, of keeping a reasonably steady course through waters that not only run very deep, but keep ramifying into separate channels, all of which lead away from the main stream.

If we ask ourselves what are the most distinctive features about the little thing we call a "word" — and it's not a question that we very often do ask ourselves — I think we shall find that the two most outstanding are these. First, a word, whether spoken or written, has a remarkable, even paradoxical, quality — namely that it both goes out and remains where it was to start with. "Word" means, of course, not simply the ink marks on the paper or the sound in the air. There is also the meaning of the word. Without that, it would not be a word but merely ink marks or noise: And when a word is read or heard, that meaning goes out — goes out to another mind, or to many other minds. But all the same, this exodus does not leave the speaker or writer any poorer. He still has the meaning nestling inside him just as snugly as he had before he let it go.

The second feature is already implicit in the first. In addition to the element in it that is perceptible to the senses — ink or sound — the word has a second element, inasmuch as it expresses or symbolizes, or what you will, something that is *not* perceptible to the senses, the something that is called its meaning.

"Expresses, or symbolizes, or what you will." By putting it in that delightfully casual way, I was, of course, skimming over the surface of some of those deep waters that I have alluded to. Just this question of what exactly is meant by such terms as "symbol" and "symbolize" has attracted a great deal of attention in many different quarters, especially in the last fifty or sixty years. It has perhaps been examined most extensively in connection with literary expression, and most intensively in connection with poetry. Now, in that latter connection, you will generally find symbolism being dealt with on the basis of perceived resemblance or likeness. In some way or other, a symbol is "like" what it symbolizes. Whether or no, as Coleridge held, it is also *part* of what it symbolizes is a further question; but a symbol's relation to what it stands for is certainly, in some manner, a relation of likeness or a development from that relation. For instance, in the domain of rhetoric or literary criticism, it is often related to other indirect ways of conveying meaning, such as the metaphor and the simile. In the simile it is pointed out, you frankly and grammatically aver that *A* is like *B*: my love is like a red rose, and so on. In the metaphor, you short-circuit the process, and perhaps move a step away from prose and into poetry, by leaving out any express reference to likeness: my love is a rose. But finally, you can go a step further than that and simply write a poem about a rose, but in such a way that everyone knows that what you are in fact writing about, that what you *mean*, is not simply a rose but also a woman. That is a simple and very transparent example of a symbol, and it is easy to see how it is based on a relation of likeness or — as the lady's family circle might prefer to put it — of imputed likeness. Actually, that remark was not just a would-be humorous reflection, but a rather important one, since it reminds us of something that we should never forget: namely that, if words are indeed symbols, they are symbols not of *things* but of *meanings* — not of something physical but essentially of something mental.

But the problem soon moves beyond that into realms where, although it is obvious that a poem, or something in one, is intended symbolically, it is no longer clear *what* it is that is being symbolized — Blake's "tyger", the French Symbolists; I need not stop to give examples. And here the conclusion that has been arrived at is that it is a mistake to try to be clear about what is symbolized and that to do so is to misunderstand the very nature of a genuine symbol. Whatever it is that is being expressed by a symbol, that symbol was the only possible way of expressing it. If there were any other way of expressing it, it would not be a true, a *primary* symbol. Or, putting it another way, if the "it" that is expressed by a symbol could be expressed in any other way, then it cannot be the kind of "it" that needs the mystery of symbolism to make it manifest.

Aristotle defined words as "symbols of soul experiences", and it seems clear that if individual words are indeed symbols, then they are certainly "primary" symbols in the sense just indicated. This is so because any attempt to explain in words how words come to *be* symbols, or just what symbolizing means in that case, is merely using what are already symbols to explain symbols. It is therefore not *explanation*, but merely *substitution*. In fact, the objection to this process is very similar to Coleridge's objection to the philosophy of science as it prevailed in his day — and still largely does in our own. That philosophy, he said, is based on the false assumption that phenomena (that is, everything perceptible to the senses) can be explained by other phenomena. You can split up the infinitesimal particles, but when you have finished doing that, the problem of how the particles came into existence in the first place remains. It is, with another hat on, the same old problem that you started out to explain — the problem of how the world came into existence. Claiming to investigate origin, all you have really done is to discern rearrangements. (Let me add that, in Henri Corbin's "The Concept of Comparative Philosophy", I recently came across what seems to me to be a very good definition of the word "phenomenon": "The phenomenon is that which shows itself, that which is apparent and which in its appearance shows forth something which can reveal itself therein only by remaining concealed beneath the appearance.")

In much the same unsatisfactory way, the literary approach to symbol — and through that to meaning — hardly reaches down to the problem of meaning itself, of meaning as such; rather, it deals, at a later stage, with the problem of two different levels of meaning — the literal on the one hand and the metaphorical or figurative meaning on the other. It is good training, and very needful training, for the sort of imagination that is needed for the anterior problem that I am trying to get at, but it hardly touches the problem itself. I mean that *any* word is the symbol of its meaning. It is the fact that words are *primary symbols* — symbols that you can't get behind, or not in that way; it is the fact that they are what Paul Ricoeur has called "fundamental symbols of consciousness". Such symbols, to paraphrase Corbin, are "things which can reveal themselves only by remaining concealed..."

Perhaps one could say that such fundamental symbols — words — must therefore be based on the principle not of *likeness*, but of *revelation*. However that may be, is there any way you *can* get behind them? Here it is worth noticing that, as I have said, while a great deal of attention has been bestowed in the last few decades on the second of the two features which, I suggested, characterize words as such (that is, their symbolic function), almost none has been given to the first — the remarkable fact, you will remember, that a word as such, or its meaning as such, both goes out and remains where it originated. This restricted approach was not always the fashion. One of the things that I discovered in that quest I mentioned was that, from time to time in the centuries of our era that preceded the sixteenth or seventeenth, a great deal of attention had been bestowed on just that feature. Thus, while I got a great deal of light on the second feature from a number of relatively recent writers, it was only when I went further back and ventured to look into some of the thinking done on the subject by such minds as St. Augustine, John Scotus Erigena, Thomas Aquinas, and St. Bonaventura that I began to get some light on the first feature and, at the same time, to realize two things: first, how essential that same light is for any insight at all into — well, let me say into words as fundamental symbols of consciousness; and second, how that same light could begin to illuminate my underlying problem of the relation between words and the Word.

You may wonder why one should have to go so far back to find anything approaching a convincing psychology of fundamental symbolism. I wondered myself. Perhaps it was because those writers had not yet had the bandage of Cartesian and Kantian dogma drawn across their eyes and were free, therefore, from undue obsession with the physical brain. I am not going into that. What I do want to do, if I can manage it, is to present some of that unfamiliar psychology in summary form, so that you can reflect further on it if you are minded to do so. You find the substance of it in a good many places: St. Augustine's treatise on *The Trinity* is one of them, and there is a good deal of it in Aquinas's *Summa*, especially in the early *Questions*. A particularly memorable moment for me was the moment when I discovered that Aquinas had also taken the trouble to produce a separate short treatise entitled *The Difference between the Divine Word and the Human* (*De Differentia Divini Verbi et Humani*).

The psychology in question differs from modern linguistics in the sense that it begins its investigation into the word at a much earlier stage in its life, or even just before its birth. The spoken or uttered word is seen as the conclusion of an interior process, during which it first took form as an "inner" word (*verbum interius*), an entity not yet belonging or clothed in any sound, real or imagined. The exponents of this psychology speak of a "memory word", of a *verbum cordis* or "heart word", and finally of the "intellect word" that finds vent in actual utterance — *vox*, the voice or sounded word. The reasoning is close, elaborate, conscientious. In fact, one gets the impression that the will or the ability to think really strenuously is something that we have since rather lost hold of. I can only sketch inadequately the general picture that is left in the mind after studying it to the best of one's ability. It is a picture of the memory as a sort of womb in the human psyche. Impressions from the senses are received into that womb, and the mere fact that it retains them instead of letting them go as soon as they appear allows the first embryonic appearance of a word or name — the *memory-word*. Received further into the light of the intellect, this *memory-word* becomes the *heart-word*, but it is only when the intellect acts on it — acts formatively on or in it — that it opens into the *intellect-word*, and is ready to be born into physical existence as a voiced or uttered word.

Of course, to get the full force of it, you have to realize that all this is not conceived as a purely subjective process. Psychology in those days had not yet become the physiology in disguise that it mostly is today. The form or species of an object, which in the active intelligence makes possible its naming, was identical to the form or species of the object itself in what we should call the "outer" world. "There is one principle which produces the object of perception and the same principle at the other pole produces the contemplation of that object." That was how Coleridge was to put it many years later; but earlier thinkers did not need a Coleridge to preach it to them, because they took it for granted.

The point I want to draw attention to is the circumstance that the context in which you find this psychology expounded so carefully and in such detail — whether it is St. Augustine on the Trinity or Aquinas distinguishing between the divine Word and the human, or some other — is usually a sustained endeavour to help the reader grasp by analogy the existential relation between the Father and the Son in Christian theology. St. Thomas Aquinas is not content simply to produce the first two lines of his wonderful Corpus Christi hymn:

> *Verbum supernum prodiens*
> *Nec Patris linquens dexteram...*
> The supernal Word proceeding
> And yet not leaving the right hand of the Father...

He must find some way, as a philosopher, of helping his readers grasp in their imaginations the appallingly difficult notion — difficult because it flouts the fundamental law of contradiction on which all strictly logical thought is based — the notion of a thing or being proceeding or going out and yet remaining where it was. And this he does by saying in effect: *Look, you find this an impossible notion to accept about your Creator. But think carefully, look very carefully into yourselves, and you will see how it is something that happens every time an ordinary human word is engendered.*

Rather strangely perhaps, I have come to the conclusion that in our day this analogy, or more than analogy, between the divine Word and the human can be more helpful in the inverse direction: that is, beginning with the divine Word, the Logos at the root of all creation, and passing thence to the mystery of language. I do not, of course, mean by that that the Christian mystery of the Son proceeding from the Father, and yet remaining with the Father, is the easier one to grasp — only that in contemplating it we are at least forced to realize that we *are* confronting a mystery: the primary mystery of the unmanifest being made manifest. And in the twentieth century, that is perhaps a rather wholesome experience. In any case, I am convinced that that is the only profitable frame of mind in which to approach this problem of words as *primary* symbols. More specifically, such an approach mitigates our tendency to over-emphasize the factor of likeness in building our concept of symbol — of likeness between one created thing and another. It suggests that, if we must think in terms of likeness or similitude, we should strive rather to conceive the kind of likeness that may subsist between the generated and the generant, to conceive of the manifest being in some manner the "image" of the unmanifest.

But now, if we do presume to try to fix our attention on such issues as the unmanifest becoming manifest, as the invisible transpiring through the visible which it has brought into being — or let us say (since that is what we have come to mean by the word "nature") as the supernatural taking form as the natural — then we are thinking about what can equally well be called "revelation". And I have come to believe that on that subject, very much as is the case with symbol and symbolism, one way of getting our thinking out of the straitjacket in which the general mental development of the last few hundred years has constricted it is to explore some of the older writers. It is interesting that there are passages in those writers where, when the topic is the true nature of words or language, it is not always immediately clear whether they are really referring to language in general or to the language of Scripture. There is a sentence in St. Bonaventura which makes more explicit the relation between the two as they felt it. He speaks of the Word as "the multiform wisdom of God, which is hidden [*occultatur*] in all knowledge and in all nature but is clearly passed down to us [the word is *traditur*, from which we get *tradition*] in the sacred writing". Some sense remained as late as the nineteenth century of this special significance of the language of

Scripture actually *as* language, as revelatory word and not merely as information about past revelation. This is reflected incidentally in the recent history of the word *hermeneutics*. Hermeneutics means, roughly speaking "interpretation", and until a few decades ago it always signified interpretation of the language of the Bible. It is only in the last few decades that its meaning has been extended (often with the omission of the final *s* — *Hermeneutic*) to cover the interpretation of language and, especially, the element of symbolism in language in general.

Is there then something special that we can lay our hands on that differentiates the language of Scripture from any other known language? If we limit ourselves for the moment to the Old Testament, I can think of at least two things. First, the predominant part played in it by prophecy — and here again I am thinking not simply of the fact that the Old Testament does contain a large number of prophecies, but also of a certain quality in the Hebrew tongue which seems somehow to integrate the substance of prophecy with the very structure, even the grammatical structures, of the language. Here I have to confess that I am no Hebrew scholar, but it does seem clear, from such investigation as I have been able to make, that the Hebrew verb is a very different matter from ours, inasmuch as, to the extent that it can be said to have a past and a future tense, it uses the *future* tense for history and the *past* for prophecy — a notion which is at least not *less* difficult to grasp than that other one, which we have already looked at, of a going out which is at the same time a remaining where you were.

Eighteenth- and nineteenth-century controversy in the realm of hermeneutics tended to focus on the issue of what was called “verbal inspiration”: whether the words of Holy Writ should be regarded as divinely dictated, so that every word must be taken as literally true and accurate, or whether the writers were indeed divinely inspired but wrote under the impulse of that inspiration what their own minds and imaginations directed them to write. I have specified the eighteenth- and nineteenth-centuries, but I suppose that issue is still a live one between those who may perhaps be called hard-line fundamentalists on the one hand and, on the other, the great body of those who, without being fundamentalists, for one reason or another regard the Bible as probably the most important book in the world. The second group, to which I belong, is of course heavily in the majority, but because the opinions that divide the two are, whether devoutly or contemptuously, often entertained with great confidence, I prefer not to ignore the first group, and my contention is that, if what one is trying to arrive at is a viable concept of revelation, that cleavage of opinion can really be ignored. The reason for this lies in the very nature of language, the very nature of a word, of which I tried to say something at the beginning. Surely a word is only a word at all if it has three characteristics. There must surely be a sound or a mark, the sound or mark must be capable of conveying meaning, and the meaning must go out and be received by a listening or reading mind. And in deciding whether or not revelation has occurred, we cannot ignore the third characteristic any more than we can ignore the other two. It is clear, is it not, that if what we mean by “the Bible” is simply a pound of ink and paper and pasteboard, then it is not revelation. It is at most potential revelation.

Perhaps it has been a clearer perception of this simple fact that has led to the broadening of the scope of hermeneutics from biblical language into the problem of language in general, with a corresponding theological feedback into the nature of biblical language itself. Whether you believe in verbal inspiration or not, if you are willing to *reflect* at all on language, or on any particular language, you cannot just leave out what happens at the receiving end.

My experience here is of a growing consensus of opinion, converging from many different points of view, that if its fundamentally symbolical nature is omitted from our understanding of language, if we forget that words are primary symbols of consciousness, then in the end we simply fail to apprehend it as meaning. For meaning, as distinct from mere information, always has an element of revelation in it. Hence the continually increasing attention that has been paid in my time to the whole realm of symbol and symbolism. If however, what I have previously suggested is correct, then the light which that attention could throw on the subject has been obscured, or certainly limited, by excessive concentration on the principle of likeness or resemblance as the key to the nature of the symbol. That is what has led (in association with the concept of "metaphor") to the prevailing assumption that a statement must be *either* symbolical *or* literal. Literal meaning, it is assumed, cannot at the same time be symbolical. Whereas, if Coleridge was right in holding that a genuine symbol is not merely parallel to but actually "a *part* of the reality it represents", then that is a false dichotomy. And of course on the falsity of that dichotomy hangs the justification of the typological interpretation of Old Testament history which has formed such a substantial part of the whole Christian tradition, and of which the carvings and the glass in almost any Gothic cathedral amount to something like an encyclopedia.

Are there any pointers to a way of transcending our limited understanding of the nature of symbol and, in particular, of the essentially symbolical nature of the word? In trying to answer that, I must revert for a moment to that acutely elaborated medieval distinction between the Divine Word and the human to which I referred at the start. The inner word is always something at the same time proceeding from the intellect and remaining within the intellect. But what does it rely on for its origin? It relies for its origin on the memory. It has to crystallize, so to speak, around some grain of sense perception given from outside itself and retained in itself. Whereas the Divine Word is self-generating. What the memory is to the human word the Creator himself, God the Father, is to the Divine Word. If I venture to reflect on the problem of meaning in language in terms of this kind of psychology, I find myself led on into a number of consequential reflections. Thus memory differs from its Creator in the fact that it is not permanent. It fades with time. In the same way, and no doubt for that reason, language fades. As has often been pointed out, words — or the living meanings in them — fade with the repeated use that they undergo with the lapse of time. Many philologists, for instance, have drawn attention to the fact that, if we look into their *history*, most words present the appearance of "fossilized metaphors". That is one of the reasons why poetry is needed as well as prose. The languages of all civilized peoples, it has been pointed out, have undergone a process of "sedimentation". It is not so much meaning that they present us with now as the husks of meaning. There is, however, a means by which the faded words, the fossilized metaphors, can be revivified, so that meaning again shines through them, so that language once again begins to reveal something behind or beyond its merely sensuous references. And that something is, precisely, the *act* of using language and the *faculty* of apprehending it as a tissue of symbols. In the case of religion, it is in much the same way — and, indeed, it is in close association with that very process of sedimentation — that what began as revelation fades into tradition. And here again the only known remedy for sedimentation appears to be the way of symbol. For tradition to re-acquire the pristine energy, so to speak, of revelation, it needs to be apprehended not *only* as historical record but *also* as a symbol. Herein, as I see it, lies the importance of what is generally called "typology" — a principle of interpretation, or hermeneutic, which, like symbolism, has been receiving more and more serious attention in the last hundred or hundred-and-fifty years. (The Oxford Dictionary gives no quotation on the word earlier than the 1830s.)

But I doubt if that habit can be acquired in our time without our first arriving at a true understanding of the *nature* of symbol. So, before attempting to say anything more about typology, let me pursue one more of those consequential reflections that I have alluded to. It was pointed out that the difference between the Divine Word, originating in itself, and the human word, originating in memory, is that the memory has to have a sense-perceptible content on which to build or around which to crystallise. Is it here, possibly, that we should look for an explanation of that undue emphasis on the element of likeness, of comparison (or implied comparison), between two existent objects which has characterized our conception of a symbol ever since Aristotle first produced his definition of metaphor, putting it in terms of mathematical ratio — the perception that *a* is to *b* as *b* is to *c* — and adding that to make good metaphors is "to contemplate likeness"? And does the difference between a man-made symbol and those primary symbols given in the beginning by nature herself, those natural phenomena which are also potential *words*, lie precisely in this: that, just as the memory must have a sense-context as its nucleus, so the *human* faculty of symbolizing must have as its nucleus two manifest objects to place side by side — that it must proceed, whether, consciously or unconsciously, from simile through metaphor to symbol? Further, shall we come nearer to an understanding of such a fundamental problem as the origin of language if we make the same distinction between symbols that the medieval linguistic analysts did between the human word and the Divine — if we study the man-made symbols that we know in terms of a useful analogy with the primary symbols that we did not create (but as no more than that, because the primary Symbol-maker did *not* have to work by comparison)?

It is certain, I think, that if we are minded to take the typology of the Old Testament as more than a man-made fiction, we should have to approach the nature of symbol more in this way than in the customary one. History is interpreted typologically — or, as Erich Auerbach preferred to express it, "figuratively" — when one worldly event is interpreted through another so that the first signifies the second and the second fulfils the first. But this can only be *fact*, and not mere *fancy*, if history itself is seen, as I have suggested that words must be seen, as the supernatural incarnating in the natural. Then the second event is seen as not simply "like" the first, but, so to speak, a further and more explicit development of it. This is how the typological or figural relation between the Old Testament and the New was seen and felt by our predecessors for many centuries: ever since Augustine described Moses as *figura Christi* — as prefiguring Christ — or before that, since Paul took Ishmael and Isaac as prefiguring respectively the heirs of the old covenant and of the new.

One may perhaps go further and raise the following question: what part, then, is played by symbolism in the *New* Testament? How are the bare bones of narrative tradition raised *there* to the level of revelation? I am indebted to Robert Funk's book *Language, Hermeneutic, and the Word of God* for pointing out the crucial importance, in the Gospels, of the *parable*. Indeed, the parables recounted in the Synoptic Gospels could perhaps be said to be in the New Testament what typology is in the Old. And it is significant, from the point of view from which I have been speaking, that the parables are, frankly, similes. "Parabolic" utterance is in fact the generic title which comprises all kinds of "other-saying", from simile through allegory and metaphor to symbol. So they *are* based on likeness. But (and here again I am indebted to Professor Funk) it is likeness of a special sort. It is a likeness which explicitly points beyond likeness. The "earthly story with the heavenly meaning" looks at first sight like a very ordinary, even humdrum, worldly event, a simple event or series of events in the natural world. But then, at some point in it, the natural breaks down. Agatha Christie's Hercule Poirot might say of it that it is "the wrong shape". Poor women are indeed glad to find the dime they have lost, but they do not in fact invite all their neighbours to a party to rejoice over it. A host whose guests fail to arrive does not send out for others in the byways and hedges, still less does he drag them to his wedding feast by force, and still less again does he then punish them for not appearing in the proper morning dress. A farmer sowing expensive seed does not in fact scatter more than half of it in places where it won't grow. And so on.

An ordinary simile suggests the supernatural — that is, the supersensible — by comparing two naturals. My love is like a rose, or is a rose. They are both objects in the sense-world, but by placing them side by side the poet suggests into being the supersensible qualities of beauty, grace, blessedness, or what you will. Whereas in the parable one term of the comparison is already supersensible. "The Kingdom of Heaven is like unto..." and then comes the parable, the parallel with nature which can only be drawn by making nature itself a little unnatural, with the result that, if it "works", so to speak — "if ye will receive it" — what breaks through is not just information about the kingdom, but the Kingdom itself.

I am then led back by such reflections to the central issue of the relation between divine word and human. An ordinary human child is first born as a physical being and then begins to speak. And when he begins to speak, he is limited, as we saw, by the necessity for a fleshly memory — a nucleus around which his words can be built. May we say that, when the divine Word itself had been made flesh and began to speak, there was no such limitation — or, if there was, that it was voluntarily accepted? That the spoken word was both divine and human at the same time? And may we add that, when the divine Word began to symbolize — since the symbols themselves were both divine *and* human, since he was symbolizing out of the flesh — he was, therefore, limited on the one hand to the necessity of symbolizing by the method of comparison, but that, on the other hand, he transformed the very element of likeness into something transcending likeness? Or, if you will, that he re-transformed his symbols into what I called primary symbols — into the kind of symbols that words are in themselves? So that, if we are to think of parallel as likeness, then it is not the likeness between one subject and another that is in question, but the likeness between the generated and the generant, the kind of likeness which allows us to call the manifest an "image" of the unmanifest.

I fear that I must leave it at that. And I do so with some trepidation. Why have I given this lecture? Because it is just a fact that the assemblage of reflections I have tried to place before you has produced in me a conviction that I do now have *some* understanding at least of that opening verse of St. John's Gospel. For that reason I thought it would be well to try to share those reflections. But I am also aware that those reflections (bound up as they are with my special interests) have been jostling each other in my mind over a long period, without having hitherto been marshalled into any sort of order — and that they are by their nature not easy to communicate in such a way as to become grounds for the like conviction in others. I am sure that I cannot have altogether succeeded, but I believe (such is the importance of the subject) that it will have been worth doing if I have not altogether failed.

THE LIGHT OF THE WORLD

When man, in the exercise of his mechanical function, puts together a structure, he does it by adding one part to another, so that they lie side-by-side in space, and the whole is made up of all the parts added together. But when nature constructs, she follows a different principle — one which man also, when he is functioning not as mechanic but as artist or poet, must strive to follow. In an *organic* structure it will be found that the parts interpenetrate and, as it were, express each other in a characteristic way, and that often a single part will seem at the same time to be the whole, or to be potentially the whole. And this is the structural principle which, at all levels from the highest to the lowest, Anthroposophy reveals to us as present in the universe itself.

We know, for instance, that the substance even of the physical world consists primarily, not of some extrapolated system of atoms or nuclei or quanta or probabilities, but of a vast number of spiritual beings and the relations between them. And this is equally true of the inner world of consciousness. Anthroposophy adopts the Dionysian nomenclature[1] and speaks of three Hierarchies of such Beings: of a First Hierarchy, consisting of Thrones, Cherubim and Seraphim; of a Second Hierarchy, consisting also of three different Orders or Ranks of Beings, for whom we usually employ the Greek names, Kyriotetes, Dynameis, Exusiai, and of the third and lowest Hierarchy of Archai, Archangeloi and Angeloi. And already, at this exalted level, we find it higher still at the level of the Divine Trinity itself; where, as is so precisely stated in the Athanasian Creed, "The

Father is God, the Son is God, and the Holy Ghost is God. And yet they are not three Gods, but one God". For, on the one hand, we think of the whole of the First or highest Hierarchy — that is, of the whole trinity of Orders which it contains — as being the Hierarchy in which the Father principle is especially manifested; of the Second Hierarchy as the Hierarchy of the Son and of the Third Hierarchy as the Hierarchy of the Holy Spirit. But, on the other hand, we also find Father, Son and Spirit manifest *within* each Hierarchy. For instance, within the First Hierarchy the Order of the Thrones carries the will of the Father, while the Seraphim express the Son and the Cherubim the Holy Spirit. And so it is with the Second, and also with the Third Hierarchy, whose field of action is more the inner world of man's consciousness. Here it is the Archai, or Time-Spirits, who are the representatives of the Father.

One can put it that way; but one can also say that through the Archai the whole of the First Hierarchy enters into and works within the Third. Or rather that it *may* do so; for when it comes to the Third Hierarchy, a good deal depends on the activity and the free choices of man himself.

It follows also that in each Hierarchy you get one Order of Beings which not only expresses a Person of the Trinity, but expresses it in a special emphasized way. The Thrones are not only Father-Beings, but are Father-Beings within the Hierarchy of the Father. So also, Exusiai express the Son within the Hierarchy of the Son; and the Angels the Spirit within the Hierarchy of the Spirit.

If we now descend, from this brief glimpse at the structure of the Spiritual World itself, to man as he lives on earth, we find the like hierarchical, or organic, relation between the four principles of which he is composed — and one which needs the like mobility of thought or imagination for its comprehension. We speak of man as consisting of the four principles, Physical, Etheric, Astral and Ego.[2] And here, too, we find that we not only have these four principles, as it were, primarily and in their own right; but also, if we confine our attention to only one of them, we shall find all four in a secondary way, manifested, reflected, aspected — how you will — in that one. In the physical body, for instance, we find the Ego principle represented — where? In the blood. And in the same way we detect the astral, the etheric and the physical as present in a special way in the nerves and senses, in the glandular system, and in the bones.

And so it is with the Etheric. Here I say "Etheric" rather than "Etheric Body", because, although man certainly has an etheric body, yet this body is not insulated from the rest of the etheric — and elemental — world in the same way that the physical body is from the physical world around it. In the Four Ethers[3] of which Rudolf Steiner has said so much, we find again the four principles of which man is composed. We find physical, etheric, astral and ego in the Warmth Ether, the Light Ether, the Chemical Ether or Sound Ether and the Life Ether respectively.

Here again, in the case of the Light Ether, we get that special emphasis — of the principle within its own principle. Light Ether is the etheric *in* the etheric. Without going into the question how far it is possible to call any part of light "physical", I suppose, then, we are not far astray, if we think of this light from the sun that comes flooding in on us through our eyes, when we wake in the morning, as a sort of gateway through which our consciousness can enter into an experience of the etheric world — if we think of light as, shall I say, the etheric *par excellence*. And that is why I begin by considering our experience of light from this point of view, by considering our experience of the etheric cosmos.

We must, however, distinguish *experience* of the etheric from *ideas* we may form about the etheric before we have any experience. These ideas are likely to be — in my case they certainly were — not truly ideas about the etheric at all, but only ideas about the effects of the etheric in the physical. I well remember reading about the etheric body in Rudolf Steiner's book *Theosophy*, and getting from there the idea of the "formative forces" of which it is composed, and which keep the living physical bodies of plants and animals and men from collapsing like dead bodies. I thought of growing plants and, insensibly, there formed itself in my mind the picture of a kind of swelling, an expanding or inflating force — something like what happens when you blow up a bicycle tyre! This really remained with me for years, and I was often much troubled by various allusions to the etheric in other contexts — lectures and so forth — which did not seem to square with it. Particularly, when I was told that the etheric forces work *inward* from the periphery. This seemed to suggest that my previous imagination contained the opposite of the truth, and that I ought really to be thinking, not of expansion from within, but rather a kind of *suction* from without. But of course that was no nearer the truth; because I was really thinking all the time, not of etheric forces but of physical forces.

It is indeed very difficult for minds — trained, as ours have mostly been, to assume that there is nothing between a physical force, at one extreme, and an abstract idea at the other — to learn to imagine, or to realize in experience, something which is a force, and yet not a physical force; something whose influence is inward from the periphery, not outward from the centre; and yet which works upon that centre expansively and not contractingly. But when one *has* overcome this obstacle, at least in some degree; when one has begun, in some dim way, to realize the etheric as etheric, then one begins to move forward into a kind of new and more intimate relationship with the world of plants. One begins, for instance, to feel, like a sort of tenderness in one's own heart, the infinite delicacy and tenderness that hovers about the growing point of the commonest weed. And at the same time — or it may well be later — it may come about that one will begin to feel a new, and again an intimate, relation with the light itself. One begins to perceive, or rather to feel, that the light itself — this light from the sun that comes to us through the senses — is etheric and that the etheric is a kind of light.

And this is a very deeply moving experience. Much deeper than mere observation. It goes to the roots of one's being, like the breath of life itself. One will begin to feel that the light is not only outside in space, but also within oneself. Indeed there are sure to be occasions when, for brief periods, one is aware, not only of seeing or feeling the light, but also of breathing it. Breathing it in and out, but especially in. Only a much more intimate kind of breathing — so that one will feel at times that one is *in* the light, not only as our bodies are in water when they swim, not only as they are in the air we breathe, but rather as we speak, in that significant English idiom, of people being *in* love. If one had to find a single word in which to sum up the more subjective aspect of the experience I am speaking of, there is only one word that could be used; and that is — *joy*. The sort of joy that we see made manifest in the sunlight dancing on the water. Deep draughts of pure joy, which obliterate, while they last, all anxiety, all sorrow, all considerations of karma, and even all memory of such things. A joy so uplifting and, if I may use the word, so thoroughgoing, that, however short a time it lasts, it will leave some enduring effects behind it. It may indeed somewhat affect the whole personality — with reverberations even into the sphere of physical health. It may bring a new and more intimate contact with the forces of growth and adolescence in us, so that we find ourselves developing a new strength to support our burdens, and a new energy for devising our tasks and carrying them through. In a word, it may lead to something which could perhaps be described, without altogether overstating it, as — Rejuvenation.

Let us suppose that, with the effects of this new and joyous light of perception in us, we choose to turn our attention to some of the great writings of the past; it may be to one or more of the Mystics — or it may be to the New Testament itself. What sort of experience shall we have? We shall have read Rudolf Steiner's description, in the Cassel lectures on the Gospel of St. John, of how, when the blood flowed from the Cross on Golgotha, it was much more than a merely physical event. How there was then a change in the aura of the Earth itself, so that, from being a mere planet, a mere receiver of light from the sun, it began itself to emit light. "Earth began to glow," he says, "first astrally and visible only to the seer, but in future ages the astral light will become physical light and the earth will be a luminous body — a Sun-body".[4] And now we may well feel that something has happened, like a cracking of the hard rind of a seed by the new life stirring within it; as if a stone had been rolled away, not only from the tomb of our own sense-bound thinking, but from the whole historical development of Christianity. And we shall feel a sort of astonishment, when we reflect on the sombre and gloomy thing which has been made of Christianity — perhaps by the Protestant confession as a whole, but certainly by all manner of narrow, evangelical sects, which have sprung up in the West in the last two or three centuries. We shall feel this astonishment, when we read, for instance, in St. John's Gospel, certain utterances of the Son of Man, such as: "I am come that ye might have life, and that ye might have it more abundantly", or: "These words have I spoken unto you, that my joy might remain in you, and that your joy might be full." Above all, we may feel that we now understand in a new and triumphant way those solemn words of the Christ: "I AM THE LIGHT OF THE WORLD."

Those five pregnant words "the light of the world" were uttered by Christ Jesus on three occasions, two of them recorded in St. John and one in St. Matthew.[5] Rudolf Steiner often pointed out that the Gospels were not composed or arranged in any haphazard way. If we wish to deepen our understanding of any particular event or utterance, we must always also observe exactly whereabouts in the narrative it is recorded: what came before and what followed after.

The Eighth Chapter of St. John's Gospel opens with the coming of Christ to the Temple in the early morning —

after the Feast of Tabernacles, which was celebrated with lighted candles. It describes how, while He was teaching the multitude, the Pharisees brought to Him a woman who had just been taken in adultery — "in the very act", as her accusers eagerly emphasized. The narrative of this encounter is too often repeated to need repeating here. At the moment I only want to draw attention to the fact that, directly after this incident has been described — immediately after Jesus' final words to the woman (those words which are quoted rather less often than the others): "Go, and sin no more" — in the very next verse the tremendous phrase occurs:

"Then spake Jesus again unto them, saying, 'I am the light of the world; he that followeth me shall not walk in darkness, but shall have the light of life'."

Now in the ensuing dispute with the Pharisees the Christ alludes very frequently to the Father. He refers, for instance, all moral judgments to the Father:

"I judge no man. And yet, if I judge, my judgement is true; for I am not alone, but I and the Father that sent me."

And He elaborates this argument in what at first sight seems a strange — even a far-fetched way. According to the Mosaic Law, the testimony of *two* witnesses is true; therefore His, the Christ's, judgment is true — it is true because it is the judgment, not of one, but of two — of Himself and the Father.

If we bear these words in mind, and the many, many other passages in St. John's Gospel where the Christ continually distinguishes Himself from the Father, refers all power and authority to the Father, emphasizes His obedience to the Father, as to one distinct from Himself; and if we set beside them other very different utterances such as "I and the Father are one", or His answer in Chapter 14, to Philip, when Philip says to Him, "Lord, show us the Father!"[6] and if we meditate much and deeply upon them, we may hope to approach a little nearer to one of the great mysteries which St. John's Gospel seeks to reveal to us. The other mystery is the mystery of light — and the two are most intimately connected. That is why, before I return to the light, I want to say a little more about the Father-being, as we read of Him in St. John's Gospel.

I have said that there were many, many other passages; and indeed the words "the Father" recur so frequently throughout the Gospel that they positively seem to ring through its pages, like the note of a gong struck over and over again and coming clear upon our ears through all the other sounds. In the early part of the gospel Jesus speaks more of His having come *down* from the Father, having been sent by the Father, doing the works of the Father, and so forth. Towards the end, however, He begins to speak of going *to* the Father; and it is then that His disciples fail to understand Him.

Rudolf Steiner has spoken of this failure and has pointed out that they failed to understand that, when the Christ spoke of the Father, He was really speaking of — what? Of *death*. When He said: "I came forth from the Father and am come into the world", it was really as if He said: "I came forth from death, that is from death in its true form, from the Life-Father". Only afterwards did it flash upon His disciples "that the world, as it surrounds them, is the outer expression of the Father and that the most significant feature in the outer world, its greatest maya or illusion, is equally the expression of the Father; that death is the name of the Father".[7]

These are startling words; but I believe there is a road along which we can try to penetrate somewhat into their meaning. The ordinary conscious experience of a living being, that is, of a being in this world of maya, always has two sides to it, an inner and an outer. No matter what it may be of which I am conscious — whether it is of houses and trees, or whether it is only of memories, or whether it is of the light itself, the physical or etheric light, there is always the duality, the subjective-objective duality, which is signified by the word "of". There is, on the outer side, that *of* which I am conscious, and, on the inner side, that in me which *is* conscious. I can never at any moment be conscious of that innermost in me which is actually "doing the business of being conscious". If I *say* I am conscious of it, I am deceiving myself — for I necessarily presuppose a yet more inner innermost, namely the "I" which is saying so. We get, in fact, what the philosophers call "an infinite regress".

But where the philosophers speak of an infinite regress, we speak of astral and ego; of the divine Hierarchies; and of the Father in us. For we assume that, besides the ordinary experience of human beings today, a different kind of experience is possible. We think that the part of us which *is* conscious — as distinct from the parts *of* which we are conscious — is not just a sort of phantom subject of the grammatical sentence "I am conscious of...", but a Being in a world of Beings. And it is that world which we call the astral world, and, at a further stage, the spiritual world. Thus, the difficulty still remains; but it has ceased to be merely logical and has become — awful. For it follows from what I have said, that to penetrate into the astral is to turn what by its very nature is an *inner* — what for ordinary experience is indeed inwardness itself — into an *outer*; into something like an environment. It involves — to use a very crude and perhaps rather offensive expression — a sort of turning inside out.

Now those who have read much of what Rudolf Steiner has written and spoken about man's life between death and a new birth, will know that it is precisely in such terms that he often describes the experience of the dead. He says that, whereas on earth we feel ourselves as looking out from a centre to a periphery, after death it is the other way. We feel the periphery as ourselves, and we look inwards to a centre. It is the centre which is now the "environment". This is very nearly unimaginable; and it is unimaginable, because it is the experience, not of the living but of the dead.

This break between the experience characteristic of the living and the experience characteristic of the dead — with the abruptness, the sharpness, the bitterness which it involves — does not lie between the physical and the etheric. It lies between the etheric and the astral. Physical and etheric are, both together, our outer world. Astral and ego are the inner.

If, therefore, a man who had penetrated to some extent into the etheric world, that soundless realm of interweaving, ever-changing forms — a world of joyous light, but a soundless world (and a colourless one) — wished to go further and penetrate into the realm where the Divine Word is not only seen, but also *heard* — namely, into the astral world — he would have to do — what? He would first have to die! Either he would have to die in the ordinary physical sense, or he would have to go through an experience very near to death, on the way of initiation. In one way or another he would have to take the great leap in the dark. He would have to cross the Threshold.

It is important to realize this. Not that penetration to etheric vision or experience is unimportant. On the contrary it represents, in our age above all, a real victory over Ahriman[8] and, as such, is a matter for unqualified rejoicing. It may well be that the whole future of Science depends on it. But it is also very important to realize its limitation. Because, if things *should* have happened in the order I have been supposing (and it is by no means inevitable that they should); if we have first acquired, or perhaps have been granted by that "natural clairvoyance" which Rudolf Steiner foretold for many in the second half of this century, some measure of etheric vision, and if we then seek to progress beyond it, *without* making this abrupt break, this reversal of our whole attitude to life, we shall merely deceive ourselves. We shall never actually know the astral world. We shall at best know the *effects* of the astral in the etheric — that is, the Chemical or Sound Ether; just as we may formerly have recognized the effects of the etheric in the physical, without really *knowing* the etheric itself; that is, without actually experiencing it in our own etheric hearts — or glands.

Now this duality I have been speaking of, this awful contrast between an inner and an outer world, besides concealing the mystery of the Father, and of death — has very much to do with the mystery of light and the mystery of the sun. For it was through the sun that it was gradually brought about. Read the first few lectures of the other Course on the Gospel of St. John,[9] and you will realize how the opening words: "In the Beginning was the Word, and the Word was with God, and the

Word was God... In it was life and the life was the light of men" — take us back to the remote past, before the separation of the sun from the earth, before "Lemuria". There was then *only* what, from our point of view, if we could be suddenly be transported back into it, we should feel to be an "inner" world; and the "life", which was in the Word, was not the organic, physical and etheric, life, which we contemplate as life today (contemplate rather than experience) — but the "life which *we* only know as death", or (to use Rudolf Steiner's phrase which I recently quoted) "the Life-Father". And when *light* first began to shine forth as a manifestation of this life, this spirit-life, it was not the outer sunlight we know. That is why the Book of Genesis records the creation of light as having taken place before the creation of the sun and moon — which, if it is taken superficially — is nonsense.

The Lectures last referred to contain a description of how light, as we see it, only began long after the separation of the Sun, when the sunlight, as an outer phenomenon, began to be dimly perceived by man through the fogs of Atlantis. This, then, was how the inner first became outer; how the *life* became the *light* of men. This was also the beginning of sense-perception in anything like the mode of today. But even then, it was not until a long time after this that the perceptions of the senses, and that contrast between outer and inner which they mediate, grew sharp and clear, as they are now. Elsewhere Dr. Steiner has described how, in the long course of our own Post-Atlantean cycle of ages, man's experience of the sun has undergone further changes. First, as we have seen, it was changed from an inner experience to an experience received through the senses. But since then it has gradually altered from a direct experience of the Divine *in* sense-perception into an experience of *mere* sense-perception. The Ancient Persians, he said, beheld the sun as the divine Bearer of light; the Ancient Egyptians as the divine Bearer of life; the Greeks received the sun — I say the sun, but in their case it was rather the whole surrounding sphere of the sun-filled ether — as a *soul* experience; they felt it as the divine Bearer of love. That is, of course, of that aphrodisian love, which is the potency of organic life on its way through the soul. The Greeks, he said, felt the sun as the divine Bearer of Eros. It has been left for the man of our time to feel it as the physical begetter of physical, organic life.

Now let us turn to the second occasion in St. John's Gospel, where those words "The light of the world" occur. It is at the beginning of the Ninth Chapter. Jesus sees the man who was born blind. His disciples ask Him whether this is retribution for the man's own sins or the sins of his parents, and Jesus answers: "Neither — it was in order that the works of God should be made manifest in him." And now, once more there come those five brief amazing words. For He continues: "As long as I am in the world, I am the light of the world." And then He makes clay by mixing His spittle with the earth and anoints the blind man's eyes with the clay; and He tells him to go and wash in the Pool of Siloam; and the man goes and washes, and thereupon his sight is restored.

I cannot go fully into the account of this miracle; but anyone who studies it carefully — with the events and utterances which follow it — will notice several things. He will notice, for instance, that the first words which the blind man himself is recorded as saying after he is healed are the words "I am". He will observe that the writer goes out of his way to translate the Hebrew name SILOAM which he says means "sent forth" — it was clearly a spring of water sent forth from the earth; and he will mark the Christ's words to the Pharisees, when they are disputing with Him afterwards about the miracle:

"For judgment I am come into this world, that they which see not might see, and that they which see might be made blind."

And then he will perhaps ask himself: What did the Christ really mean by those words: "That the works of God should be made manifest *in* him"? Remembering that one of the first "works of God" was the creation of light; remembering that *krima*, the word used for the English "judgment" has rather more the meaning of "distinguishing" or "discriminating" than of condemning, I think myself that both the miracle itself and the Evangelist's account of it are meant, with the words which follow, above all to emphasize the distinction between the outer light of the world and the inner: between the outer light from the sun and the inner light, which is sent forth from a source or spring within man itself, as it was sent forth in the beginning from the Father — who also spoke the words I AM, and, in doing so, revealed His holiest name.

I suppose the real question is, how seriously one intends to take these things. Only, our truest and inmost intentions are not always the ones that are best known to us. It may even happen that we first learn of our own intentions, not from within, but from without, from the things which happen to us. For light is not the only thing which has been mysteriously externalized — changed from subject into object. If we really accept the doctrine of Karma, we must also believe that the things which happen to us, apparently by accident, are not just accidents — are not even really external to us — but are actually part of us, in something the same way that the visiting insects are part of the blossom they fertilize. And this belief may become rather more than a belief: it may begin to be realized as a *positive* experience, precisely then, when that other experience which contains the bitterness of death — the experience of the Threshold — I will not say, approaches us, but at least comes into view on the horizon. And this intimate relation between the inner life and the outer event is something which we shall find we can decidedly foster and cherish by meditation.

There are today hundreds of thousands — perhaps I should say millions — of people all over the world, to whom things are happening, which are very, very bitter. I am not thinking only of the violence and physical privation, which are as yet outside the experience of most of us here. There are other ways in which the consciousness soul has to meet the assaults of the world. It is, for instance, within my knowledge that there are people within this Movement who feel that they have just about reached the end of their tether; who really do not know which way to turn, to whom life appears to be one long series of seemingly meaningless frustrations; people for whom, in their inmost souls — or what they as yet feel to be such — life really does, in one way or another, wear the mask of something like a living death. To such people it is not the province of a lecturer, and I am not qualified, to speak emotional words of comfort in tribulation. I do, however, feel impelled to quote one short, dry — perhaps even harsh — sentence of Rudolf Steiner's. It is this: "It is an indispensable condition of initiation that we should not wish things were otherwise." It is a short sentence, but it will bear long reflection.

I do not mean, by quoting it, to encourage anyone who feels despair to infer from that that he is a very important person, for whom initiation is only just around the corner. But all tribulation involves a kind of dying; and what matters is, not whether the next one, or the next three or four or five, of our many deaths is to be a physical death or an initiation death experienced in the body — but the inner attitude we gradually learn to adopt towards death. Christ, in accomplishing the Mystery of Golgotha, opened the way of initiation to all who truly seek Him. Physical death also is a crossing of the threshold, if we are prepared for it; and indeed we cross it every night when we go to sleep. And yet it depends on our attitude to it, on the strength we have, or have not, developed, whether we really do cross it, or whether we merely — sleep.

In the old conflict between those who represent Christianity as a religion of sorrow and gloom, which tells us only that this world is a Vale of Tears, and that it is absolutely necessary to be miserable now, because that is the only way of being happy later on — and those who represent it as being primarily a religion of comfort and joy — my own sympathies are all with the latter. But it has to be admitted that there are a good many passages in the Gospels which it is pretty difficult for us to get round. Take, for instance, the parable of Dives and Lazarus. It ends with Dives in Hell and Lazarus in Heaven. Yet it is nowhere even hinted that Lazarus was in any way a better, or a more loving, man than Dives —

only, as Abraham expressly states, that he was more wretched. Or take the Beatitudes, as we find them recorded in St. Matthew and St. Luke. The overall impression is pretty uncompromising. Blessed are they that mourn! Blessed are ye that hunger now… Blessed are ye when men shall hate you… Blessed are ye that weep now, for ye shall laugh! And so on, up to the final climax of the terrible Ninth Beatitude: "Blessed are ye, when men shall revile you and persecute you and say all manner of evil against you, falsely, for My sake: for great is your reward in Heaven!"

What are we to do with these very plain words? Are we just to pretend they are not there? To ignore them, and select others which we like better? Let us rather reflect that it is immediately after these very Beatitudes, as they are given in St. Matthew, that we come upon the Third of the three utterances of the Christ concerning the Light of the World. And then perhaps we shall understand to whom, and in what crisis, they are addressed.

Firstly, let me briefly recall the other two. The first followed immediately after the incident of the accused woman. She had just committed adultery. In her soul, therefore, she knew something — and, at that time, in Palestine, there must certainly have been among the bystanders many Hellenizing Jews, who knew something — of the power of the Eros content of the joy-bringing light. And here it is necessary to pause for a moment and ask a question which, in our particular phase of society, has become rather uncomfortably esoteric. Why is adultery prohibited by the Seventh Commandment? For the Decalogue is not, as the man of our time has been adroitly diverted into believing, an accidentally preserved list of primitive tribal taboos. It is, on the contrary, the framework, the scantlings — rather the blueprint — for man's own voluntary co-operation with the First, Second and Third Hierarchies in their age-long labour of constructing a human Ego out of divine materials.

When we commit adultery, in an effort to snatch the glory of the Eros-bearing light for ourselves, we surrender the conscious ego, which normally controls our actions, to the unconscious Father-forces of procreation in the physical body. We relapse, as it were, into the First Hierarchy, rather as — according to Solovyev[10] — the individual animal rejoins the group-soul in the act of copulation. When we consummate a marriage — I mean a true marriage — we make indeed the same surrender; but now the Father mitigates and balances the surrender — humanizes it, if you prefer — by tentatively asserting His more recent sovereignty in the astral and ego organization — in the conscious ego itself; whether, as at first, from Sinai, with thunder and the threat of savage penalties; or whether, as now, from His throne in the free will of each individual who determines, and in course of time effects, that the mutual consequence of the act shall be at least life-long. Through the First Hierarchy the Father reigns in the outer world, which includes our own physical bodies and their processes. Through the Time-spirits, who are His representatives in the Third Hierarchy, He will reign in the inner world of man's consciousness. Therefore these Time-spirits — the Archai — are also called Spirits of Personality.

In placing immediately after this incident the naming of Himself by the Christ as the Light of the World, it is clear to me that the Evangelist* intended to underline the distinction between the false light of the world and the true. He is indicating that, for Ego-men, the way to the Father is not the backward way through Eros and orgasm, but the journey on, which leads through death. In recording it again, during the healing of the man born blind, we have seen that he brought out the contrast between the outer light and the inner. The *third* of the three occasions on which these words occur — this time in the Gospel of St. Matthew — is during the Sermon on the Mount, immediately after the Beatitudes. But this time the setting is different. This time Jesus is no longer addressing the multitude. He is alone with His own — with His disciples, who need no such instruction in discrimination. They have been "so long time with Him", as He once reminded Philip, and have so often seen the true Light of the world — the light from the source *within* — shining from His countenance, that they need no education in distinguishing that Light from any other light. Instead, therefore, He first prepares them by endeavouring to build up in them, through those uncompromising Beatitudes, the kind of attitude to the deathly bitterness of tribulation, which I have already mentioned — the attitude which can detach itself from strong feelings and treat them as a means to an end; which does not wish disaster away; which can even accept it as a blessing. And then, after He has prepared

* I mean, of course — as anyone without clairvoyant knowledge must mean — the actual compiler or compilers of the gospel as we have it in the Canon. It was Rudolf Steiner who first convinced me that the gospels yield their deepest secrets to those who ponder the familiar text, rather than to those who lose themselves in the mazes of textual criticism; which, in the case of the *Pericope adulterae* (John VII, 53 — VII, 11), has a long history stretching back to Jerome and Augustine.

them in this way, He speaks the Five Words. But this time He speaks them a little differently. This time He does not say "*I am* the light of the world". This time He makes the terrifying, or the sublimely exalting, revelation. This time He says "*Ye are* the light of the world". And again "Ye are the salt of the earth!" And immediately afterwards He instructs them in the *Our Father*, the Lord's Prayer — the prayer which — except, perhaps, for one half-sentence — He could Himself join them in saying.

What did he mean by such words? He, who also said: "The Kingdom of God is within you"? He, who also said: "The Father in Me, and I in you"? The "salt" of the earth is its essence, its true being; and it is this essence, which in future is to be the light of the cosmos — gradually taking the place of the sun. When, therefore, He told His disciples that they were the light of the world, He was in effect saying to them: Once the Word was spoken by the Father, and the Word was the source of the true, the Father-Life, and the Life was the source of Light. And henceforth that Light, that Life, that Word and that Father are *in you*! "The Father in Me, and I in you!"

And what is He saying to us? He is saying the same thing; but He is also saying: The change in the earth's aura, which took place at the time of Golgotha, depends, if it is to grow and brighten, or even if it is to continue at all, on a change in *man's* aura. It depends on whether there will be enough souls of men struggling somehow on towards a time when they will not merely *enjoy* the light of the world, but will actually *be* it.

There are many of Rudolf Steiner's writings, which will take us on from here, and which will carry our thoughts into that astral region, where the light is experienced from within. We may take, for instance, the four printed Lectures, *Mysteries of the East and of Christianity*, particularly the description of the Sun at Midnight, and the account there given of the soul at night, looking down upon its own etheric and physical bodies and feeling itself as the sun which is warming and illumining them. Or *The Inner Nature of Man and Life Between Death and Rebirth*; where the emphasis is rather on the relationship which it is possible for us to have with the dead, precisely in that inner world. Or one may seek to study the relationship of this astral light to speech. Although we do not yet *shine* from within, we do already speak the word from within ourselves; and if we could really follow language back to its source, back to what is called the "Lost Word", we should come also to the source of light.

If, after penetrating to the source of light and uniting ourselves with it, we then return, and open our eyes, like the man born blind, to the outer etheric light, then above all is there a true rejoicing in the light. For I do well to rejoice in the etheric light, if I am so related to it as to be aware all the time that "I", that is, the Father in me, am the true source of it; and not the blazing sun out there in space, which is now no more than a hollow reflector. When we absorb the light from without, we absorb also the fallen Bearer of the Light. We take Lucifer[11] into our souls, and he gives us his strength and his enthusiasm, in exchange for a seat on the Father's throne in us. When we ourselves go *out* into the light from within the light — that is, from beneath the Father's throne in us — then, too, Lucifer gives us his strength and his joy; but now it is as a free gift, as a thank-offering for his redemption. And just as he brought *Eros* to the Greeks, so he brings us *Agapé* — namely, the love whose well-spring is rather compassion, but whose intensity is desire. And, with that, he brings also — not so much that *rejuvenation*, of which mention was made earlier, but rather something, which is very like rejuvenation, but also very unlike it — the first, firm beginnings of something which could more properly be described as — *resurrection*. All this he can do, because he himself has fulfilled, in us, his old longing to rise again as the Holy Spirit.

The source of the light cannot experience the light objectively. It *is* the light. That is why, to one on the very verge, the very threshold, of union with it, the true spiritual world — the Supreme Identity, the Inwardness itself — looks, not like light, but like a darkness and a death. This is also the secret of the link between the many references to the light in St. John's Gospel and the still more numerous references to the Father. For the Father is the *source*. Indeed, that is what we mean by calling Him Father.

And in those references we can find, if we seek it, a sure touchstone for detecting the presence of Lucifer, there, where he has his last, and perhaps his best chance for concealing it from us. That is, when he chooses to hide himself, like a maggot in an apple, in the very core of the high impulse of Johannine Christianity. Seated on the Father's throne in us, Lucifer will glibly and readily say: "I and the Father are one", hoping thereby to deceive us into mistaking him for the Christ. For those are the very words of the Christ. But Lucifer will never say the other thing. Lucifer will never say — as the true Christ said over and over again, according to the testimony of St. John: "I and the Father are *two*." Because his pride will not allow it; and because in any case he prefers to keep mum about the Father.

Rudolf Steiner often spoke of the time, from about 1930 onward, as a period in which the faculty of etheric vision would become more and more widespread. He pointed also to the middle of this century as a time in which there would be "violent breakings in of the new" from many directions. Perhaps therefore, just at this juncture in the life of the Twentieth Century and of this Movement, it may not be unimportant that we should come to distinguish more and more clearly between the outer light and the inner; between the etheric light and the astral light; between the conquest of Ahriman and the redemption of Lucifer; between the light in and for itself and the Source of the light in the Alpha and Omega, in the Word of the Father.

OWEN BARFIELD AND THE ORIGIN OF LANGUAGE

ARISTOTLE ONCE ADMONISHED his hearers to "call no man happy until he is dead". When people hear that I think they generally assume that it was simply a piece of ordinary pessimism, signifying that it is better to be dead than alive. That is not actually what he meant. In the original context he was trying to define the meaning of 'happiness,' happiness meaning not just a state of mind which you enjoy for an hour or two, or a day or two, but something that applies to a whole life. Perhaps the word 'blessedness' would be more appropriate. Because it applies only to a whole life, you could only really decide whether a man is happy or not after he is dead. Well, I mention that because it occurred to me that, if Aristotle had been asked about the choice of a human subject for a biographical lecture he might very well have laid down the same rule; and I notice that the sponsors of this series,[1] in all the other lectures, *have* observed that rule inasmuch as all the other subjects *have* completed their lives. There is another difference, and it is one that involves a certain amount of embarrassment. In every other case the subject of the lecture was one person, the lecturer another. Here they are both one and the same human being. That does arouse a certain element of embarrassment, and I have come to the conclusion that I can mitigate it a little by following the previous lecturers in the practice of referring to the Subject in the third person. I hope you will approve.

It happens that the actual moment when the Subject of this lecture was first made aware that it is possible to enjoy language *as such* — the very nature of language — can be identified very precisely. The scene is a school-room in the few minutes before the master comes in to take a lesson in Latin syntax, and the textbooks from which the homework has been prepared are lying open on the desks. The practice here was to illustrate the points in syntax by quotations from an actual Latin author. I think, at the risk of overburdening you with detail, I will tell you exactly what it was, even to the extent of using the blackboard. The point was to illustrate the fact that in Latin the accusative case is used to express duration of time. The sentence was: *Cato, octoginta annos natus, excessit e vita* (Cato died aged 80) and, for the student, the only word in the quotation that really mattered was the word *annos*. Nevertheless the boy sitting next to him suddenly observed: "Cato, at the age of 80, *walked out of life* — that's rather nice!" or words to that effect.

You would be mistaken if you imagined that at the time the Subject was deeply impressed by his friend's sensitivity, or anything of that sort. If anything he was rather irritated and inclined to think the man must be, in the language of those days, "rather an ass". But somehow it stuck. It must have done. Otherwise why has it gone on recurring to his memory at intervals throughout a rather long life? You see, what this friend — by the way the Subject was 11 or 12 years old and so was his friend — what this friend (whose name incidentally was *Cecil Harwood*[2]) was drawing attention to, because it tickled his fancy, was a *metaphor*. You can say "Cato died". You can also say "Cato walked out of life". Well, of course the Subject himself was familiar with other metaphors, with figurative language, figures of speech; but it had never occurred to him before that it was possible to *enjoy* them, to relish them, for their own sake. That is the proper moment to identify, if you want to place the origin of the Subject's interest in, and feeling for, the nature of language.

Some years elapsed before the Subject himself acquired the habit of enjoying metaphors, and when he did, it was of course mainly the kind which form such an important part of lyric poetry. They would bear, not merely reading and enjoying. One could somehow dwell on them. It might be a diffuse, rich metaphor, like Shelley's calling on the West Wind to "make me thy lyre even as the forest is" or it might be a highly condensed, startling, even paradoxical, brief metaphor like Milton's description of the venal clergy as "Blind mouths that scarce themselves know how to hold a sheep hook". He became rather fascinated with them.

The world in which the Subject was growing up was the world of Wells and Shaw. The old Victorian confidence in unlimited progress was still going strong. It was a few years before Wells published his *Outline of History*. There was a new world in front of us; mankind had begun to move on and on and up and up, and to control the outer world with an ever-increasing multitude of gadgets, and everything was to be wonderful. What was not mentioned so often, although it was regarded as equally certain, was that, at the end of the whole process, the entire universe would crumble or freeze into a mere conglomeration of inanimate matter. It was — for anybody who really took a long view — you could say a pretty hopeless perspective. Well the Subject was somewhere between the ages of 17 and 20, I think, when he definitely concluded that lyric poetry was perhaps one of the best things in life, and certainly the most hopeful thing, in the prevailing materialistic climate of opinion in which he was being brought up; and furthermore that the *metaphors* in lyric poetry were what constituted the principal substance of it. It was not just a matter moreover of enjoying lyric poetry, the world became a profounder and a more meaningful place when seen through eyes that had been reading poetry. That was perhaps the most important thing of all. Poetry had the power to change one's consciousness a little. I will return to that, but first I want to say something about another point of view from which the whole business of metaphor can be approached, one which also began to attract his attention, and that is, the part it seems to have played in the historical development of language.

One thing that is noticeable about metaphors is that, if they are used too often, or if the *same one* is used too often, it fades away. It fades away as a metaphor and turns into a straightforward meaning. For example, at some time in the past someone wanted to say that he had tried every expedient he could think of, and he thought he would put it in a figurative way, make a little picture of it, say it in images. So he said: "I've left no stone unturned." And no doubt his hearers had the pleasure of forming a little picture to themselves of a man with a hoe or a pickaxe. But the metaphor has been used so often since then that the man with the pickaxe has disappeared; nobody bothers to imagine him any more. The metaphor has turned into what is sometimes called a 'trope', which is a verbal convention rather than a figurative expression; another name for it is 'cliché'. And a second thing about metaphors is that they don't necessarily need a whole sentence for their embodiment;

a single word may be a metaphor. For example, again, to 'walk out of' is to depart from; 'Cato walked out of life' or you could say: 'Cato departed from life' and then the single word 'depart' can be used as a metaphor for 'to die'. It has been used so very, very often that the word 'departed' has become practically a synonym for 'dead', perhaps not so much now as 70 years ago. It isn't quite so common now to refer to the 'dear departed' either on tombstones or elsewhere as it was 70 years ago.

A third thing: a metaphor may be a material picture of a material content. A snail "carries its house on its back" is an example of such a metaphor. But it can also be an *immaterial picture* (after all, all visual imagery is made up of material components): it may be a *material* image of an *immaterial* content. When Shelley speaks of the West Wind making him its lyre, he is drawing a material picture of an immaterial relation, a mental or spiritual relation between himself and the world of nature, a relation of inspiration, as it were. This second kind of metaphor is by far the most important, and it is this kind of figurative language that, as our Subject was now beginning to discover, has played such an enormous part in the whole history of language, and also, as we shall see, in the history of *theories* about language, including theories about the origin of language.

For some considerable time before the Subject was born a lot of people had been pointing out (John Locke, Emerson, Max Müller, Anatole France, Jeremy Bentham are only a few of them) that not only do a great many of the words in any modern language consist of just such faded, or petrified, or fossilised, metaphors, but that this is true of all those words which comprise what Bentham called the "immaterial vocabulary". Immaterial meanings apparently began their life in that way, that is by having purely material meanings, which were then extended by metaphor. When we speak of "grasping an idea", is 'grasp' a metaphor or is it a literal word? Well, let's make sure we are not being metaphorical by speaking instead of 'conceiving' an idea. All right, but if you look into the word 'conceive,' you come on a Latin word which also meant at one time 'to grasp' in a bodily sense, 'to take hold of,' and so you can go on and very interesting it was, at all events to the Subject.

But there is one point about all this, that it is easy enough to say now, but which it took the Subject a long time to become fully aware of. This conclusion: that all words with an immaterial meaning, however simple or however refined and abstract (and of course there are thousands and thousands of them: 'mind,' 'love,' 'hate,' 'ugliness,' 'obligation,' 'analyse,' 'progress,' 'motivation,' 'liberation,' 'departmentalisation,' etc., etc.) this conclusion, that they all arose out of what were originally mere signs for visible objects and events, was based on certain unstated assumptions concerning the nature of primitive man. I mean the view that he had ascended from the condition of a mindless animal. It was a view that had already begun to gain currency in the 18th century and had later been popularised and riveted on the whole cultural climate of the West by the Darwinian theory of evolution. If Darwin was right (and at the time the Subject was born in 1898 no one dreamed of suggesting that he might not be right), if he was right, the first words uttered by primitive man must have been mere signs for the physical objects and events by which he was surrounded. And it would follow from this that immaterial meanings could only have been imported by using those simple signs later on as metaphors, as images of the second kind, images where the material picture expressed an immaterial content, a content of which man was somehow, in some mysterious way beginning to become aware. Max Müller in particular talked of a definite stage of evolution or perhaps of pre-history, during which this process was going on. He called it the "metaphorical period".

Now let us go back to what I began with, the experience that can come from reading poetry. For some reason the Subject felt a strong impulse, not merely to go on enjoying the experience, but to examine it. Perhaps it was because, while he felt sure it was one of the best things in life, he was conditioned by the whole intellectual climate in which he was brought up, to suspect that somehow it might all be a subjective illusion. I spoke of that sense of an increase of wisdom or knowledge as an abiding result of the change of consciousness poetry brings. What if it were all just an illusion? Perhaps it was for that reason, or perhaps it was because he just happened to have a poking and prying kind of mind. Whatever it was, in the year 1922 (I think it was) he chose the language of poetry as a subject for a thesis to be submitted for a minor post-graduate degree. Much later, in 1928, this was published as a book under the title *Poetic Diction*. I'm afraid I must try very briefly to summarize the contents of that book, or perhaps better say its two conclusions. I don't see any way of getting along without it. They were as follows:

First, that the appreciation of lyric poetry brings about, in however small a degree, a change of consciousness, a change in the direction of a slight increase of knowledge, of wisdom. The pleasure we feel in it is, from the point of view of that book, less important than the change. It lasts while we feel the change is going on. After that the pleasure doesn't last, but the change does, or it may do so.

The second conclusion was that the same experience, the change of consciousness and the pleasure in the change, can be aroused by other kinds of language than the language of lyric poetry. Almost any kind of language in fact that is expressing a consciousness essentially different from our own. More particularly it can be aroused by a language which is at an earlier stage of development than the one that is our own, because it is the nature of language to grow less figurative, less and less couched in terms of imagery, as it grows older. We notice, we *relish* figurative quality in older language, and we experience this figurative element in the same way that we experience a metaphor before it has faded or before it has become fossilised. That is also the way in which we experience those new metaphors which poets make for us. But it does not follow from this (and this is where most of the philologists of the 19th century and the early twentieth have really made their mistake), it does *not* follow from this that that figurative element, that presence of living imagery, that we find in earlier language was *made*, invented, created by the individual genius of a poet. On the contrary, it couldn't have been. It was simply *there* in the language as such; it was a 'given' kind of meaning, a 'given' kind of imagery. I am doing the best I can to epitomise the main argument of the book, and I realise it is not very satisfactory, but perhaps you can see that it entails a kind of critique of that theory of the origin of meanings (especially immaterial meanings) that I've just been speaking of, I mean the theory that they originated in the creation of metaphors by some individual person. The book pokes a little fun at Max Müller, pointing out that his notion of 'metaphorical period' necessitates the strange hypothesis that at a certain stage in its evolution the human race broke out into a kind of rash of poets. Perhaps I might quote a couple of sentences: "In other words, although when he moves backwards through the history of language, he finds it becoming more and more *figurative* with every step, yet he has no hesitation in assuming a period — still further back — when it was not figurative at all! To supply, therefore, the missing link in his chain of linguistic evolution, he proceeds to people what he calls the 'infancy of society' with an exalted race of amateur poets."

Does all this indicate fairly clearly what had been happening to the Subject? He started off by trying to examine as objectively as possible a certain change in his own consciousness which could be brought about by reading poetry. In the result he found himself saddled, as it were, with a theory of a long-term change in the consciousness of humanity as a whole, a change which can really only be described as an 'evolution of consciousness'.

So much for the contrast between early language and later language. What about the Origin of Language? It was a subject on which a great many theories had been put forward in the fifty-odd years or so preceding the birth of the Subject. There had been an outburst, a rather wild outburst, of speculation in the latter half of the 19th century. Most of it had died away by the time he was born and began to look around him, but there were still a few surviving reverberations. All those speculations about the origin of language were based on the assumption to which I have already referred, namely the emergence of human consciousness from a purely animal one, from a consciousness to which any notion of meaning was inapplicable. The human being, it was assumed, first awoke to self-awareness to find himself surrounded by a world of sharply defined objects; and that self-awareness gradually increased as he learned to control and manipulate these objects in the course of the struggle for existence, struggle for survival. For purposes of that struggle he needed tools of all kinds that he had to invent, and the most useful of all the tools he invented or stumbled on in the course of that struggle was speech. It was also the most effective one in raising him above the level of the animal kingdom. All that part of it was taken for granted and anyone who had anything to say about the origin of language was expected to come up with some new way of explaining how grunts or other animal noises somehow or other developed into words. You probably know something about the kind of theories that were put forward. One theory was that it all arose out of human beings trying to imitate noises in the world around them, noises made by animals or wind, or water. That was sometimes jocularly called the 'Bow-wow theory.' Another one was that he was supposed to have uttered an exclamation at something happening to him. You said 'Oh' or 'Ah' and so forth: and out of that you gradually formed meaningful words. That was jocularly referred to as the 'Pooh pooh! theory.'

Well, although it's very clear to him now, it took the Subject some time to realize how totally incompatible all this was with his own speculative notions about the nature of language in its early stages. If the figurative, or let's say the imaginal, meaning in the earliest words was really 'given', and was not something added to them by an individual speaker (which is what happens when a metaphor is invented), then there must have been going on, not only a different kind of thinking but a different kind of perceiving. The picture quality, the given meanings must have been present not only in the perceiver but also in what he perceived; it must have been present in fact in the world about him. There must have been a kind of participation between perceiver and perceived, between man and nature. That is something we no longer experience, only get an occasional glimpse of its quality through the creative imagination of a modern painter or poet.

If you can grant this, you see language as originating in that participation, so that in the earliest stages of all it would have to be described as nature speaking through man, rather than man speaking about nature; and you see the subsequent development of language as evincing the gradual diminution of that participation as time went on. The early book I have just mentioned, *Poetic Diction*, went only as far as *suggesting* this concept of participation between man and nature. It was only much later, after a gap of which I shall say something shortly, that it was developed more fully in a book called *Saving the Appearances*, where the term "original participation" was used to distinguish it from the kind of participation, similar in quality, though not in immediate origin, of which we get these glimpses in poetry and art. It was possible, accordingly, to include in that book a short chapter on the origin of language as distinct from its historical development. Except that a good many years ago he did give a lecture on the origin of language in this building,[3] of which I can find no record at all. Really only a faithful Darwinian can speculate about the *origin* of language, because he is convinced that it was *added*, at some stage of evolution, to a consciousness which was previously altogether inarticulate. It is different when you have become convinced that the human psyche (somewhat like a child, at first in the womb then afterwards at the breast) gradually *drew forth its own meaning* from the meaning of its environment; that man was, so to say, spoken into being before he himself began to speak. In the chapter of the book, *Saving the Appearances*, just referred to, the author complained that to ask about the origin of language is "rather like asking about the origin of origin".[4]

It was in 1922 or possibly the end of 1921, that the Subject first heard of Rudolf Steiner, and began to read some of his books and lectures. He approached them with an attitude of caution, even of suspicion; particularly he was put off by a certain residual aroma of the Theosophical Society, which was rather noticeable in those days. He had recently begun working on the thesis, afterwards published as *Poetic Diction*, but you would be quite wrong if you imagined him confidently confronting the orthodox picture of an exclusively biological evolution with a totally different picture of his own. The Darwinian story, the Darwinian fantasy as I am now inclined to call it, was about as firmly riveted on his imagination as on everyone else's; and of course Rudolf Steiner's picture of evolution is startlingly and, on first acquaintance, disconcertingly different therefrom. So, looking back on that time, he seems to recall that his first really positive, really concrete response to what I would call the 'content' of Anthroposophy was rather strangely similar to that older response to poetry, or rather perhaps to language out of which the idea of the book

Poetic Diction first arose. That had begun, you may remember, with the discovery that the forms of language created by poets produced a certain change in consciousness, a change that was both pleasurable, and more than pleasurable — followed by the further discovery that older forms of language could produce a similar change, as it were of their own accord, without the help of the poet, without the help of art. He now found, simply as a matter of experience, that there was also a third source from which that sort of change of consciousness could originate.

The often surprising things that Rudolf Steiner reported with such confidence as the findings of his spiritual research, *acted* on him in the same way as did poetic or figurative language. Whatever else they were, they were (in those memorable words of Cecil Harwood) "rather nice". Yet in this case it was certainly not a literary or linguistic experience. He was reading Steiner in English translation and in those days many of the translations then available were, to say the least of it, not models of literary excellence. I thought that might raise a laugh! I must pause for a moment to disclaim any intention of ridiculing them. In those early days of the Movement[5] in this country there were two or three people only who somehow kept the translations going and kept us up with what was happening. There was the weekly *News Sheet* coming out in German, which was reproduced here almost the day after, and all the time the great body of lectures was being steadily translated and the store in the library steadily added to, so as to make it possible for people like myself, who was then no German scholar, to make an acquaintance with the corpus of Anthroposophy. Ours is a tremendous debt. I wouldn't want to laugh at those translations for a moment. But it was just a fact that it couldn't be called a literary experience. Yes, in that case, it was the content, irrespective of the language that, so to speak, did the trick. But it was the same trick, the same sort of change of consciousness as in the other two cases. As in the other two cases, so in this, belief or unbelief were irrelevant. The change *happened*. It was something that was *there*.

Well, that seems to have been how it began. But of course he couldn't continue long in that rather dilettante approach to Anthroposophy. What followed then in the relation between the Subject and Anthroposophy, was probably not very different from what has followed in innumerable other cases: first of all resistance, then gradual acceptance, with the one changing into the other by innumerable gradations of conviction, ending in a firm conviction that the findings of Rudolf Steiner's spiritual research are far and away our most reliable avenue in the direction of truth.

It would make a long story to go into all that, and it is not quite the story I am here to tell. Perhaps the greatest difficulty was the same one which had led to his original impulse to examine the nature of poetic experience: an ingrained suspicion of self-deception. He had imbibed from the whole of his 20th century environment a suspicion, almost a conviction, that *any* theory implying that the world as a whole has any meaning, let alone a spiritual source, *must* be due to subjective wish-fulfilment. He recalls, in this connection, how very welcome (and for that very reason how *suspect*) it was to him when he discovered the central piece in Rudolf Steiner's picture of evolution occupied by the Christian Incarnation. Also how well, you could almost say how precisely, it fitted in with his own halting notion of the development of meaning in language. A good deal later he was to give some account of that in a lecture entitled "Philology and the Incarnation" which has been printed in the *Anthroposophical Quarterly* among other places.[6]

One might, I suppose, have expected it to be otherwise. One might have expected the Subject to say to himself: "I have been suspecting for some time that there has been something like an evolution of consciousness going on, though nobody else much seems to have tumbled to it. Here is a man who obviously knows exactly what he is talking about and who bases everything he has got to say on precisely such an evolution. This is the man for me." Actually it wasn't quite like that. The two processes, acquainting himself with more and more Anthroposophy and trying to develop and to embody his own ideas, went on side by side for quite a long time. Years I should say, rather than months, went by before he clearly and explicitly and intimately connected his own way of putting certain things with the terminology he found in Steiner. For example, Rudolf Steiner begins many of his lectures on a great variety of subjects by observing that human beings many, many years ago had a kind of consciousness very different from our own. Sometimes he terms it "atavistic clairvoyance", sometimes he characterizes it in other ways. It strikes me now as odd that the Subject had been studying Anthroposophy fairly intensely and for quite a time before he could say to himself in so many words: "This Atavistic Clairvoyance he speaks of is none other than that figurative consciousness and awareness of meaning in the environment, of meaning entering *into* man rather than coming *out* of him, that I have been all along trying to point to; the only difference of course, being that I *end* with it, I have been labouring to establish from very different grounds that there must have been such a consciousness. Steiner simply starts from it, affirms on the basis of his own direct perception that there in fact was such a kind of consciousness, and then he builds on that as his foundation."

I don't know if I have done right, or done what was expected of me, in concentrating as heavily as I have done on subjective mental experience. In any case I expect it's time now to turn rather to externals. What, for instance, was the fate of the two books that I have referred to? *Poetic Diction* was published at the worst possible moment for a book of that kind, just before the beginning of the 1930s, which saw a quite violent reaction in literary circles against anything in the nature of romanticism, anything of that nature, anything connected with it. So the book was praised here and there, but sales (I speak of sales as a pointer to distribution rather than from the financial aspect) — sales soon fell to a mere trickle. It didn't do even as well as another book that I haven't mentioned, published a year or two earlier, *History in English Words*.

Meanwhile the Subject, for economic and other reasons, entered the profession of the law and virtually ceased pretending to be an author. He did not cease to be an Anthroposophist, and it was during that period that he managed to produce a few lectures and a number of articles for Anthroposophical periodicals, many of which were subsequently collected and published in 1944, in a volume called *Romanticism Comes of Age*. He was also, still more occasionally, in fact very rarely indeed, being asked to give a talk or read a paper to outside circles. One of these papers, called "Poetic Diction and Legal Fiction"[7] was printed in a volume of *Essays Presented to Charles Williams* and had rather momentous consequences, which I shall mention in a minute or two.

Meanwhile during this rather lengthy *pralaya*[8] in the literary life of the Subject changes had naturally been going on outside, changes in the general climate of opinion, one of them being a sort of romantic reaction against anti-romanticism which was a great help. In 1952, at the suggestion of the publishers, a second edition of *Poetic Diction* was published and the trickle turned into — I won't say a cataract, but into a recognisable little brooklet, which has continued to flow happily. A year or two later it appeared in paperback in America with a Preface by an American poet, in which he observed, among other things, that the select few to whom the book had long been known had always regarded it "not only as a secret book but even as a sacred book". That was rather gratifying.

The *paralaya* drew at last towards a close and in its later stages, when other pressures began to lighten a bit, the Subject was at last able to produce, in 1956, the other book which I have referred to, *Saving the Appearances*. It was a very different book from *Poetic Diction*, though I believe that the same substance is there in it. I should like to mention at this point that the Subject's own feelings about all his books is that he has simply gone on saying the same thing over and over again! But whereas *Poetic Diction* is about the language of poetry, though it ends up, so to speak, by inferring an evolution of consciousness, *Saving the Appearances* is wholly about the evolution of consciousness, and therefore is also about the evolution of the earth itself. That the two evolutions are really one and the same is part of the argument of the book. Whereas in the earlier book an acknowledgement is made to Steiner in the Introduction, in the later one he is definitely established at a certain point in the text as a key figure in the theory of that evolution, if indeed not in that evolution itself. Nevertheless it is not an exposition of Anthroposophy, and because there is so much of the Subject's own in it, the full extent of its indebtedness is very likely not apparent. It is possibly something of this sort that the Chairman had in his mind in the beginning in the kind remarks he made. The two are so inextricably mixed. But let me now have a shot at it. I can give you one single example. Judging by the letters that the Subject receives and occasional references in other people's books and articles, and by some other indications, the concepts of 'original participation' and 'final participation' (or perhaps the choice of that particular terminology) have been of some considerable importance to quite a few people. I don't think that he would ever have been able to evolve those concepts, or that terminology or however you call it, if the evolutionary relation between macrocosm and microcosm which is the marrow of Anthroposophy, had not become to him, during the *pralaya*, something more than an abstract idea, something more like an actual experience, though no doubt a very rudimentary one; and I am convinced that that would never have come about except as the result of considerable meditation on the nature of eurhythmy[9] and of a long, long love affair with the little book called the *Calendar of the Soul*.[10]

It was not only in the narrow world of literary criticism that the intellectual climate had been changing. The word 'semantic' had recently come into use, and in its early days it had a much richer and more living significance than it has come to have now that it has been taken over by the analysts. In particular (this applies especially to America) an increasing number of people from a number of different points of view had started to interest themselves rather intensively in that problem of a metaphorical element in language, the figurative element in language, especially in its relation to myth, and in the light thrown by all that on the early consciousness of human beings. Arising from that, they were becoming interested aesthetically, philosophically and so on in Symbolism of all sorts. They included, besides philologists, theologians and perhaps an occasional scientist or two. There was even a new name for it: Hermeneutics.

It happened somewhere around 1963 that a graduate student in an American university who was taking part in a seminar, discovered that paper on "Poetic Diction and Legal Fiction" that I referred to earlier and introduced it to the class and his professor. This led to their looking into other books of mine, and a little later (I should have said 'his' — the first time I have slipped up!) to the Subject being invited to America as a Visiting Professor. You probably all recall or have heard of how surprised Molière's Monsieur Jourdain was when he discovered that he had been speaking 'prose' all his life without knowing it. The Subject was equally surprised, when he got to America, to find that he was regarded in the appropriate circles, as an expert, even something of an authority, in a department of academic study of which he had never heard!

There was another set of circumstances also in his favour. The teaching staff at a good many universities were beginning to feel that the subjects they taught were too departmentalised, too much divided up into separate watertight compartments. Either you studied philosophy in Room 516 or you studied psychology in Room 990, or you studied literature in Room 1078. Yet the subjects themselves overlapped. There was a growing impulse towards the development of what are called 'inter-disciplinary' programmes. For that purpose the kind of books and articles the Subject had been producing were, I suppose, corn in Egypt. Anyway, during the next ten years he found himself a visiting professor at a number of different American universities, each time with a different title. Here he was a professor of language and philosophy, there of philosophy and religion, there again English and American literature, or it might be simply professor of philosophy. They don't do things by halves over there. And of course it worked both ways. The books got him the appointments and the appointments reacted on the reputation of the books. They are now certainly ten times better known on the other side of the Atlantic than on this. In saying this I do not forget that ten times nought is nought — and ten times one is still only ten.

What else is there to say? There were three or four later books in addition to those I have mentioned — the last one a fairly lengthy study of the philosophy of S. T. Coleridge, whom I have not previously referred to (you can't get everything into a lecture), but to whom the Subject owes a very heavy debt indeed. But you don't want a Bibliography. Let me rather, speaking in this building, say a word or two more about the relation of his books and articles to the Spiritual Science of Rudolf

Steiner; I mean in externals — to which I am confining myself in this part of my lecture. Experience seems to indicate that readers react in one of three different ways. One class of them (and of course I am referring to *favourably disposed* readers) says: "This Barfield is a deep one — says a lot of interesting things — has 'meaningful insights' — What a pity he goes and spoils it all by continually dragging in that man Steiner!" The second class (rather more rationally, I consider) says something like: "If anyone as thoughtful and insightful as this man appears to be lays such startling emphasis on Steiner, there is probably something in it. One ought to look into it." But they don't. They have got all they want, or all they are prepared to take, from Barfield. And then there is the third class, who argue in the same way as the second class — but who then *do* go on and take the trouble to encounter Steiner for themselves. A smaller class, I should say, than either of the other two, but not quite negligible. Some of them have become serious students of Anthroposophy in a private way; a few of the younger ones have gone into institutions such as Waldorf schools[11] for a career, and I gather quite a number in the last few years have found their way to Emerson College[12] over here.

Perhaps it is because the books are not specially *aimed* at the younger generation that it seems to be rather specially the younger generation to whom they appeal most effectively. Children do not like being addressed as children, and the books for the most part take the form of argument between supposedly 'mature' minds. Yet more often than not it is the young who respond. *Saving the Appearances* was, or so I was told, on sale in a Hippy bookshop in San Francisco shortly after the American paperback appeared. In the universities it tends to be the young who introduce them to their teachers rather than the other way round. I can give you two examples. A few years ago the Subject received a letter from a Professor in a well-known Canadian University, introducing himself as a reader, who told him that this habit in the young was sometimes found disconcerting to their teachers. The students would start throwing Barfield at them — and they had never heard of Barfield! It was such a nuisance, he said, that in more than one university the younger members of the Faculty were coaching the older ones in what they called "Barfield-readiness". Again: at the height of the Student Protest period, when some of the students were insisting on running the whole show themselves (including settling the curriculum), at Berkeley in California they instituted a credit course in Barfield. It lasted for one term.

How important is all this? Many anthroposophists attach little or no importance to the academic milieu. They feel it is too far gone in arid intellectualism. They hold — and I think I agree with them — that, if anything like a break-through occurs in the acceptance of Spiritual Science (and surely there must be such a break-through before long, if our civilization is to survive) it will not be the academic world where it first appears. I think I agree with them. But I think it must be important that the message, and the legacy, of Rudolf Steiner should have its representatives, in book or in person, in the academic world *as well* as elsewhere. There is moreover no doubt that this was Dr Steiner's own strong desire. For these and other reasons, then, maybe the Subject has not altogether wasted his energies and his time. The time may even come — and is probably not far distant — when Aristotle will feel justified in describing him as "happy".

EDITOR'S NOTES

FORM IN POETRY

1 A refrain in the song "Sigh, no more, ladies, sigh no more" in *Much Ado About Nothing* (Act 2, Scene 3).
2 A refrain in the English folksong "The Frog and the Mouse" in which a frog woos a mouse to marry him.

GREEK THOUGHT IN ENGLISH WORDS

1 This passage can be translated "...when he spoke of the ability to reason [or the reasoning part of the human soul] or contrasted mind and knowledge with conventional opinion [or common sense]".
2 Greek. "Analagous" or "proportionate".
3 Greek. Transliterated "methodos", with a meaning of "following after" or "pursuit" and given the meaning of "pursuit of knowledge" by Plato (and hence of the mode of pursuing knowledge in later philosophy and science).
4 Greek. Transliterated "mousikós". "Musical" had the meaning of the types of activity performed under guidance from the Muses, for example lyric poetry accompanied by music. As used by Plato it referred especially to the rational, and perhaps more inward, content of the poetry, rather than the elements of rhythm and melody typically associated with music. See especially the *Republic*, Books 2 and 3, 376e–403c.
5 This is translated in the Loeb Classical Library edition as "The criterion of truth arose indeed from the senses, yet was not in the senses: the judge of things was, they held, the mind — they thought that it alone deserves credence, because it alone perceives that which is eternally simple and uniform and true to its own quality. This thing they call the Idea, a name already given it by Plato; we can correctly term it form" (LCL 268, trans. H. Rackham).
6 Latin. "Where are you going, Muse?" From Horace's *Odes*, Book 3, third ode.
7 Latin. Literally "cause without which not", the condition of possibility for the coming into effect of a final cause, or *causa causans*.
8 Latin. Literally "causing cause", the intentional reason of a being or object; the final cause or telos in Aristotelian terms.

GIORDANO BRUNO AND THE SURVIVAL OF LEARNING

1 A description of the *rückschau* (retrospect), which Rudolf Steiner advised anyone engaged in esoteric training to carry out before sleep, as self-interrogation of the correctness in all senses of the student's activity, as a means of strengthening the imaginative powers of the soul by the exact picturing of details, and ultimately for the transforming of ordinary memory into a spiritual seeing of past events, relating to oneself and in time also to others. Remembering events in inverse order frees the student's thinking from its dependence on sense-perceptible processes, which Steiner says is necessary for entry to the astral plane, the plane of consciousness, separate from the physical, where events run in the opposite direction to that in the physical world.

2 Barfield's conclusions in these regards are given in an appendix to *What Coleridge Thought*, "Polar Logic" (Oxford: Barfield Press, 2014, pp. 247–267).

3 See in particular Chapter X, "The Evolution of Phenomena", of *Saving the Appearances*, for an outline of the distinction between the history of ideas and the evolution of consciousness. An excerpt from that chapter: "A history of thought, as such, amounts to a dialectical or syllogistic process, the thoughts of one age arising discursively out of, challenging, and modifying the thoughts and discoveries of the previous one. [...] Many indications suggest that, in addition to the dialectical history of ideas there are forces at work beneath the threshold of argument in the evolution even of modern consciousness" (Oxford: Barfield Press, 2011, 3rd edition, pp. 72–73). This is noteworthy given that modern consciousness, as its evolution has continued, has been shaped by dialectical process to a greater degree than past forms of consciousness.

4 There can be no real doubt that this is a reference to C. S. Lewis.

5 The prologue runs in part:

can this cockpit hold
The vasty fields of France? or may we cram
Within this wooden O the very casques
That did affright the air at Agincourt?
O, pardon! since a crooked figure may
Attest in little place a million;
And let us, ciphers to this great accompt,
On your imaginary forces work.
Suppose within the girdle of these walls
Are now confined two mighty monarchies,
Whose high upreared and abutting fronts
The perilous narrow ocean parts asunder:
Piece out our imperfections with your thoughts...
(11–23)

6 Barfield writes briefly on Coleridge's treatment of the topic of the passive fancy and its relation to memory, and the role it plays in the distinction between fancy and imagination, in *What Coleridge Thought*, Chapter VII, "Imagination and Fancy (2)" (Oxford: Barfield Press, 2014, pp. 117–118). An excerpt from this passage: "This linking of it with *memory* indicates fancy's playing a part in the genesis of consciousness at an altogether earlier stage than literature could be concerned with. Besides 'playing with' the fixities and definites that are given to it, fancy has evidently taken a hand in producing them — in rendering them the very fixities they are. [...] In its debased form [fancy] is, as passive fancy, more or less identical with precisely those characteristics of human perception, which it is the function of imagination (by modifying perception) to overcome..."

TWO KINDS OF FORGETTING

1 This was delivered as a lecture at the Graduate School of Drew University, New Jersey.
2 See "Greek Thought in English Words" note 2.
3 See "Greek Thought in English Words" note 3.
4 This refers to a public debate which arose after C. P. Snow's lecture "The Two Cultures", published in 1959, in which Snow described a mutual dismissal by scientists and technicians on one side and literary intellectuals on the other, as well as a lack of communication and mutual comprehensibility. Snow criticized British education for valuing literary education to the detriment of the scientific. F. R. Leavis, the University of Cambridge literary critic, was the most prominent of Snow's respondents in the debate.
5 Greek. "Koinos logos", meaning common reason.
6 Greek. "Idia phronesis", meaning practical wisdom, individual prudence, with undertones of private calculation.

THE RIDDLE OF THE SPHINX

1 Latin. "Bridge of asses [i.e. fools]", commonly used metaphorically to denote a problem arising early within a field of study which severely tests the inability of an inexperienced person.
2 See "Two Kinds of Forgetting", note 4
3 Ernst Cassirer (1874–1945), German philosopher who, through investigation of natural language and myth, concluded that man is a "symbolic animal".
4 Greek. It can be translated as "man-centred" or "human-centred". Anthropocentrism has been defined as "regarding man as the central fact of creation". In respect of incarnate, anatomically modern man

such as existed prior to the scientific revolution, the perception that corresponds to anthropocentrism was, Barfield writes, that "both the somatic and the psychic components of the 'self' were assumed to be, and felt as if, connected by invisible and immaterial threads with the world of 'not-self' that lay outside them. The whole organism was one of many points of concentration of a field of forces, and of the beings from whom the forces emanated, rather than one object placed among other objects in a void" (*The Rediscovery of Meaning*, 2nd ed., Oxford, England: Barfield Press, 2013, p. 233).

5 Greek. "Person-centred". The contrast with the anthropocentric cosmos (see note 4) is based on an understanding of the "person" as the single individual possessing a body and mind, and determined by physiology and sense-perception. In the essay "Self and Reality", Barfield describes the person-centred cosmos as understood by those who perceive the world in that way as consisting of a "'public' world of objects outside us and existing independently of us, on the one hand, and the 'private' world of our thoughts and feelings, on the other", of which "the former is 'real' in a way that the latter is not" (*The Rediscovery of Meaning*, 2nd ed., Oxford, England: Barfield Press, 2013, p. 233).

6 French. "Treason of the learned". A betrayal of intellectual, artistic or moral standards by intellectuals.

GOETHE AND EVOLUTION

1 *Urphänomen* may also be translated as "primal phenomenon".

2 This is probably best translated as "sensual-supersensual" but could also be translated as "sensory-supernatural".

RUDOLF STEINER'S CONCEPT OF MIND

1 Latin. "To be is to be perceived." George Berkeley's summary of his own immaterialist or subjective idealist philosophy, which Barfield occasionally contrasted with Steiner's objective idealism.

2 E. R. Clay explicated the 'specious present' as follows: "The relation of experience to time has not been profoundly studied. Its objects are given as being of the present, but the part of time referred to by the datum is a very different thing from the conterminous of the past and future which philosophy denotes by the name Present. The present to which the datum refers is really a part of the past — a recent past — delusively given as being a time that intervenes between the past and the future." William James wrote of the specious present that it was "the short duration of which we are immediately and incessantly sensible".

3 This essay was first published in *The Faithful Thinker*, described by Barfield as "a volume of essays by various writers on Steiner, his work and the posthumous development of his work, which appeared on the centenary of his birth, in 1961" (ed. A. C. Harwood, London: Hodder and Stoughton).

THE MANY AND THE ONE

1 This lecture was delivered to a conference organised by the Lindisfarne Association at Crestone, Colorado in 1982. A recording of the lecture was published in audiocassette format, which is not readily available; this is its first printed publication, based on Barfield's manuscript. The essay title has been added by the editor of this book.

2 French, "lived world". The term has an origin in the work of the philosopher Edmund Husserl (in German, *Lebenswelt*), meaning the world as it appears, as given, to the observation of those who experience it in the same way, on the basis of which they can construct their knowledge of it. Barfield's "collective representations" can be taken as another term expressing this experience.

3 Barfield writes at greater length about these two stages of initiation, in other than anthroposophical terms, in the essay "Imagination and Inspiration" (*The Rediscovery of Meaning*, 2nd ed., Oxford, England: Barfield Press, 2013, pp. 160–188).

4 Latin, literally translated, "nature naturing". As defined by Coleridge, "the sum or aggregate of the powers inferred as the sufficient causes of the forms (which by Aristotle and his followers were called the substantial forms) is nature in the active sense, or *natura naturans*".

5 Latin, literally translated, "nature natured". As variously defined by Coleridge, "the aggregate of phenomena ponderable and imponderable, is called nature in the passive sense — in the language of the old schools, *natura naturata*" and "the sum total of the facts and phenomena of the senses".

6 For a further description of the etheric realm as such, see within "The Light of the World" note 2. For a description of each of the four ethers, see "The Light of the World" note 3.

7 Latin, "mind moves matter."

8 Greek, variously translatable as "rational seeds", "seminal reasons", "germinal principles". In Philo's conceptualisation, these were the thoughts of the Logos, a being differentiable from God, which brought forth the physical world. Broadly the *logos spermatikoi* was conceptualised to account for the continuation of fundamental transformation, and the observation of potentiality, in nature after God's creative deed.

9 French, "agreed-upon fable". The phrase was used by Rudolf Steiner to describe conventional historiography.

ISRAEL AND THE MICHAEL IMPULSE

1 I.e. the Archangel Michael.

2 Steiner's found, in broad accordance with the teaching of Abbot Trithemius of Sponheim (1462–1516), that seven archangels cyclically assume the rulership or leadership of humanity's evolution, each for periods of between 300 and 350 years. The rulership of Michael, archangel of the Sun, which may last until c. 2400 A.D., was preceded by that of Gabriel, archangel of the Moon (1510–1879), and will be followed that of Oriphiel, archangel of Saturn.

3 The phrase "Intellectual Soul" is used by Steiner to refer to the operation of the self as it thinks about the sense-perceptible objects around itself. As a corollary, it augments its sense of itself *as* a self, as a being separate from the rest of nature. However, while separate from the natural objects around it, the intellectual soul does participate intellectually in the being of nature, through perception of and meditation on the intelligence within nature. This member of the soul was the object of evolution especially from the period of Greek philosophy up till the period of the scholastic theologians.

4 *Nous Poieticus* and *Intellectus Agens* may both be translated as "active mind", *Nous Patheticus* and *Intellectus Possibilis* may both be translated as "passive mind". The change in meaning which is referred to, illustrating the emergence from prior participation in nature, may be illustrated by the following passge from *Saving the Appearances* (3rd ed. Oxford, England: Barfield Press, 2011: p. 113): "there is a sinewy quality in Aristotle's νοῦς ποιητικός and νοῦς παθητικός (*nous poieticus* and *nous patheticus*), which has already faded somewhat from their Latin equivalents *intellectus agens* and *intellectus possibilis*. The *nous* of which Aristotle spoke and thought was clearly less subjective than Aquinas's *intellectus*; and when he deals with the problem of perception, he polarizes not merely the mind, but the world itself, without explanation or apology, into the two verbs (*poiein* and *paschein*, 'to do and 'to suffer')".

5 The phrase "Third Post-Atlantean Epoch" requires an explanation of each of its words in reverse order.

Steiner stated on the basis of his spiritual research that during the period of earthly evolution preceding the current one, most of humanity lived on the continent known as Atlantis, situated where the Atlantic Ocean now is. This period concluded with a great upheaval. Evolutionary patterns already present in humanity during the Atlantean period, such as an increasing involvement with the physical world perceived by the senses to the relative exclusion of spiritual perception, and the concomitant development of an independent capacity for thought and feeling, have continued and intensified throughout the course of the current, post-Atlantean, period. Steiner stated that the destiny of post-Atlantean humanity is the conquest of the physical world, in some moral and physical form or other, by its own faculties. The essential purpose in this destiny, however, is the development of soul faculties, not directly inspired by the spiritual world, of human thinking and feeling, which may be carried once again to the spiritual world. This purpose has been carried forward through a number of distinct historical epochs within the post-Atlantean period, of which there are to be seven in total lasting approximately 2500 years each.

The Third Post-Atlantean Epoch (also called the Egyto-Chaldaean-Babylonian epoch, 2907 B.C–747 B.C.) was marked by a diminution of direct access to the spiritual world, and by the first growths of that intellectual engagement with the material world which became later ascendant. Nature was experienced as imagery (of the spiritual), in the way Barfield notes in this article, to a great extent because vision of the spiritual world itself had grown dim.

6 This episode appears in the Book of Numbers, Chapter 25. Steiner's explanation of Phinehas' importance is given in the lecture cycle *The Gospel of St. Mark* (Steiner's Collected Works 139), Lecture 8. Available online at: https://rsarchive.org/Lectures/GA139/English/AP1986/19120922p01.html, accessed 9th November 2022.

7 Steiner's Collected Works 122. Translated by Dorothy Lenn with the help of Owen Barfield. Available online: https://rsarchive.org/Lectures/GA122/English/APC1959/19100817p02.html, accessed 9th November 2022.

8 Four plays written by Rudolf Steiner from 1910 till 1913 about the spiritual development of a group of individuals linked by their karma across a number of incarnations.

THE NATURE OF MEANING

1 Latin. Translatable as "the names of the gods", "names are gods" and within this context as "names as revelations of the gods".

2 A reference to philosophers in the school of logical positivism, in particular the linguistic analysts. Barfield is referring, without explicit mention of it, particularly to an argument of Gilbert Ryle's in *The Concept of Mind* (1950).

3 Another warmer and (to paraphrase Barfield) "experiential" depiction of the Jewish Law is contained in the essay "The Psalms of David", in *The Rediscovery of Meaning* (Oxford: Barfield Press, 3rd edition, 2013, pp. 351–366).

4 Matthew 13:10–23; Mark 4:10–20; Luke 8:9–15.

5 Barfield practised as a solicitor.

JULIAN THE APOSTATE

1 Gore Vidal's novel *Julian*, now the most famous literary account of the life, was published in 1964, three years after this lecture was published.

EQUITY

1 The lecture series translated as *World Economy* by Owen Barfield and T. Gordon Jones is currently available in the volume titled *Rethinking Economics: Lectures and Seminars on World Economics* (Great Barrington, MA: SteinerBooks, 2013: pp. 1–182).

2 Lecture 5, "Production and Consumption", delivered in Dornach 28th July, 1922. *Rethinking Economics*, op. cit.: pp. 54–66.

3 The fourth post-Atlantean period (also called the Graeco-Latin period), is distinguished by the process of the final completion of the separation, which had been taking shape throughout previous post-Atlantean development, of the earthly human soul from the spiritual world. Concomitant with this was a strengthening of the wholly intellectual way of knowing which had commenced in the third post-Atlantean period, with concepts and ideas now thoroughly superseding a spiritually inspired understanding of phenomena in all spheres of knowledge. The coming of Christ on earth in this period was essential, in assuring the continued presence of the spiritual world, even as it was beyond perception to all but initiates.

For background on the post-Atlantean period as a whole, see note 5, "Israel and the Michael Impulse".

4 The present fifth post-Atlantean epoch is characterised above all by a global, material civilization based on natural science. In a dualistic relation with that pronounced tendency, there has persisted as an undercurrent a spiritual life of devotion and deep feeling (as exemplified in literary romanticism or the development of the law of equity) which has nevertheless failed to permeate the methods and results of natural science. The goal of evolution in this period is the renewed perception by each individual of spiritual facts, fully cognised by the intellectual and feeling qualities gained in this and the fourth post-Atlantean period. This epoch will last until the 36th century A.D.

For background on the post-Atlantean period as a whole, see note 5, "Israel and the Michael Impulse".

5 Currently published as *Towards Social Renewal* (London: Rudolf Steiner Press, 1999).

6 The other systems within the State, as explained by Rudolf Steiner, are the spiritual-cultural sphere whose ideal is Liberty since it is peculiarly the domain of the individual; and the economic sphere

whose ideal is Fraternity since everyone is involved in its activity. Given these realities, while the three systems do indeed interpenetrate, these other two systems may legitimately sidestep or ignore the State, or overflow its borders, whereas the political-legal sphere is the domain of the state *per se*.

7 The human being has a threefold nature in a number of respects: as having the soul faculties of thinking, feeling and willing, and as having body, spirit and soul. His threefold nature is most thoroughly interpenetrated in the physical body, which has three separate but interdependent systems: the nervous-sensory system, the respiratory system including the heart and lungs, and the metabolic system including the stomach. These can be imaginatively linked with the cultural-spiritual sphere, the political-legal sphere and the economic sphere respectively of the state.

8 The Law of Property Act 1925

WHY REINCARNATION?

1 Latin. "What always, everywhere and by everyone [has been believed]." The phrase was originally used within the Catholic Church to express resistance to weakening in the teaching of its doctrine.

THE LIGHT OF THE WORLD

1 Dionysus the Pseudo-Areopagite (fl. late 5th century — early 6th century A.D.) wrote *De Coelesti Hierarchia* (Of the celestial hierarchy). This nomenclature was also adopted by St Thomas Aquinas.

2 These four principles are not exclusive to man, and each one can be found in other entities also.

The physical refers to what obeys the laws of physics as discovered by natural science. The physical body can be distinguished conceptually from the mineral body, which is the body as apparent to normal sense-perception. However, the human body as apparent to normal sense-perception is composed of mineral substance and obeys physical laws, and can be called a physical-mineral body.

The etheric can be conceived of most simply as the life-force, which functions to preserve life in physical bodies also in the plant and animal kingdoms. The etheric realm functions in various respects that counteract the effect of gravity in the physical realm, so that Ernst Lehrs, a student of Rudolf Steiner, refers to it in his book *Man or Matter* in an introductory way simply as "Levity", though it has other properties in addition to this. Higher beings act within the etheric to create the various forms of life, so that the etheric body can also be regarded as forming the physical body, however this should be distinguished from the etheric *per se*.

The astral is the realm of consciousness as such and indeed of emotion, which humans share with the animal kingdom. Later within this article Barfield, for that reason, identifies the astral principle within the human body with the nerves and senses.

The ego is what makes the human a self-conscious being, allowing him to think of himself as an 'I'. This capacity is had in common only with higher spiritual beings. This property of the human allows him to make moral judgments.

3 Warmth Ether, uniquely among the ethers, is also present in the physical world as the element Fire, resulting in processes such as drying, melting, combustion, and digestion, which cause physical bodies to lose form, necessary in order that they can be acted upon by the other ethers.

Light Ether acts by a drawing-out of centric, earthbound matter, which can be envisaged pictorially in the growth of plants by their orientation to the sun. It is also active in the human act of thinking. That objective ideas present in natural forms are identical with the concepts formed of them by man is also the working of the Light Ether.

Chemical or Sound Ether acts by preserving or creating separate parts or differentiations within natural phenomena, even as a unity is sustained within those beings. The example of a chemical compound, containing different atomic elements within itself, gives it one of its names, while the example of a music, in which different notes in a mathematical relationship create a whole, gives the other.

Life Ether allows the creation of individual living bodies in the plant, animal and human kingdoms. This it does by allowing a holistic consistency throughout the being and creating an exterior or skin in accordance with the being's inherent form. This makes interaction with other parts of nature safe. In the absence of direct experience of this ether, it is the most subtle of them, since unlike the others it is not perceptible in inorganic nature, but can be inferred through the nature of living beings.

4 In Lecture XIII of these 1909 lectures, presently published as *The Gospel of John and its Relation to Other Gospels* (GA 112). The quotations in Barfield's lecture are from the 1933 edition, available online at https://rsarchive.org/Lectures/GA112/English/PLH1933/index.html, accessed 30th November 2022.

5 John 8:12 and 9:5; Matthew 5:14

6 "Have I been so long time with you, and yet hast thou not known me, Philip? he that hath seen me hath seen the Father; and how sayest thou then, Shew us the Father?" (14:9)

7 Op. cit., Lecture XIII.

8 Ahriman can be described as the spirit of materialism. He has also been called Satan and Mephistopheles. Rudolf Steiner called him Ahriman in modern times, which was the name used by the Zoroastrians for the spirit who opposed the Spirit of Light. Vision or experience of the etheric is a victory over Ahriman since it is a recognition of the spiritual in nature, which he wishes should not be recognised by man.

It is critical to note that Ahriman and other beings such as Lucifer who seek to pervert the course of cosmic evolution, at a certain point failed to complete the individual evolution that was potentially open to them, rather than being created *ex nihilio* as negative spirits. They seek therefore either to prevent or delay further evolution (Lucifer) or to speed it up unsustainably (Ahriman), with results that humans justifiably experience as evil. Their function within cosmic evolution, in spite of their own goals, is to allow humankind to meet challenges in developing its loving, creative capacities while also using its free-will.

9 Delivered in Hamburg in 1908 and published as *The Gospel of St John* (Collected Works 103).

10 Vladimir Solovyov, in *The Meaning of Love*, for an edition of which Barfield wrote an introduction (Great Barrington: Lindisfarne Books 1985).

11 A rebellious spiritual being who has worked to bring man out of alignment with his divinely intended evolution. Lucifer has made it possible for man to have a free and fully independent consciousness. However, his work has been within the astral body, rather than the divine, controlling Ego, which has left man prey to illusion. Besides those emotions noted by Barfield of enthusiasm and self-enjoyment, being subject to illusion has implanted made man subject to fear. Due to Lucifer's influence, man can make free decisions within the earthly realm, disregarding other spiritual influences. The result of this was man's condensation into the earth and solidity. He has therefore become prey to death. A pictorial portrayal of his activity is given in the story in Genesis of the Fall and the expulsion from Eden. He is to be distinguished from Ahriman, also called Satan (see note 8).

OWEN BARFIELD AND THE ORIGIN OF LANGUAGE

1 This lecture was delivered as part of a series about pioneers of anthroposophy in Britain at the Rudolf Steiner Hall, in London, on 26th July, 1977.

2 Cecil Harwood (1898–1975), educationalist and writer. General Secretary of the Anthroposophical Society in Great Britain, 1937–1974. He was involved in setting up the first Waldorf school in

England. A lifelong friend of Barfield. Through Harwood's future wife, Daphne, he and Barfield became aware of Rudolf Steiner.

3 See note 1.

4 *Saving the Appearances*, Chapter XVIII. The passage continues that the "roots [of speech] are the echo of nature herself sounding in man. Or rather, they are the echo of what sounded and fashioned in both of them at the same time."

5 A reference to the anthroposophical movement.

6 Reprinted in *The Rediscovery of Meaning, and Other Essays* (2nd ed., Oxford, England: Barfield Press, 2013: pp. 338–350).

7 Reprinted in *The Rediscovery of Meaning, and Other Essays* (2nd ed., Oxford, England: Barfield Press, 2013: pp. 63–93).

8 A word taken from Hindu cosmology to denote a period of non-manifestation or inactivity between periods of cosmic evolution. It has been compared to the plant when it takes the form of a seed. It is to be taken in this context partly as a humorous, self-ironical reference.

9 Eurythmy is an art of bodily movement, superficially similar to dancing, accompanied by speech (usually a recited poem) or music. The gestures in eurhythmy aim to restore a feeling of the primordial gestures by which world-creation occurred, within eurhythmic performers and also spectators. These whole-bodily gestures are related to the sounds on which human speech relies. Eurhythmy was conceived by Rudolf Steiner in 1911.

10 The *Calendar of the Soul* is a collection of fifty-two verses, one for each week of the year, which is intended to make the reader conscious of the seasons' role in consciousness and to deepen her relationship with these developments. It was first published by Steiner in 1912. Barfield translated these verses, which he published under the title *The Year Participated* (1985), which remains in print.

11 Elementary (primary) schools based on an understanding of children and associated pedagogy developed by Rudolf Steiner. The three soul faculties of thinking, feeling, and willing each receive attention, with artistic and practical activities intended to develop the last two faculties an essential part of education.

12 Founded as an education centre for young adults in 1962, based on anthroposophy and situated in Sussex.

PUBLISHED WORKS BY OWEN BARFIELD

	First published
Books by Owen Barfield	
The Silver Trumpet	1925
History in English Words	1926
Poetic Diction: A Study in Meaning	1928
Romanticism Comes of Age	1944
This Ever Diverse Pair	1950
Saving the Appearances: A Study in Idolatry	1957
Worlds Apart: A Dialogue of the 1960's	1963
Unancestral Voice	1965
Speaker's Meaning	1967
What Coleridge Thought	1971
The Rediscovery of Meaning, and Other Essays	1977
History, Guilt and Habit	1979
Orpheus: A Poetic Drama	1983
Owen Barfield on C. S. Lewis	1989
Night Operation	2008
Eager Spring	2008
The Rose on the Ash-Heap	2009
The Tower: Major Poems and Plays	2021
The Riddle of the Sphinx: Essays	2023
Translations and edited works of Rudolf Steiner	
World Economy: The Formation of a Science of World-Economics (trans. with T. Gordon-Jones)	1936
Anthroposophy: An Introduction	1961
The Case for Anthroposophy	1970
Guidance in Esoteric Training (trans. with Charles Davy)	1972
The Year Participated: being Rudolf Steiner's *Calendar of the Soul* translated and paraphrased for an English ear	1985
Edited works by other authors	
Man and Animal: Their Essential Differences, by Hermann Poppelbaum	1960
The Voice of Cecil Harwood	1979

Milton Keynes UK
Ingram Content Group UK Ltd.
UKHW012042250424
441772UK00001B/72

9 780956 942357